NEUE NATIONALGALERIE

Refurbishment of an Architectural Icon

BERLIN

Published by Arne Maibohm
for the Federal Office for
Building and Regional Planning

Bundesamt
für Bauwesen und
Raumordnung

jovis

Acknowledgments

The Federal Office for Building and Regional Planning wishes to thank the
Federal Government Commissioner for Culture and the Media,
the Stiftung Preußischer Kulturbesitz, the Staatliche Museen zu Berlin,
and the Neue Nationalgalerie for the trust they have shown in
implementing the general overhaul.

Special thanks go to all planners and implementing parties,
specifically David Chipperfield Architects. The project could only be completed
through the trust and commitment of all its participants.

Our warmest thanks go to Dirk Lohan and the family of Mies van der Rohe
for their faithful collaboration and consulting, to Norbert Heuler representing the
Berlin Monument Authority for his invaluable support,
and to Fritz Neumeyer for contributing his expertise on Mies van der Rohe.

My personal thanks go to Annett Miethke for her constant support and to the
entire BBR team – Katrin Bauer, Michaela Bauer, Arminius van Cleve, Jörg Fliegner,
Jana Galinowski, Tobias Heide, Angela Kauls, Norbert Klövekorn, Katja Kühn,
Andrea Lipka, Susanne Manthey, Gertrud Matthes, Mark Moammer,
Alexander Niederhaus, Anke Offermann, Ulli Precht, Birgit Rössig, Andreas Schubert,
Sandra Völp, and Till Waninger for their immense commitment to the task;
also to Christina Haak, Joachim Jäger, Nils Lanatowitz, and Alexander Tietze
for the impetus they added to the project;
to Michael Freytag, Björn Löbe, Kerstin Rohrbach, and Mathias Stieb
for their willpower and endurance;
and to Britta and Béla for their heartfelt support during our long journey.

– The long-awaited moment has arrived! –
Arne Maibohm

Table of contents

Implementation

Petra Wesseler

Preface

Around 60 years ago, Ludwig Mies van der Rohe was commissioned to plan the Neue Nationalgalerie at Berlin's Kulturforum. The result was an outstanding, unique new building. Today, the museum is regarded as an architectural icon of worldwide renown, as well as the culmination of the architect's oeuvre. The project to carry out its general overhaul can equally be described as outstanding and unique. It was commissioned by the Stiftung Preußischer Kulturbesitz and recently completed under the supervision of the Federal Office for Building and Regional Planning. After almost 50 years of intensive use, the aim was to sustainably refurbish the building fabric, while integrating contemporary museum requirements, and at the same time taking essential heritage preservation aspects into account. David Chipperfield Architects developed a refurbishing concept that envisaged a respectful approach to the architectural heritage and integrated the necessary additions with sensitivity.

The general overhaul involved mastering a wide range of significant challenges, all under the guiding principle of "As much Mies as possible." For instance, one special task was refurbishing the steel and glass facade of the exhibition hall, above all the procurement of new glazing with the original dimensions of 3.43 × 5.40 meters. At the time of the refurbishing work, such oversized panes were only produced in China and had to be imported by ship.

Another unique aspect was the relocation of over 1,400 valuable paintings and the dismantling of around 35,000 individual original building elements from the Neue Nationalgalerie at the start of the general overhaul. These were carefully charted, inventorized, and stored for later reinstallation.

Exceptional circumstances dominated the later stages of the general overhaul: from the spring of 2020 onward, the COVID-19 pandemic gripped the entire world, with consequences for all fields of life and work, including the building site at the Neue Nationalgalerie.

I would like to thank all those who contributed to the success of the general overhaul under these challenging conditions. The cooperation between everyone involved, while focusing on the goal of refurbishing an icon of Modernity, was an immeasurable factor in the project's success. This documentation is aimed at honoring the extremely constructive and, in a positive sense, combative path toward that goal.

President
of the Federal Office for Building and Regional Planning

Hermann Parzinger

Foreword

For a number of years, the Stiftung Preußischer Kulturbesitz has been focusing its attention on the Kulturforum. Before that, the immediate post-reunification period had seen all of our efforts concentrated on the restoration and contemporary extension of the Museum Island. In the meantime, the Tiergarten district's famous architectural monuments of postwar Modernity had grown old and needed refurbishment. The now concluded general overhaul of Mies van der Rohe's Neue Nationalgalerie represents a major milestone that will attract worldwide attention. Plans are already progressing at full steam to refurbish Scharoun's "Book-Ship" diagonally opposite. And finally, the future extension of the Nationalgalerie according to plans by Herzog & de Meuron will continue to develop the Kulturforum into a lively venue for the arts and culture.

Since its opening in 1968, the Mies building has been in constant use, so its comprehensive refurbishment and technical modernization was essential. Furthermore, today's museum operations place different demands on a highly frequented building compared to former times. Everyone involved in this undertaking approached this gem of architectural history with the utmost respect and maximum attention. I am grateful to David Chipperfield Architects, the Federal Office for Building and Regional Planning, all the planners involved, and the implementing companies for that commitment. They have been extremely diligent in making the building fit for the decades ahead. I would like to thank the Federal Government Commissioner for Culture and the Media, Monika Grütters, and the Budget Committee of the German Bundestag for providing the necessary funds, as well as the Berlin Monument Authority for its constructive cooperation.

The result is mesmerizing. One could almost claim that the brilliance of Mies's architecture has never been more evident than today. This steel and glass architecture captivates us all with its radical precision and clarity. While at the time of its construction, the Neue Nationalgalerie was a recessed building in the midst of a wasteland, its serene power is now palpable in a changing urban environment.

For over fifty years, the Neue Nationalgalerie has shaped Berlin's cultural life with its legendary exhibitions. I wish the building and its collection an equally great future. The stage is now set.

President
of the Stiftung Preußischer Kulturbesitz

Jörg Haspel

Foreword

Since 2001, Ludwig Mies van der Rohe has been represented in the list of UNESCO World Cultural Heritage with his exquisitely preserved and restored Villa Tugendhat in Brno (Czechia), which was built in 1929/30. The architect's achievements and works have helped shape 20th-century architectural history around the world, although only one of his buildings has gained official recognition as UNESCO World Heritage. Nothing he produced in the regions he focused on, namely Germany and the USA, is registered in the list of World Heritage. By contrast, other heroes of classic Modernity, such as Walter Gropius, with three World Heritage sites in Germany alone, or more recently Le Corbusier, with 17 entries worldwide, are far more prominently represented.

The Neue Nationalgalerie, which opened in Berlin in 1968, is regarded as a key monument of what is known as the International Style. It is an icon of Modernity worldwide and the crowning piece of Mies's late work. Only a stone's throw from his former studio at Am Karlsbad, the last Bauhaus Director, who emigrated to the USA in 1938, was commissioned by the Berlin Senate to design the concluding piece and climax of a series of support-free, universally usable hall structures that began with the Crown Hall in Chicago (1956).

Over the years, the Neue Nationalgalerie at the Kulturforum has aged, needing refurbishment, valorisation in terms of monument preservation, and enhancement for contemporary museum operations. It is an immeasurable achievement of the Staatliche Museen zu Berlin–Stiftung Preußischer Kulturbesitz, the Federal Office for Building and Regional Planning, and David Chipperfield Architects, as well as all the project participants, to have initiated and implemented the required preservation and modernizing measures with the utmost care and the greatest respect for this surviving masterpiece. The phrase "less is more" that is attributed to Mies also proved to be a suitable guideline for this project, even going as far as accepting imperfections. The building has not only maintained its world status as an incunabulum of Modernity, but has also been the subject of world-class preservation work.

President
of the German National Committee of ICOMOS

David Chipperfield

Foreword

Any restoration project must be guided by a clear philosophical framework within which technical and formal issues can be approached and solutions developed. The complex issues raised during the process of repair often entail contradictory concerns and challenges. Problems related to the present physical condition are measured not only against the priorities of the original design or intentions, but also in consideration of the status of modifications made since and any inherent defects. The task of restoring Ludwig Mies van der Rohe's work involved some particularly fascinating challenges. The relatively young building, which lacks the more conventional monumental status familiar to older structures, nevertheless carries intense meaning–not least as a significant work by one of the most influential architects of the 20th century–alongside other complexities. As an architectural manifesto in itself, the directness and simplicity of the constructive composition is fundamental to the singular idea of the building. The restoration could not therefore be regarded from the dispassionate distance of technical solutions alone, for even the technical elements touch its very soul.

Alongside the privilege of working across time in dialogue with an architectural hero, we have enjoyed the opportunity to consider the physical stuff of architecture in a coherent and intelligent environment with others who share a belief in the importance of the building, both as an icon of modern architecture and in terms of its significance in the complex social, political and emotional history of Berlin itself.

Behind every intervention on the Neue Nationalgalerie, there lies a substantial body of rigorous analysis and exploration, aided by the input of consultants and collaborators, and distilled through debate and mediation. The outcome represents a deep respect not only for the building, but also for the idea of the building, invisibly restoring its original, optimistic spirit, which reminds us of the physical and social power of architecture.

Architect

MONUMENT

Dirk Lohan

Learning from
the Sixties

When considering how Ludwig Mies van der Rohe took on the Neue Nationalgalerie project in Berlin, it is important to understand why the city of Berlin virtually laid the construction task at his feet. Until his emigration to the USA in 1938, Mies had lived in Berlin for 33 years, becoming famous in the 1920s as an avant-garde architect. Interestingly, apart from his early classicist buildings, he had constructed no important Modern buildings in the city apart from the small Lemke House. However, his concepts for the high-rise glass buildings at Friedrichstrasse Station, which were never built, made him world-famous.

Unlike in Berlin, his career in Chicago was marked by solid successes, especially in the 1950s, with buildings for the Illinois Institute of Technology, above all the Crown Hall (1956) for the Architecture College, as well as the Lake Shore Drive Apartments (1951) in Chicago (Fig. 1), and the Seagram Building (1958) in Park Avenue, New York. Not only his achievements after World War II are important, but also his interest in clear structures, which he sought to express in architecture. In the USA, he studied the materials of steel and glass very intensively, sounding out their architectural potential.

The idea of designing large, broadly spanning halls interested him during that period, resulting in various plans for event and exhibition spaces. In the early 1950s, he designed an administrative building for the Bacardi company in Santiago de Cuba. The building consisted of a large, support-free hall on a granite-clad podium accommodating the floor below. The roof of the hall was planned as a concrete coffered ceiling, since there was no steel in Cuba. The building was fully planned when Fidel Castro came to power and announced the nationalization of large-scale private property. That naturally meant the end of the Cuban project, but the underlying idea remained important to Mies. He revised the project to create a steel-roofed hall for the major 19th-century art collection of the German industrialist Georg Schäfer. The building was planned for construction in Schweinfurt. However, it was never built because the City of Berlin enquired whether Mies

1

could design a building for the still divided city. Mies was immediately enthusiastic about the opportunity, since he had never constructed an important building in Berlin before. Thus, he asked Georg Schäfer to forgo the plans for his Schweinfurt museum, to which the industrialist graciously agreed. In this way, Mies was finally able to work on a museum of modern art, a subject that had interested him for decades. The museum demanded considerably larger dimensions than the previous designs and was constructed in a very short time.

Valuable role in a German-American coproduction

I was involved in the project from the outset and, as it progressed, became the responsible staff member for my grandfather Mies van der Rohe. I was also based in Chicago, but traveled regularly to Berlin during the construction period in the 1960s, assuming the overall artistic management as Mies's representative. The entire planning and construction process was carried out as a combination of American methods and German models. The Chicago office produced a set of architectural drawings illustrating all of Mies's aesthetic and architectural requirements. The other plans, for instance for the air conditioning, electrical, and sanitary systems, including the load-bearing plans, were taken over by selected offices in Berlin. I coordinated the implementation together with the Senate Building Administration. The Construction Office of the Senate Building Administration, led by the experienced Building Manager Peter Neuendorff, took over all the tasks that we could not supervise from Chicago. Naturally, all tender offers and quotes

1 Ludwig Mies van der Rohe, 860–880 Lake Shore Drive Apartments, Chicago, 1951

were negotiated and awarded in Berlin. Since the project represented a demanding cultural task, the best firms in West Berlin were contracted for implementation wherever possible.

Our own architectural planning was influenced by the Museum of Modern Art (MoMA) in New York, which experienced several extensions and conversions during that period. The MoMA was regarded as the leading museum of modern art. We received extensive information from the renowned electrical engineer Edison Price, who was involved in work on the MoMA, concerning the best wall and painting illumination to ensure good lighting for the artworks. The collaboration with many experts during this period was very successful. There were no disagreements, although occasionally, presumably on grounds of costs, compromises were necessary with respect to the quality of the final product.

Since its completion in 1968, the Neue Nationalgalerie has been famous for ambitious, innovative exhibitions on art and artists. The building has not undergone any comprehensive structural measures since the day it opened. Following an assessment of the existing structure between 2009 and 2011, it became clear that fundamental refurbishment was required to remove certain deficiencies. Over time, the demands of the Stiftung Preußischer Kulturbesitz, which had not been the original client, became more clearly defined. After the other museums on the Museum Island had been completed, it became possible to fund the Neue Nationalgalerie's refurbishment. Around that time, in early 2012, I was asked to collaborate as a consultant architect and represent Mies's joint heirs.

2

2 Dirk Lohan during a meeting to inspect surface samples at the building site of the Neue Nationalgalerie, 2016

Applying the original experience to the new project

It was a great joy and honor for me to participate in the general overhaul (Fig. 2). When does an architect get the chance to work on such an important project for a second time 50 years later? Another exciting factor was integrating Mies's copyrights, which enjoy far more attention in Germany than in the USA, for example. My first task in the process was to secure the participation of an experienced and suitable architect for the project. Several architectural offices were invited to an application interview. It is no great surprise that the Berlin office of David Chipperfield was selected–above all due to its successful refurbishment of the Neues Museum on the capital's Museum Island. When I visited the Neues Museum, I was particularly impressed by the fact that not all the scars of World War II had been plastered over, instead very gently showing the general public here and there what the building had experienced. The fact made me personally optimistic that David Chipperfield's team would adopt the same approach to Mies's monument, the Neue Nationalgalerie.

Intensive study of Mies's work was an important element of the tasks carried out by David Chipperfield Architects. Time and again, it was surprising in meetings to see letters or documents that I had written and worked on in the 1960s. In addition to the architectural copyright of the Neue Nationalgalerie, the planning process focused on monument-preservation considerations. The aim of the general overhaul was to improve certain functions and technical systems, while ensuring that such renovation measures always harmonized with preservation concerns.

Study trip to consolidate good collaboration

One important step in the planning process was a study trip to Chicago, where many of Mies's buildings from the 1950s and 1960s have also been refurbished and others are still awaiting such measures. The traveling party included the senior architects at the David Chipperfield office, Martin Reichert, Alexander Schwarz, Eberhard Veit, and Michael Freytag, as well as the representatives of the Berlin Monument Authority, Prof. Dr. Jörg Haspel and Norbert Heuler, and representatives of the Staatliche Museen zu Berlin, Dr. Joachim Jäger, Director of the Neue Nationalgalerie, and Willy Athenstädt from the Construction Planning Office. The group also included Prof. Dr. Fritz Neumeyer, Consultant to the Federal Office of Building and Regional Planning (BBR), Sven Seehawer, Partner at the project-steering company KVL Bauconsult GmbH, and Arne Maibohm, the BBR Project Manager. We visited various buildings by Mies, discussed their condition, and met a number of architects who worked on their refurbishment. The trip and the exchange of experience between experts was very helpful, while also aiding future collaboration (Fig. 4). Over the years, I have had to attend many meetings in

Berlin. Today, I can say that the cooperation was successful and we were always able to find joint solutions through constructive collaboration.

The following building sections required decisions on important construction measures:

Expanding the storage spaces

The only significant change to the floor plan of the Neue Nationalgalerie was to expand the storage spaces in the basement. Originally, there had only been a few small rooms for storing paintings and sculptures to the east of the staircase hall, which proved to be completely inadequate over the years (Fig. 6). Thus, the first measure for the general overhaul was to expand the basement along Potsdamer Strasse. The extension is situated beneath the terrace of the building's podium and is invisible as an architectural amendment.

Underground connection to the new museum building

A second measure to the basement was intensively discussed, but has not yet been planned in detail: an underground connection to the new museum building by Herzog & de Meuron at the Kulturforum. I believe that such a connection between the two museums, running beneath Sigismundstrasse, is an extremely difficult architectural solution, because the Neue Nationalgalerie features an important and impressive main entrance, which should be experienced by all visitors. However, it will only be possible to assess the idea fully in later stages of planning.

Sculpture garden

The permanent exhibition spaces of the Neue Nationalgalerie are mainly located on the western side of the property, in the basement. A long glass wall affords a view of the spacious garden, which had once been filled with a wealth of sculptures and lush vegetation (Fig. 3). Unfortunately, the garden has been neglected over the decades and the bushes and trees have been left to grow wild. Their roots have raised and displaced some of the granite slabs on the ground. A careful garden preservation survey addressed the deficits at length and in detail. We discussed it intensively and largely accepted its proposals, allowing the garden to be newly planted in its original form. Essentially, the survey recommended that the sculpture garden's vegetation should be renewed using the original varieties, as well as cleaning the ground and wall slabs, before relaying them.

3

The connection between the exhibition spaces and this green open space had been very important to Mies. Many of his projects have repeatedly established a relationship between the architecture, art, and nature. 50 years ago, I myself worked very intensively on the garden's planning and am very happy that it has regained its original quality.

Glass hall facade

The large exhibition hall on the museum's podium is a steel coffered roof, supported on each side by two peripheral columns. The exhibition space itself is framed by room-high glass facades that have posed a number of problems over the years. The entire glazing consisted of single panes, which entailed certain disadvantages with respect to thermal insulation. Furthermore, the air conditioning system in the museum was unable to maintain the constant humidity of 50 percent. On cold winter days, the humidity produced condensation on the glazing and ran down part of the windows. We encountered the same problem with glass facades in Mies's earlier buildings in the USA.

It also became apparent that the steel frames did not always have a sufficient expansion tolerance for the outdoor temperature changes. The problem was considered in depth and discussed with experts. Another problem was that the large-scale window-pane formats of 3.43 × 5.40 meters were only available from a single factory in the world, namely in China. Everyone involved agreed that it was unacceptable to divide the glazing with new bars, so we were forced to order the glass panes from China. Since we did not wish to make the elegant window frames any larger or more bulky, we ultimately decided

3 View into the sculpture garden before refurbishment, 2014

4

5

6

4 Examining original
plans at the Ludwig Mies
van der Rohe Archive,
Museum of Modern Art,
New York, 2012

5 Testing the retro-
fitted LED lighting in the
sampling room, 2018

6 Painting depot with
sliding wall system before
refurbishment, 2014

to laminate only two large panes together in each frame to create safety glass. This ensured a certain degree of insulation and also preserved the original window frames and their dimensions. Furthermore, an improved air conditioning system will ventilate the window panes more actively than before. I am very optimistic that the technical solution will prove successful in the coming years. My compliments to all the experts involved in this respect.

Lighting for the paintings

Another highly technical problem was illumination for the galleries and paintings on the walls. 50 years ago, the lighting system in the exhibition spaces had been conceived on the basis of experience at the MoMA in New York. Nevertheless, it became evident that today's demands for artificial light have grown, especially with respect to the authentic presentation of original colors. Over the last five decades, much has changed in this field and new methods and lamps have been developed. We especially sought to illuminate art exhibitions in a way that was as similar to natural light as possible. At the same time, it was important to light the walls without creating so-called hotspots. To investigate these questions, various full-scale modern lighting systems were assembled and assessed in the special exhibition rooms of the Kulturforum (Fig. 5). This fascinating and important study was only possible through cooperation between various experts. In future, the exhibition spaces, above all in the basement, will enjoy much better lighting. The damaging red proportion of the former light bulbs will no longer discolor the paintings.

Installation of an expanded cloakroom

The original building of the Neue Nationalgalerie had two cloakrooms, which very quickly proved to be too small. They were accommodated in the two wooden units in the exhibition hall behind the descending stairs. The toilet facilities were situated in the basement, so that using both functions required considerable movement back and forth. Thus, David Chipperfield Architects proposed installing new, larger cloakroom facilities in the basement, directly opposite the toilet entrances, in a former depot for artworks. This new cloakroom provides sufficient space for hanging up coats and bags. The area is enclosed by walls, so no significant changes to the architecture were required, while the improvement will no doubt be welcomed.

Administration rooms

The administrative rooms had already been slightly neglected during the original planning, since the Stiftung Preußischer Kulturbesitz took over the management of the Neue Nationalgalerie at a relatively late stage, while Werner Haftmann was only appointed the museum's Director towards the end of the construction period. Although our Chicago office presented plans by Mies including furniture, decisions on their implementation were repeatedly postponed, until the new Director was ultimately able to assume responsibility for the matter. Our plans had envisaged rooms equipped with the famous furniture by Mies and additional wooden tables for meetings and workplaces of all kinds. As far as I recall, some of the furniture pieces were to be custom-made. Thus, deliveries were delayed and by the time the museum was opened, the rooms had not been furnished entirely as Mies has intended.

The different use of the large reception area, which had been planned directly to the south behind a large glass wall, is especially disappointing (Fig. 7). We wanted to give this space a certain radiance, as expressed in the architecture and the furnishing. Unfortunately, no doubt also on grounds of costs, a different solution was ultimately adopted, which undermined the aesthetic quality of this office zone. I very much hope that after the refurbishment, the reception area will largely resemble Mies's original vision.

Good teamwork

The project was developed between 2009 and 2011, followed by planning measures from 2012 to 2015. The substantial refurbishing work on the Neue Nationalgalerie began in 2016, costing around 140 million Euros. The long period and the financial investment show how fundamentally and thoroughly this monument of Modern architecture was

7

refurbished and improved 50 years after its construction. I would particularly like to highlight the care and preservation diligence with which this important project was implemented. Such results are only possible when all participants, especially the responsible decision-makers, work hand in hand and accept the necessary decisions from all sides. In this respect, I would especially like to highlight the contribution by Dr. Joachim Jäger, Director of the Neue Nationalgalerie, Arne Maibohm, Project Manager at the BBR, and Martin Reichert, Partner at David Chipperfield Architects. The many discussions were always held in the spirit of preserving a great piece of architecture. Finally, I would like to thank David Chipperfield personally for setting the tone in which we all worked on this monument of Modern architecture. In addition to these main protagonists, numerous consultants and experts have contributed to the success of this general overhaul. I can assure you all that were he still alive, Ludwig Mies van der Rohe would have warmly welcomed this thorough refurbishment of his final work.

7   View from the exhibition space into the Director's offices after refurbishment, 2021

Fritz Neumeyer

Refurbishing an icon

Viewed from the inside
and outside

As a Mies expert, I was able to contribute to the general overhaul of the Neue National-galerie and acted as a consultant in matters of architectural theory and monument preservation. The work lasting almost ten years provided a unique opportunity to regard the world-class building from a new perspective. During the overhaul measures, the building was dismantled to its shell construction, which astounded me in several ways: the roof itself, its size resembling a football pitch (Fig. 1); the structural framework directly connected to the massive steel girders of the coffered roof (Fig. 2); looking at the foot of the supports on which the 1,200-ton roof rests and is attached using twelve screws at its bearings (Fig. 3); seeing the revealed and remarkably simple wooden structure of the exhibition walls (Fig. 4); the terrace, after removing the granite slabs, which revealed a grid of undergrowth beneath the slab joints (Fig. 5) and so on. The dismantling measures required during the refurbishing work impressively showed how Mies defined the building's formal appearance down to the interior fittings using the canon of elementary statements. They are decisive in contributing to the effect of a coherent, unshakeable, harmonious unity.

Above all, I regarded my consulting task as highlighting the qualities and principles of Mies's architecture, which define the unique character and greatness of the building. That includes expressing these values to those involved during concrete tasks for the building, both in planning and during the practical implementation of refurbishing measures, which was almost unnecessary in view of the exceptionally qualified team of experts, who all shared a high affinity for Mies.

1 Roof inspection, 2017

2 Scaffolding beneath
the coffered ceiling, 2019

The fact that the museum had required refurbishing 50 years after being opened is not only the consequence of its intensive use, but also because the structural maintenance it received was not always able to do justice to this singular building. For instance, the halved and joined glass panes were born out of the necessity to replace the broken, single cast-glass panes, which had dimensions that were unable to cope with temperature and wind stresses, and were no longer manufactured in the same way. They demonstrate how the building's maintenance has encountered problems in attempting to uphold its aesthetic requirements.

However, not only obvious makeshift solutions, which were also apparent elsewhere–for instance with respect to the cabling–but also regular structural maintenance measures in the past were unable to uphold the structural and aesthetic standards of Mies's architecture. One example is the silicon sealant used on the terrace in the early 1980s. It was applied beneath the granite slabs and fixed to the facade using sheet metal screwed to the existing steel profiles, together with permanently elastic joints. This crude solution considerably undermined the clarity of the steel facade structure at its foot and was an eyesore to everyone who knew how meticulously Mies worked on the formal solution of structural ideas. Under the premise of abstraction in Modern architecture, Mies was well aware of the great significance of joining elements to form a unity. A high degree of conceptual clarity and craftsman's precision is therefore required when applying measures to Mies's architecture. Without such careful joining, the harmony of the individual elements remains fragmentary and prevents the building from being perceived as an impressive architectural unity. The clarity of the structure, the sense of proportions, and the architectural coherence between individual elements to form a unity is a hallmark of Mies, as is the impeccable execution.

Two key aspects have made the Neue Nationalgalerie a unique icon of 20th-century architecture: firstly the expressed synthesis of art and engineering, of classical form and Modern construction; and secondly the incomparable scale of expansiveness and openness that Mies achieved in the hall's floor plan. The Berlin museum is a unique manifestation of Mies's architectural and aesthetic conquest of steel and glass construction, developed on American soil, and the realization of the incomparable scope of spatial freedom that only those materials can achieve.

Eight supports placed at outer edges of the large roof plate create a load-bearing structure that ensures a support-free interior with the maximum possible spatial freedom of movement and flexibility of use. The transparent steel structure rests upon a massive stone base with an expansive terrace. This concise architectural opposition alone inspires associations with a temple podium and conjures up the image of a columned building majestically enthroned upon an inviting base, making it visible from afar and announcing itself as a public building. The classical and the Modern, monumentality and transparency, are interwoven in a way that is unparalleled in the 20th century.

3

4

5

3 Excavated foot
of a roof column, 2017

4 Revealed wooden
structure of the exhibition
walls, 2016

5 Grid of joints grown
under the granite slabs on
the terrace, 2016

MONUMENT

In Berlin, Mies achieved his life ambition as an architect, namely to transform engineering into architecture and elevate the structure of the steel skeleton to the level of an architectural order. He pursued this design ambition with a consistency that surpasses all his other buildings in terms of its structural development down to the smallest detail–also with respect to the clarity of the classical overtones he applied. Formally, the fact that the supports are actually "columns," and nominally described as such in the building plans, is an indication of this approach.

The Neue Nationalgalerie–the last building by Mies and one he was unable to inspect after its completion–is also the climax and conclusion of a development in cultivation and refinement with respect to the aesthetic potential of steel structures, on which Mies had worked for decades in Chicago. It formulates the philosophy of a steel skeleton that has been used in almost every building since the late 19th century, in the form of the industrially standardized steel girder, the T- or double-T-profile, going beyond its technical presence and transcending it into an architectural carrier of significance with intellectual expressive possibilities. Mies used steel profiles to develop "classical" corner solutions that would have pleased Brunelleschi; similarly, in the facades of his high-rise buildings, Mies discovered the pilasters of the industrial age, by making steel girders rise up as formally structuring elements between the windows. No other architect was able to elevate this basically banal construction material to the status of a defining building element, conveying upon it the monumental dignity and noble elegance of the classical architectural form.

Mies gave the eight steel columns, which have deliberately been moved to the outer-most edges of the roof plate and support the enormous coffered roof of almost 65 × 65 meters, capital-like, concise bearings and a slightly slanting, upwardly narrowing form. This formal detail of *entasis*, as is characteristic of classical columns, required considerable efforts and extremely precise welding work, affording the columns both elegance and tectonic, expressive power. The capital and *entasis* are key elements in achieving the impression that the coffered roof hovers, representing a further special technical feat. The individual segments are calculated separately, tailored with a curvature and welded together to raise the roof plate accordingly, thereby preventing sagging at its centre and sinking corners, as well as giving the visual impression of being horizontal.

This great building is not only architecturally striking due to its structural uniqueness, but also equally through its unparalleled spatial aesthetics. Mies based the design on a spatial composition that transforms the act of entering the building and walking through it into a *promenade architecturale*, offering a unique experience of the area. It begins by ascending the open-air steps onto the granite-covered podium, its terrace raised from the regular street level to form an urban space. In the urban-planning wilderness with the presumptuous name "Kulturforum," it is the only place that invites one to wander about aimlessly and sit in the open air, thereby fulfilling the urban-planning role of a centre.

Upon walking beneath the massive coffered roof, one's path leads past the steel columns that support it. One has already arrived at a spatial layer that can be perceived as an interior space, while still belonging to the outdoors. On entering the great hall, this logic of impressions is inverted, since one is in an interior with the mood of an outdoor space. The hall gains this unique, apparently paradoxical atmosphere through the fact that the outside world is visually omnipresent, yet acoustically excluded. The space exudes a sense of generosity, inner expanse, freedom, festivity, and affirmation, thereby drawing visitors for a moment out of their world, while keeping them in the midst of their urban environment, which creates the perfect backdrop for viewing the artworks. The space's simultaneous inward *and* outward orientation invites one to contemplate, reorganizes attention and thereby becomes a marvelous, challenging location for the presentation of art.

Freestanding stairs lead down from the hall to the basement into a broad foyer with entrances to the exhibition spaces, which can be freely organized using moveable partition walls. The exhibition spaces have their point of reference in the adjoining sculpture garden. As an enclosed space within an outdoor setting, also as an open-air exhibition area, it forms a complementary conclusion to the sequence of walkable areas. The fact that in earlier design plans, the grid of the flooring slabs in the interior smoothly continued into the courtyard highlights the intended spatial continuity between the two areas. All in all, Mies created an architecturally defined museum landscape leading from an open expanse to a closed spatial form and back again. It offers a morphological series of spaces, each with its own value, ranging from the omnipresence of the outside world in the interior to the intimate exhibition cabinet and the silent seclusion of a *hortus conclusus*.

Recently, it has been impossible to enter the sculpture garden since this undermined the air conditioning system. Opening the doors to the garden had considerable effects on the climate of the indoor rooms in the exhibition area and led to temperature jumps that are no longer tolerable according to today's preservation standards. However, removing access to the courtyard from the museum experience strongly contradicts Mies's concept of connecting the enjoyment of art to free movement and specific spatial perception. Regaining the accessibility of the sculpture garden and therefore making the spatial interrelationships conceived by Mies tangible in their entirety was therefore a special goal. The improvements to the climate in the entrance areas have this goal in mind. All three doors will provide access, albeit not without limitation–to avoid the considerable consequences of having to install a climate lock: This will only be possible with outdoor temperatures over 15 degrees Celsius. If outdoor temperatures exceed 25 degrees Celsius, the museum climate will be protected by only using one door to enter the garden.

I regard the intact nature of the spatial and formal autonomy of the building's appearance as a maxim and criterion for all measures carried out on it. The intact nature of the surfaces and the legibility of the edges and profiles, both outside and indoors, are essential for the building's architectural and spatial effect. Materiality, construction profiles, and proportions form an inseparable, precisely balanced structural unity that is highly sensitive even to minor disturbances. The combination of materials chosen by Mies–steel and glass, Tinos marble, Striegau granite, and brown oak–is a key aspect of the museum's specific spatial quality.

The untouchability of the base is another essential factor. Building measures of any kind, such as apertures, extensions, and fixed advertising boards, undermine the autonomy and aura of distance that guarantee the building's spatial effect. The planning and implementation of structural measures for the overhaul followed those criteria, as did the extension to the depot spaces beneath the terrace. The most significant measure in the base section was the essential wheelchair-friendly ramp on the southeastern outdoor steps.

6

6 Black pine trees at the foot of the northwest stairs, 2009

The spatial effect of the building was also to be enhanced by the installation of sculptural artworks, as well as the placement of sculptures and installations on the terrace. In the case of the Neue Nationalgalerie, Mies integrated the well-calculated tension arising between the sculptures and the architecture, as in many of his other buildings and projects, as a method of spatial staggering. Mies's plan gave clear instructions on the placement of sculptures, in the same way as he carefully defined areas for planting vegetation. Even the podium for the sculpture by Henry Moore was designed by Mies.

As can be seen on all photo collages, drawings, and also the model of the museum, all the sculptures Mies intended to include were *figurative* and never *abstract*. For Mies, who believed in the aesthetic principle of mutual enhancement through complementary opposites, sculptures produced in an abstract geometric physical language, which also applies to the general nature of architecture, could not develop an especially tense relationship with a building and therefore had a rather redundant effect.

From 2003 to 2010, the large, steel sculpture by Barnett Newman (a copy of the "Broken Obelisk"), which was placed in a central location in front of the entrance (!), had a geometric formal language and competed with the scale of the building itself. It miniaturized the architecture, especially the columns, and considerably undermined the building's appearance through its placement right in front of the main axis. I have also pointed out another misplaced work, namely the black pines by Ben Wagin planted as a green artwork in the 1970s. The two trees stood directly at the bottom of the double-flighted steps that offer a majestic ascent to the podium on the northwestern side (Fig. 6). The overhanging branches of the evergreen pines constricted the space in front of the steps on the Kulturforum side. They obstructed the open view of the inviting steps and thereby undermined the anticipation of approaching the building from that direction. The fact that in the opposite direction, the descent from the expansive terrace via these spacious steps ended in front of these trees was no less frustrating.

Needless to say, technical improvements to maintain and facilitate museum operations, including the interests of preserving the building's original condition and the restoration of its original appearance, could not be carried out without measures to the building fabric. These include the installation of a new cloakroom in the basement and the establishment of a museum shop, as well as the redesign of the cafe according to a concept by David Chipperfield Architects.

The other side of the coin is that restoring the building's original condition can also mean the continued existence of fundamental problems from the time of its construction. The considerable improvement in the air conditioning system and the thermally optimized composite safety glass can only reduce condensation during wintry weather, but not completely prevent it. The reinstallation of curtains that had originally surrounded three sides of the hall was decided on for reasons of monument preservation–although I have my reservations. During the original construction work, the Berlin Senate developed technical equipment that included curtains to provide sun protection. As Dirk Lohan has reported, Mies was not enthusiastic for obvious reasons. A facade made entirely of glass, which makes the presence of the outside world an aesthetic experience inside the building, is conceptually incompatible with a system that subsequently blinds it out–if only for some of the time–using a more or less transparent textile wall. At the time, I considered the decision to close up the magnificent, transparent space of the exhibition hall with curtains on three sides (no curtains were suspended on the entrance side due to the revolving doors) to be a massive limitation of the spatial experience, and only acceptable as an extreme exception. Mies accepted the curtains *nolens volens* in 1966. In a letter on February 28, he expressed the well-meaning hope that it might, "pleasantly enhance the architectural appearance of the great hall," although it, "should by no means undermine the building's clarity." The hoped-for enhancement to the architecture was not forthcoming. At the bottom, the curtains billowed up from the windows due to the air that was blown in from the floor vents; higher up, they stuck to the condensation on the large glass panes in frosty weather. Nor were heavier and therefore even less transparent curtains a viable solution.

In 1989, the curtains were completely removed for the solo exhibition by Ulrich Rückriem, also because the technical mechanism for moving the large curtain bands along its rails was prone to breaking down. I believe the installation of new curtains is only acceptable if its underlying drawbacks can be solved. Furthermore, the architecture's transparency should not be sacrificed as a result. Thus, while examining fabric samples, a textile with a high degree of transparency was chosen, so that even when the curtains are drawn, the relationship between interior and exterior spaces is not completely interrupted and the construction of the load-bearing structure remains legible in its entirety.

The question to what extent, in addition to the restoration of the original appearance, building measures to improve the building structure and museum technology should also affect the atmosphere, led to lively discussions. Terrazzo flooring had originally been intended for the public area in the basement. Instead, a fitted carpet in a color corresponding to the granite was laid in 1968. The carpet, which had the disadvantage of needing replacement on a regular basis due to soiling and wear, gave the exhibition space a muted, peaceful room atmosphere, which combines with the exhibition walls covered either in burlap or woodchip wallpaper to create an almost homely mood. This characteristic grew with its years of use and was further strengthened by the relatively warm lighting using wall washers and down lights. The special room atmosphere–which no longer conforms to today's aesthetics of presenting artworks in a museum–was respected by the preservation authority as a quality of the monument. The carpet was renewed, the walls retained a lightly textured surface that recalled the original, while the lighting, which now uses LED technology, was adjusted to resemble the light's distribution and temperature at the time of the building's construction.

7

I believe these decisions are right: firstly because respective contemporary presentation aesthetics for visual arts change as time passes; secondly, because Mies's building, with its own aesthetics dedicated to contemplation, rather than today's event culture, can represent a significant enrichment to the current museum landscape. The great hall has also proved to be successful for over half a century as a location of exceptionally diverse utilization, which suggests that the spatial freedom Mies created will continue to provide a unique, first-class architectural framework for artistic events in the future (Fig. 7). In this Berlin building, Mies has created a specific synthesis of spatial experience and the enjoyment of art, one that no other 20th-century museum building can match.

7   Upper hall after
refurbishment, 2020

Alexander Schwarz

Preserve the aura
or regain an image?

Considerations on
the restoration of the Neue Nationalgalerie

The restoration of the Neue Nationalgalerie is a matter of Modernity and permanence. The question is: How romantic is the Modern icon, its substance incorporating the novel of its permanence? Modernity genuinely has the tendency to want to be new and Modern compared to the critical mass of the other, the non-Modern, which the Modern cannot itself create, but nevertheless requires for its narrative, for its story, for its novel, for the dialectic of its reality. Yet what happens if Modernity ceases to be new, if it becomes additive, joining the ranks of the other, the non-new, thereby ceasing to be narrative and therefore romantic? A Modernity that breaks its promise of endless youth, its narrative decaying into addition, leads to inhospitality–and that is perhaps the dilemma of Modern architecture. One has to make it new again, at least generating the image of the moment of its exceptional newness, to make it hospitable again.

Is the Neue Nationalgalerie a Modern building in that sense? In other words: How much of the critical mass of the no longer new other has it incorporated from the very beginning? Is it classical enough to still be romantic after 50 years, or has its permanence made it inhospitable? The answer appears to be: one can find elements of both. The permanence of its existence reveals both, the classical and that which has become un-Modern, the temple and the carpet. And they both belong to the monument, to an icon of Modernity. The museum is a building that serves both art and the general public. And as an icon of Modernity, it is very much both an exhibit and a museum. The preservation of its fabric and its function are equally relevant, like a Stradivarius, which should not only have as many original parts as possible, but should also play louder than an orchestral *forte*; nor should one be able to see that for this purpose, the violin-maker has spent years taking it apart, restoring individual parts, and reassembling it. Just as the Stradivarius makes it possible for the tone to carry, unfold, and fill the Philharmonic, the museum must allow the art to carry, unfold, and fill the space.

1 Günter Figal, *Einfach-heit – Über eine Schale von Young-Jae Lee*, Freiburg, 2014 [trans.].

2 Ibid., p. 35 [trans.].

3 Ibid., p. 35f. [trans.].

4 Martin Heidegger, "The Origin of the Work of Art", in id.: *Off the Beaten Track*, Julian Young, Kenneth Haynes (eds., trans.), Cambridge University Press, 2002, p. 24.

5 Günter Figal, *Ando. Raum, Architektur, Moderne*, Freiburg, 2017, p. 17ff. [trans.].

6 Ibid., p. 148.

The Neue Nationalgalerie is perhaps not an ideal museum. Nevertheless, it is an ideal building. The architecture does not tend towards the dialectic and is in that sense not Modern. Despite "top and bottom," "open and closed," despite the "podium and temple," "sticks and stones," there is less emphasis on duality, on one thing and another, and instead more on the "higher unity," as Mies calls it.

It is not about the number two, but about the number one. It is about the square. The square design deals with ideals, universality, absolutes, non-referentiality, singularity, rather than dualities or multiplicities, which are still always something different. The Neue Nationalgalerie is singular in the sense Günter Figal describes in his book *Einfachheit – Über eine Schale von Young-Jae Lee:*[1] something that must rely on the "existence of the work, its specific aesthetic appearance."[2] The building "is the pure realization of the aesthetic appearance. It is simple appearance and therefore also the appearance of simplicity–appearance that does not challenge one to understand."[3] The Neue Nationalgalerie is primary. Thus the spatial experience is also primary beneath the square roof, raised up by eight columns to open up a space that reaches out into the openness around it, equally in all four cardinal directions. A pantheon of the horizontal, not the vertical, open not to the sky, but on all sides towards the world surrounding it.

In its reduction, its simplicity, the museum is by no means immaterial. Its material is just especially dense and therefore highly relevant. In "The Origin of the Work of Art", Martin Heidegger writes, "the temple work, in setting up a world, does not let the material disappear; rather, it allows it to come forth for the very first time, to come forth, that is, into the open of the world of the work. The rock comes to bear and to rest and so first becomes rock; the metal comes to glitter and shimmer, the colors to shine, the sounds to ring, the word to speak. All this comes forth as the work sets itself back into the massiveness and heaviness of the stone, into the firmness and flexibility of the wood, into the hardness and gleam of the ore, into the lightening and darkening of color, into the ringing of sound, and the naming power of the word."[4] The quote also applies to the Neue Nationalgalerie, its hidden sensuousness in the material, what it expresses in the material, and what it represents "as a place, as an open space, as an expanse."[5] It thereby proves itself "permanently of today:"[6] a definition both of space and of Modernity that Günter Figal proposes in his book *Ando. Raum, Architektur, Moderne.*

Spatially, its singularity means the absence of content, without which the building cannot be understood, but would be somewhere else and not at the site of the building; and temporally, its singularity means the building should not be regarded as a step in a development towards a goal to be achieved in the future, since, "what is still to be cannot simply be itself. Accordingly, the understanding of Modernity that was a guiding principle of the Bauhaus program would only be revealed when Modernity is experienced no longer historically, but spatially, as the space of Modernity, as space that is simply experienced and lived today, and also as its inherent timelessness. What could enable this experience of Modernity more than Modern architecture, spatial art, especially when its buildings teach simply being here, by dissolving the 'now' of the moment and the present in the simple 'here', sometimes even making it disappear? And which architecture could be more clearly Modern than a relaxed Modernity that simply demonstrates the timelessness of today?"[7]

By that logic, the Modern space is not a temporal phenomenon, but a spatial quality. In "being here," it is always of today and singular, i.e. liberated from speaking of something that it is not, here. In being by itself, it gives the art the chance to find itself inside it. In that sense, Mies shows us a different Modernity that suffices in itself and thereby avoids the narcissistic urge of dialectic Modernity that needs to be new and different. The radiance, the blossoming out from within, leads to a network of aesthetic and ethical categories that can be regarded as anti-Modern or other-Modern. For instance the stance of Frei Otto would be typically Modern: "What is beautiful is not necessarily also good. Beautiful is not the same as good. Beautiful can sometimes be horrible and ugly can be good [...]. What I mean is that today, we do not need to be taught what is beautiful in architecture."[8] That is certainly a far cry from Mies's position. And it is interesting that of all things, it is cable-supported construction, which was a key aspect of Frei Otto's work, that represents the possibility to circumvent the dilemma, since in it, forces can only move in the direction of the cables, meaning that form, aesthetic appearance, and truth all come together to create one entity almost by themselves, without architectural intention. The same cannot be said for the roof of the Neue Nationalgalerie, as can be seen in the criticism of the uneconomic structure and the "senseless" heaviness it causes. Naturally, it is clear that the Doric-like weight of the steel structure, its other-Modernity, and material presence is decisive for the edifice and its striving for perfection. At Mies's inaugural speech in 1938, which closes with a presumed quote from St. Augustine, he reveals a stance of interwoven truth and beauty: "We want [...] an order where every thing has its place. And we want to give each thing what it deserves according to its nature. We want to do this in a perfect way so that the world of our creation begins to blossom from inside outwards. We do not wish for anything more. Indeed we cannot do any more. The goal and purpose of our work is nowhere more accurately described than in the deep words of St. Augustine: 'The beautiful is the glory of truth.'"[9] Two years earlier, Martin Heidegger described this non-dialectic radiance or blossoming from inside, the beautiful appearance of the essential, as follows: "In this way self concealing being becomes illuminated. Light of this kind sets its shining into the work. The shining that is set into the work is the beautiful. Beauty is one way in which truth as unconcealment comes to presence."[10]

For buildings such as the Neue Nationalgalerie, which are restored as monuments, it is decisive that they remain themselves and are not replaced by something that is identical to them. At best, the identical incorporates what has already been expressed, everything that has been transformed into information and digitized. Everything that has not been said, probably very many hidden things, are lost through the reproduction. In time, it

7 Ibid., p. 164.

8 Frei Otto, "Ethik, Architektur, Innovation", speech at the XXI. World Architecture Congress on July 25, 2002 in Berlin, full text printed in: Winfried Nerdinger (ed.), *Frei Otto. Das Gesamtwerk: Leicht bauen, natürlich gestalten*, Basel, Boston, Berlin, 2005, here p. 125–128 [trans.].

9 Fritz Neumeyer, *Mies van der Rohe. Das kunstlose Wort: Gedanken zur Baukunst*, Berlin, 1986, p. 279f. [trans.].

10 Martin Heidegger, "The Origin of the Work of Art", in id.: *Off the Beaten Track*, Julian Young, Kenneth Haynes (eds., trans.), Cambridge University Press, 2002, p. 32.

11 Martin Heidegger, *Poetry, Language, Thought*, trans. Albert Hofstadter, New York: Harper and Row, 1971, p. 219.

12 Martin Heidegger, "The Origin of the Work of Art", in id.: *Off the Beaten Track*, Julian Young, Kenneth Haynes (eds., trans.), Cambridge University Press, 2002, p. 21.

13 Gunny Harboe, "Restoring Mies. Experiences from the Illinois Institute of Technology in Chicago", conference: *Form versus Function: Mies und das Museum*, Berlin, 27./28.11.2014.

14 Martin Heidegger, "The Origin of the Work of Art", in id.: *Off the Beaten Track*, Julian Young, Kenneth Haynes (eds., trans.), Cambridge University Press, 2002, p. 20.

Translation of a lecture presented to the symposium: *Raum – Zeit – Odyssee. Die Aktualität von Mies' Architekturdenken,* February 28, 2020, Mies van der Rohe Haus, Berlin.

becomes dull, as a substitute of what it has replaced, but is not. With respect to what it has replaced, the result is an ultimate silence.

Heidegger again: "The same banishes all zeal always to level what is different into the equal or identical. The same gathers what is distinct into an original being-at-one. The equal, on the contrary, disperses them into the dull unity of mere uniformity."[11]

Above all, Modern buildings are often replaced by their identical images when they are restored, with the explanation that the material is irrelevant because it is industrially manufactured and therefore inherently reproducible. Typically for our digital age, the argument overlooks the unique aspect that buildings remain permanently in one place. The material is not only imbued with the narrative of having been built here, but also, as time passes, with the narrative of having been here and having been itself.

We believe that the decisive aspect for the restoration of Mies's Neue Nationalgalerie is preserving it materially as far as possible, even if its material has broken its Modern promise of eternal youth. It is by no means a building of intellectual Modernity that must be new, and is instead a building that is especially with itself. It pertains to the number one, the square, and has over time by no means become inhospitable or un-Modern.

The Neue Nationalgalerie is an ideal building the way Heidegger describes in "The Origin of the Work of Art": "Standing there, the temple first gives to things their look, and to men their outlook on themselves. This view remains open as long as the work is a work, as long as the god has not fled from it."[12]

"Do you lose God if you have to change the detail?"[13] Gunny Harboe asks in his contribution "Restoring Mies," referring to Mies's statement that "God is in the detail." I would adapt the question for the restoration of the Neue Nationalgalerie and say: God is in the material. It is hidden there in the Heidegger sense. One cannot see it, let alone depict it. But it not only defines the architectural experience, but also ensures that the museum functions as a building that serves art. The non-depictable, sensuous dignity of the material is decisive not only for the restoration, but also generally for the joy of the architectural experience.

If not before, as soon as the material has been transformed into its likeness, the god has fled from it. There are many restorations that transform a building into a likeness. However, Heidegger states: "A building, a Greek temple, portrays nothing."[14] Thus, a building that portrays something–even if it portrays itself–ceases to be a building. At least–according to Figal–it would no longer be a Modern one.

Bernhard Furrer

The monument
and its image

"Thou shalt not make unto thee any graven image or any likeness *of any thing* that *is* in heaven above, or that *is* in the earth beneath, or that *is* in the water under earth."[1] This law forms part of the first of the Ten Commandments that God, through Moses, bestowed upon the people of Israel after their exodus from Egypt. The Swiss author Max Frisch picks up on the commandment: "God tells us: Thou shalt not make unto thee any graven image. It no doubt also applies to the following: God as the living entity in every person, that which is not tangible. It is a sin that we commit, and is committed against us, almost incessantly–apart from when we love."[2]

The soul, the living being of a person, is not detectable. It is an unfathomable secret that is constantly transforming and perceived differently by all people. Thus it should not be held onto, as the commandment states. A fixed idea of the nature of a person does not do justice to the complexity of his constant changes. The same applies to the body in which the nature of a person is revealed and reflected. It only expresses the transforming spiritual nature in a highly inaccurate way and differently for all observers. And yet we constantly fall into the trap of believing that the essence of a person can be grasped through their external appearance, of which we make a firmly fixed image for ourselves. The fact that the spiritual essence and physical being of a person, with its constant changes, cannot be completely grasped or captured in a precise concept means all the more that depictions such as paintings or photographs are unable even to come close to that person's complexity. They are always individually characterized, simplifying interpretations and thereby ultimately distortions. At best, they only provide a rudimentary reflection of the entire person (Fig. 1).

1 *King James Bible,* Exodus 20:4.

2 Max Frisch, *Tagebuch 1946–1949*, Zurich, 1986, p. 27–32 [trans.].

1

2

1   People like to portray
a specific image of
themselves. Ludwig Mies
van der Rohe, 1956

2   Mobile phones
obscure one's own view,
drawing by Peter Gut,
2020

A "storm of images" with an inverse omen

Like people, the complexity of material reality cannot be completely grasped through a two-dimensional representation. Nevertheless, a storm of images is raging through today's world. It suggests that substantial reality can be validly represented in its materiality through the images of it that we produce. However, the picture and the depicted are never identical, as Ingrid Scheurmann shows.[3]

Many people no longer look closely at a location, do not remember its particular qualities and instead view it (so to speak) on the display of a mobile phone or camera. With its search for an effect, the photo usurps the act of seeing in the sense of inner experience, as the sociologist Siegfried Kracauer already recognized in 1927.[4] Today, photography has become a fetish. Photos are often more than mere personal memory aids. Instead, they become evidence addressed to other people: only events that have been photographed are confirmed. The representation can become more important than the event itself (Fig. 2).

It is significant that the people taking a photo somehow appear in the image themselves, since they unconsciously make numerous decisions and position the object in a specific way in the picture, thereby interpreting it. The time the photo was taken and the position of the photograph, as well as the framing and perspective, tell us much about the author. The image editing goes one important step further through the conscious influencing of perception. The right illumination can highlight elements, while others are made to disappear in the shadow. Further changes to the depicted reality using image editing are usual in photography, and completely normal in painting.

Places and buildings

Although not identical to people, buildings have remarkable parallels, since they have their own personality and a specific nature. Their intellectual and physical unity forms their own "double nature" (Georg Dehio), which is the starting point of this essay. Their nature can only be grasped if the historical fabric is investigated and other sources are called upon to approach it, in the awareness of temporality and the provisional nature of insight.

Our perception of important historical buildings and places is shaped by two-dimensional depictions, drawings, paintings, and photographs that are published over and over again in large numbers. These representations express what should be communicated: Cleverly chosen details and the skillful use of focus present a building embedded in a dense neighborhood as a freestanding building; overall proportions are changed and a particular camera position stresses specific elements (Fig. 3). Means of scene-setting are used consciously in the buildings of today's star architects on their behalf and

3 Ingrid Scheurmann, "Braucht das Bild Substanz? Stadtbild- und Denkmalpflege", in: *Konturen und Konjunkturen der Denkmalpflege. Zum Umgang mit baulichen Relikten der Vergangenheit*, Cologne, Weimar, Vienna, 2018, p. 378–392, p. 387.

4 Siegfried Kracauer, "Die Photographie", in: Inka Mülder-Bach (ed.), *Siegfried Kracauer Schriften*, 1927–1931, Vol. 2, Berlin, 1990, p. 83–98.

with exclusive rights. Anticipatory depictions of buildings, be they drawings or perspectives used to present or advertise a project, often manipulate reality to an especially pronounced extent (Fig. 4). Today's common presentation method of "rendering" sometimes differs substantially from the future reality and has a strongly seductive potential. Views of existing and planned buildings are interpretations by the image author rather than reliable witnesses.

Two-dimensional depiction is unable to capture the quintessential aspects of historical buildings, since crucial information cannot be communicated. The image cannot even come close to capturing a building. It is unable to reflect the period of its construction, nor the social, economic, and technical conditions that existed at the time, nor the cultural and financial means of the builder, the qualification of the architect, the skill of the building personnel and companies involved, the available materials–all these conditions that the building reflects are hidden. These circumstances and contributing factors condense into a unity with different contours and nuances for every observer. Furthermore, the perception of a building is not solely characterized by a visual impression, but also significantly influenced by the spatial impression, specific acoustic qualities, the tactile properties of the materials and their finish, as well as the building's specific odor. The character and nature of a building can be intuitively perceived and described, yet they are only objectively appreciable to a very limited extent.

Today's form of historical building is also characterized by the time passed since its construction. It is the result of a long series of interventions carried out during its existence. Conversions, extensions, adaptations to new practices, and renovation measures: They all form part of the work and its history. These interventions are overlayed with the traces of ageing, all the small changes that, in their entirety, influence a building for better or for worse. The traces that time has inscribed upon the building are key factors in shaping

3

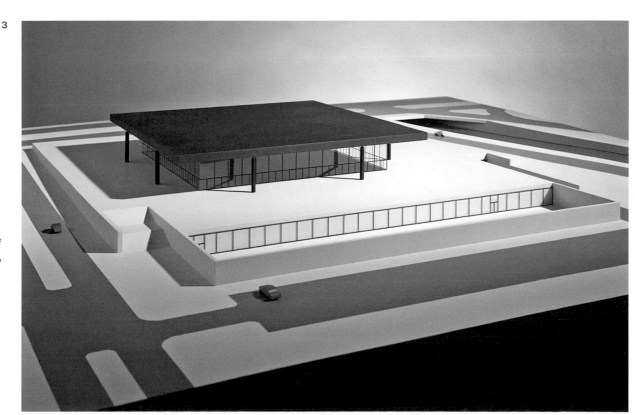

3 Architectural model of the Neue Nationalgalerie, 1963

4

its appearance; they reveal its historicity and are inseparable parts of the building. In the awareness of their individual approach, attentive visitors synthesize all these observations into an overall impression, an inner image, knowing well that in doing so, the nature of a building can only be approximated.

Thus, the historical building is much more than the above-described image, the outward appearance perceived by people. The edifice's material contains extensive recorded information on the construction process, later changes, and the influences of use. For today's and future research, the historical fabric forms the most important basis for insight and improving knowledge of the building. It is supplemented by written sources and images. While these can sometimes be unreliable, the material witnesses of the building are infallible. For instance, research on Regensburg Cathedral is based on a systematic study carried out over decades, examining the actually existent historical fabric. Only if the latter is retained can building research derive new insight, allowing future experts to check and supplement today's results.

The external appearance and, all the more, any images of it only express the essential aspects of a building as a rough approximation. For any building or place, the historical fabric is essential to become a witness of the period of its construction and the time now past. The interpretations that go with it are always individually shaped and perpetually transforming.

4 Ludwig Mies van der Rohe, design for the Neue Nationalgalerie Berlin, interior, collage, 1963

5 Bertolt Brecht, *Stories of Mr. Keuner,* Martin Chalmers (ed., trans.), San Francisco, 2001, p. 27.

6 Georg Dehio, "Denkmalschutz und Denkmalpflege im neunzehnten Jahrhundert (1905)", in: Norbert Huse (ed.): *Denkmalpflege – Deutsche Texte aus drei Jahrhunderten,* Munich, 1984, p. 139–145, p. 139ff. [trans.].

7 UNESCO, Liste du patrimoine mondial. Centre historique de Varsovie, valeur universelle exceptionnelle, brève synthèse, Critère (vi), URL: http://whc.unesco.org/fr/list/30 (accessed on August 17, 2020). In addition to the described causes of the destruction, one key aspect is the fact that, with the exception of a number of monumental buildings, the authors regarded the rebuilding work not as a reconstruction, but as a new creation inspired by the former buildings, carried out by the directly affected survivors immediately after the end of the war.

8 Walter Benjamin, "Das Kunstwerk im Zeitalter seiner technischen Reproduzierbarkeit" (first German version, 1935), in: Rolf Tiedemann and Hermann Schweppenhäuser (eds.), *Gesammelte Schriften, Vol. 1, Werkausgabe Vol. 2,* Frankfurt am Main, 1980, p. 431–469.

Nostalgic images

In his *Stories of Mr. Keuner,* Bertolt Brecht describes how we create an image of people and try to adapt them to that image: "'What do you do,' Mr. K. was asked, 'if you love someone?' 'I make a sketch of the person,' said Mr. K., 'and make sure that one comes to resemble the other.' 'Which? The sketch?' 'No,' said Mr. K., 'the person.'"[5]

The process described by Brecht can also be seen in buildings and places that have undergone a construction measure. Often, during restoration or renovation work, a monument is adapted according to the ideas of those who have an influence on the measures, the idea of the client, the architect, or the general public. The term "Bilddenkmalpflege" ("monument image preservation"), which has been in use for some time, contains this search for the harmonious and coherent. "Flaws" that upset this image should be eliminated. The monument is thereby not only subjected to more or less subtle changes, but also receives a new significance. For instance in Budapest's Buda Castle, installations from the socialist period, some of which are of architectural value and all of which are historically significant, shall be destroyed and replaced by reconstructions of earlier conditions, while the dome, which was "wrongly" reconstructed after the war, is to be replaced (Fig. 5).

The reconstruction of a building or a place is similar to the production of a three-dimensional image; in a way, it is an architectural model at a 1:1 scale. Regardless how good the documents are on which it is based, it will always remain a new creation—Georg Dehio speaks of an "impressive life-size illustration [...] according to the archaeological knowledge of the time," finding that it lacks the "rich polyphony" of the historical references.[6] A reconstruction therefore reveals much about the current period of construction and little on the period of the missing historical building. The three-dimensional image of a reconstruction is not the monument. This is also clear in the often-cited example of Warsaw old town, which was not included in the World Cultural Heritage list as a town that had developed between the 13th and 20th centuries, but as "a unique example of the almost complete reconstruction of a town that had previously been entirely destroyed" (Fig. 6).[7] Reconstruction measures carried out today are the mere fulfillment of a nostalgic yearning for the restoration of a world that is regarded as safe and sound. Furthermore, it expresses a deep mistrust towards the ability of contemporary architecture to adequately fill existing gaps.

The image of a reconstruction, its overall appearance, may on the whole resemble its lost predecessor. However, it has no "aura," a quality that Walter Benjamin regarded as essential for each work of art and which he sees in its remoteness, authenticity, and uniqueness.[8]

Fabric and appearance

When a monument is preserved and restored, it is always necessary to intervene in the delicate structure of the historical fabric. Furthermore, major changes may be unavoidable. Occasionally, the question arises whether priority should be given to the surviving materiality of the monument, including its changes, or to its image, its best possibly perceived architectural appearance. In the case of the Villa Tugendhat by Ludwig Mies van der Rohe in Brno, Czechia, such considerations lead to a situation where not only carefully preserved, but also reconstructed building elements exist side by side; on location, it is not easy to distinguish between the two approaches (Fig. 7).

When handling a building or one of its elements, the question whether the fabric, the historical materiality or the appearance, the image, should be prioritized, cannot be answered with simple recipes or outlined on the basis of general rules. It depends on the concrete case, the direction in which the work is heading. However, the preservation of the surviving elements, using the smallest possible measures, should always be the goal, and not their replacement. Respect for the surviving fabric preserves the original evidence stored within it and allows the greatest possible scope of approaches for future considerations and measures. For instance the sheet-metal covers over the flying buttresses of Bern Minster change its appearance, but protect the building's fabric (Fig. 8). In any case, such decisions should not be made by individuals according to their inclinations. Instead, they should much rather be examined and decided upon through group discourse. Stances in the debate and reasons for decisions should be documented.

5

6

7

8

9 Sigfried Giedion, *Raum, Zeit, Architektur. Die Entstehung einer neuen Tradition*, Ravensburg, 1965, p. 370 [trans.].

10 → Lohan, p. 30–39.

5 Budapest, Buda Castle, north-wing reception area, 1950s

6 Newly constructed town houses in Warsaw's old town, inspired by the destroyed buildings

7 Adjacent original and reconstructed building elements, Villa Tugendhat, Brno

8 Sheet-metal covers over the flying buttresses of Bern Minster

Ludwig Mies van der Rohe: Gallery of the 20th Century, Berlin, 1963

In 1949, the Berlin Senate founded the "Gallery of the 20th Century" in West Berlin. In 1962, the contract for the new building to accommodate the growing collections was directly awarded to the 76-year-old Mies van der Rohe. Mies emigrated to the USA in 1939 and ran an architectural office there until his death in 1969. His buildings constructed in the States have a reduced formal and structural language that is oriented toward a major figurative effect within the context of the city or the landscape. The architect's efforts to shape the perception of his buildings in a given situation through memorable, clear volumes are not limited to the overall form or the individual spaces. His attempts to achieve the perfect image go far beyond that, reaching into the smallest details. Sigfried Giedion describes how, "in the studio of Mies van der Rohe in April 1964, [he saw] on a drawing board the square modular grid of his Berlin gallery to a scale of 1:5 and on it, standing three-dimensionally, one of the supports with its cruciform cross-section."[9] Profile cross-sections and structural nodes are decisive for a building's appearance; the office of Mies van der Rohe produced many such models to a 1:1 scale.

Mies van der Rohe's concept for Berlin is based on ideas he had developed for an administrative building intended for the company Bacardi in Santiago de Cuba, which was never constructed.[10] The defining element is the support-free area, a "universal space," beneath a roof borne by eight columns, which projects broadly over the corners, above a base clad in granite slabs. This "podium temple" picks up on the basic form of the museum temple on Berlin's Museum Island. The project and its implementation are entirely aligned towards figurative quality: The memorable appearance of the roof that seems to hover over the striking base, as well as the surrounding glass walls, was more important than the function–the all-round glazing is ill-suited to exhibiting paintings, while the connection between the hall and the basement areas makes separate presentations difficult. Exhibition curators had their work cut out in the building.

The image was more important than functional aspects, not just for the architect, but also for the client. Firstly, Berlin and the Federal Republic sought a symbol with which to express a cosmopolitan, new state system. On the Kulturforum, it strived to visually demonstrate the superior Modern architecture of the West, both to its own population and to the citizens of the GDR on the other side of the nearby border. The building also had to show how West Germany commemorated those who had been driven out of the country by National Socialism, honoring them by giving them the opportunity to construct important buildings. The new building's iconographic quality is a "wanted monument" in the sense described by Alois Riegl[11]–and it has remained an icon of 20th-century architecture to this day.

According to many people and a number of architecture books, this iconic quality is reduced to the memorable appearance of a podium, a glass hall, and a hovering roof. The existence of the diverse spaces built in the basement is often overlooked in critical reception, thereby failing to take notice of the building's dual nature. These are relatively conventional areas for receiving visitors, exhibitions, administration, and depots, as well as the outdoor space of the sculpture garden. Nevertheless, they are also integral elements of the monument. A comprehensive grasp of Mies's architectural language is only possible if both spaces, the upper and the lower, are read together (Fig. 9).

The Neue Nationalgalerie: Restoration of an icon, 2015–2021

In 2009, the restoration of the Neues Museum in Berlin by David Chipperfield Architects demonstrated in exemplary fashion how the original fabric of a monument can be almost completely retained, preserved, and carefully restored despite the demanding requirements, to present an image both inside and outdoors that does without any reconstruction and refuses to satisfy the central European yearning for perfection. In 2012, with reference to that achievement and with the same goals, the architects won the "Procurement procedure for freelance services" to restore the Neue Nationalgalerie.

This goal, which the architects set themselves, could only be achieved to a greatly limited extent, since the required depth of measures was far greater than expected. During preliminary planning, after careful analysis of the building and extensive research in the surviving archive documents, it became apparent that in-situ repair and restoration was impossible. The building had to be peeled down: Almost the entire, largely intact interior fit-out and granite cladding were dismantled, stored and reassembled in their original positions. The measure was necessary because the materials on which the interior fit-out had been applied had to be replaced for technical reasons: If the floor-heating on the hall level breaks down, the floor slabs must be lifted, requiring the prior removal of the wooden structures standing on the floor. If the concrete beneath the intact granite cladding of the sculpture garden crumbles, the slabs must also be lifted for extensive repair

11 Alois Riegl, *Der moderne Denkmalkultus. Sein Wesen und seine Entstehung*, Vienna, Leipzig, 1903, p. 39.

work. To restore the reinforced-concrete shell structure or renew the building technology, the flooring in the basement and the visible elements such as wall plaster and ceiling cladding must be removed. Most of these were newly produced, raising the question of the significant materials of the time, woodchip-wallpaper and woolen carpets. The metal constructions of the roof and facades remained structurally untouched. Only the stairs and the marble cladding on the three sides of both supply shafts were retained in the exhibition hall.

Dismantling building elements always involves additional damage. This was minimized in the Neue Nationalgalerie thanks to the great caution and care with which the measures were carried out. It was important to clearly locate the large number of elements, which were restored, adapted to new requirements, and refreshed (Fig. 4, p. 273). Following the re-assembly work, each piece has now been returned to its original position.

The same architects applied the same goals to the Neues Museum, the "skin of the building" and the interior surfaces retaining all the scars of the past–making history tangible. By contrast, the Neue Nationalgalerie feels like a new building and conceals the major measures applied beneath its surface. Following its restoration, the visible surfaces seem homogenous or are entirely new elements. The passage through history is only legible to insiders.

A key reason for this difference lies in the fundamental transformation of building methods that has taken place in the past hundred years. 19th-century buildings were constructed with considerable reserves. Only a few building materials and methods, which had been known for centuries, were applied. Hardly any technical equipment was installed. Thus the buildings react "benevolently" to subsequent measures.

By contrast, post-war buildings have been optimized to the limit and have only few reserves. New materials, which often contained substances that are now known to be toxic, were used in construction. The buildings' formal perfection reacts sensitively to the smallest changes. For a long time, there was a widespread nonchalance towards structural physics, such as aspects of thermal engineering. The complex technical installations, for which replacement parts have long since become unavailable, are subject to rapid wear, while often no longer conforming to today's technical standards.

Despite this fundamental difference between 19th-century buildings and post-war edifices, the preservation principles to be applied remain identical and unchanged. Approaches and considerations on measures remain the same. The described differences can lead to different solutions in individual cases. Dismantling and re-assembling building elements, under certain circumstances even their replacement, may prove to be unavoidable, not least to ensure the monument's original use. The restoration of the Neue Nationalgalerie had the aim of continuing to fulfill the building's original purpose despite the enormous increase in functional requirements. It is remarkable that the operative unit has been preserved and the administration remains in its original rooms; even the depots have not been outsourced, instead receiving a new space in the now extended basement. The building security to operate a museum today and the technical installations required measures going far beyond usual restoration work, including extensive renewal.

12 → Reichert, "Spatial Reorganization", p. 131–139.

Following the restoration, which has been implemented with profound insight, extreme care, and enormous effort, the only visible measures on the exterior of the Neue Nationalgalerie involve the new ramp for people with limited mobility. Inside the building, only the "carefully and self-confidently" (David Chipperfield) inserted basement spaces for the cloakrooms and the museum shop in the former art depots are evident.[12] The image fits: After careful repair work on damage and thorough cleaning, the granite and marble slabs have been returned to their original location. The now restored fixed furniture is in perfect condition. Inconsistencies due to long-term use have been eliminated. Lights and smaller technical elements have been preserved. The thin, outer shell remains, while many of the load-bearing materials and the once advanced technical equipment behind it have been replaced. Traces of age and incipient patina can hardly be seen.

Thus upon reopening in 2021, the external appearance and the publicly accessible areas of the Neue Nationalgalerie remain almost identical to the original building at the time of its opening in 1968. Since then, a considerable portion of the building fabric has been removed or replaced, the age of the monument is hardly noticeable or recognizable in areas open to the public. Is that what causes the slight unease that the meticulously implemented restoration leaves us with?

9

9 View of the Neue
Nationalgalerie from the
garden, 1968

Gunny Harboe

Restoring Mies

Experiences from the
Illinois Institute of Technology

Ludwig Mies van der Rohe was one of the most influential architects of the 20th century. While he had achieved fame for his revolutionary modern design of the Barcelona Pavilion of 1929, and teaching at the Bauhaus, the Nazi regime made it difficult for him to find work in Germany. He was lured to the United States in 1938 with the offer to become the director of the architecture school at the Armour Institute of Technology (AIT) in Chicago, a city that also offered the potential for him to express his architectural theories through designing buildings.

A major opportunity arose soon after he arrived at AIT, which became the Illinois Institute of Technology (IIT) in 1940. Not only was he to head the architecture school, but he was also given the assignment to design the new, expanded campus being planned on Chicago's south side. He created numerous schemes for a six-block area that was eventually expanded to be more than twice that size. He also went on to design over twenty buildings that were realized between 1943 and 1958 when he left the school. They ranged from a simple windowless brick box for electrical switchgear to the expansive and glorious steel and glass masterwork, S.R. Crown Hall (Crown Hall) (Fig. 1). Throughout, the design vocabulary and material palette for most of the buildings was the same; exposed steel framing painted black, steel or aluminum windows, and buff brick masonry (Fig. 2). The entire campus was laid out on a 24" × 24" (61 × 61 cm) grid that unified the whole.

Mies retired as head of the school of architecture in 1958 and also lost his role as campus architect. It was a great disappointment for him not to have realized the two major buildings he had spent much time planning, the main library, and the student union building. The role of campus architect was given to the firm of Skidmore Owings and Merrill (SOM), where many former students of Mies worked. This meant that the rest of Mies's campus was completed by SOM but in a manner sympathetic to the Miesian principles already in place.

1

Construction on the campus slowed over the 1960s and ended altogether by the end of the decade. It would be another 30 years until anything new was constructed. In the meantime, the Mies campus suffered from deferred maintenance. This situation was not unique to IIT, as many universities see themselves in the business of education, sometimes to the exclusion of caring for their buildings. The campus also suffered from the social ills of the surrounding neighborhoods that were rife with poverty, gangs, drugs, and crime. IIT leadership seriously considered moving the school to the suburbs, where it had another campus. However in 1996, an extremely generous gift of $120 million was pledged by Robert and Jay Pritzker and Robert W. Galvin to reinvest in the school. While this money was not directly intended for restoring the Mies buildings, it was clear there was a new attitude towards the campus.

The reevaluation of the future of IIT resulted in several positive actions, putting the campus on a trajectory towards renewal that began in the mid-1990s and continues to this day. A master plan for the urban campus was created by Dirk Lohan, Mies's grandson, who had attended IIT and became a prominent architect in his own right. It identified the need for renovating many of the key Mies buildings as well as locating where new construction could be accommodated.

In 1996, Donna Robertson was appointed Dean of the College of Architecture and brought grand plans that included the "greening" of Crown Hall, which remained the heart and soul of the school. The movement for sustainability in architecture was in its nascent stage, and Dean Robertson was keen to incorporate these principles in the school's curriculum and the proposed building renovations.

1 Ludwig Mies van der Rohe, Crown Hall, Chicago

Crown Hall had been renovated in the 1970s by SOM. All the original polished plate glass was replaced, and the steel repainted. The large upper lights remained clear glass but the lower sandblasted glass was replaced with laminated glass that had a translucent interlayer. While it emulated the diffuse light of the original, its inside surface was very reflective, and the overall effect was just not the same.

By the late 1990s, the building's deferred maintenance problems had become acute. There was paint failure and surface corrosion inside and out. Some lights of glass had cracked due to the expansion of the steel elements and the travertine paving of the south porch was crumbling and hazardous. Something had to be done.

Dean Robertson started with a small project, the renovation of the south porch. The firm of Fujikawa Johnson was hired to oversee the work. The author, having completed a Historic Structure Report documenting the history and existing conditions of Crown Hall in 2000, was hired as the preservation consultant. Deterioration of the steel structure supporting the porch was so advanced that the entire porch had to be rebuilt. There ensued a serious discussion about switching the paving material from travertine to granite. Joe Fujikawa, who had studied under Mies and worked for him until his death in 1969, was adamant that the material should be changed to granite. The author, and others, were strongly opposed to such a change. While Mies had certainly used granite on many projects, he also loved travertine. He employed it at Farnsworth House, 860–880 Lake Shore Drive Apartments, the three apartment buildings on the east side of the campus, and Crown Hall. It would have been a big mistake to change it. The issue was resolved by the fact that Crown Hall had become a City of Chicago Landmark in 1997 and a National Historic Landmark in 2001 and changing the materials was simply unacceptable.

2

3

The university recognized the special need for raising money for the restoration of Mies's buildings on the campus, so in 2002 it created a separate fundraising and advocacy entity called The Mies Society. The first three projects identified were Wishnick Hall, Crown Hall, and Robert F. Carr Memorial Chapel of St. Savior (Carr Chapel), with the renovation of Wishnick Hall the first to be undertaken. Originally built as the main chemistry building, it was to be updated with new "state of the art" teaching labs. Holabird & Root were hired as the architects and the author was hired as a consultant to IIT for the preservation issues.

The two most challenging tasks were addressing the deterioration of the large original aluminum double-hung windows and retaining the interior layout of the open main lobby and stairways (Fig. 3). The windows were in reasonable condition, but the steel sills that they sat on were extremely corroded. The original drip edge detail on the sill had not extended out far enough and water seeped back into the gap between the steel window still and the structural "T" that was embedded in the masonry kneewall. This corroded the plug welds used to tie it all together, and the expansion of the corroded steel had deformed the sills beyond repair. To fix the problem, the aluminum windows had to be removed. Although a restoration treatment was explored, it proved to be extremely expensive and did not solve the problem of thermal bridging and poor energy performance. The solution was a replacement window made with custom extrusions that matched the original sightlines exactly. While not the most ideal solution from a purely conservation standpoint, it balanced the need for a cost-effective solution with minimal visual impact on the facade. The design problem in the lobby required meeting the new fire code which did not allow for open stairways of more than two stories. A creative solution was found that created code-compliant enclosures at the basement level and the second floor that was not visible from the main lobby.

The restoration of Crown Hall was the next project to be funded. Krueck & Sexton were selected as the architects with the author serving as preservation architect. Dean Robertson wanted the project to demonstrate as many sustainable practices as possible. A full building renovation was planned to include restoring the exterior curtain wall and upgrading all new building systems but unfortunately, only enough funding was found for the exterior restoration. As simple as that project was in concept, it was very difficult to execute.

The biggest challenge was restoring the glazing. The steel was all in need of new paint. Mies had used his preferred Detroit graphite paint which was an industrial-grade coating. It had a high lead content level which is no longer legal and so a new industrial coating by Tnemec was selected. The paint system required complete removal of the original paint down to "white metal" to achieve the best result, and therefore all the existing glazing needed to be removed. Current building codes required that the glass thickness of the large lights be increased, and the detailing of the glazing stops changed to accommodate a larger "bite" to hold the glass in place. This meant that the stops had to increase from 5/8" (1.6 cm) to 3/4" (1.9 cm). Multiple configurations were investigated and the least visually intrusive appeared to be a stop that maintained 5/8" at the outer edge and sloped up to 3/4" at the glass. There was significant concern by some on the team that the introduction of an angle, no matter how small, was a sacrilege on a Mies building. Several options were mocked up at full scale and it was clear that the angled stop was almost imperceptible and was thus selected.

The glass itself was also an issue. At the very beginning, there was a desire by some to use an insulated glass unit to improve the performance of the skin, which is almost all glass. Unfortunately, doing so would have completely changed the original delicate steel details. The question remained if there was something that might be done with the translucent glass. Dozens of different options were investigated to see if a coated or laminated option could be found that would look like the original sandblasted glass, yet have better thermal performance. Six options were mocked up at full scale in situ and in the end, it was clear that the original sandblasted glass was the only real choice. It had the added benefit of performing better thermally in some ways than the laminated options (Figs. 4, 5). With only 15 weeks to complete the project over the summer break, the construction schedule was also a challenge. While there were a few minor bumps along the way, the project was completed on time and was well received by all.

Carr Chapel, affectionately known by the students as the "God Box", was the third project funded through the Mies Society (Fig. 6). Carr Chapel is the only religious structure completed by Mies and although it was intended to be a very modest structure, he took the assignment very seriously. Mies said of it: "Too often we think about architecture in terms of the spectacular. There is nothing spectacular about this chapel; it was not meant to be spectacular. It was meant to be simple; and, in fact, it is simple. But in its simplicity it is not primitive, but noble, and in its smallness it is great, in fact, monumental. I would not have built the chapel differently if I had had a million dollars to do it." His statement clearly illustrates his attitude to his work. Simple, direct, yet monumental. It embodies the concept of "less is more" so often attributed to his work.

Like so many other buildings on the campus, Carr Chapel had not been maintained. The steel windows were corroding, the interior wood doors and paneling were stained and delaminated, and the brick masonry revealed numerous problems. Worst of all, the roof detailing had been changed and was unsightly, and not functioning properly. The available funding was limited so the restoration was undertaken in phases, beginning with the roof and exterior masonry. The roof termination was the most difficult as the original detail intended for only the outside face of a large steel channel to be visible. This did not allow for proper termination of the roof membrane at the perimeter nor any insulation. This was further exacerbated by the fact that there is only a single roof drain. The solution was to add a steel angle set back from the edge and continuously welded to the original outward-facing channel. This allowed for proper flashing and several inches of insulation with minimal visual impact. Steel windows were restored and reglazed with

4 Restored glazing,
Crown Hall

5 Facade detail,
Crown Hall after
its restoration

the clear glass on the east and sandblasted glass on the west as Mies had intended. A slight alteration was required to allow for wheelchair access through the front door by raising the grade of the sidewalk 15 cm to the level of the three large granite pavers. The interior restoration was deferred for several years but included the careful restoration of all wooden elements, cleaning of all masonry walls and concrete ceiling surfaces, and the creation of an accessible bathroom (Fig. 7). It also allowed for the removal of the large enclosure that housed the pipe organ that was installed well after the building was completed. It had blocked all the beautiful west light Mies had intended to bathe the surfaces of the plain brick sidewalls which can now be fully appreciated. Many other smaller projects have been carried out on the campus but there is still much more to do. Fundraising for restoration projects has continued, with the full restoration and renovation of Alumni Memorial Hall intended to be the next in line.

6 Ludwig Mies van der Rohe, Carr Chapel, Chicago

7 Restored interior, Carr Chapel

6

7

Gerrit Wegener

The construction history of the Neue Nationalgalerie since 1968

Ludwig Mies van der Rohe envisaged the Neue Nationalgalerie both as a prestigious exhibition building and as "a center for the enjoyment [...] of art."[1] He designed a building with attributes that he described as clarity and stringency.[2] Contrary to its apparent simplicity, the aim was to bring together the complexity of function and production into a coherent design expression. Structurally implementing that goal proved to be a great challenge, both in terms of its utilization and with respect to technical building maintenance. Nevertheless, after his first visit to the building, Walter Gropius telegraphed Mies to express how impressed he was, "both in the head and in the heart."[3] Adding to or amending existing structures runs the inherent risk of undermining that clarity and stringency. However, during its almost 50 years of use as a museum, the building was constantly forced to adapt to changing demands in terms of restoration, security technology, museum education, and curatorial requirements.

From 2009 to 2010, a comprehensive heritage-preservation examination was carried out on the building to investigate those changes and the elements of the building that had survived from the time of its construction. This investigation was further consolidated during the building measures. The responses to the presented challenges concerning the building's maintenance and its use are described in detail below with respect to the ashlar stone, the black steel structures and the glazing for the exhibition hall.

1 Ludwig Mies van der Rohe, "A Museum For a Small City", in: Architectural Forum, Vol. 78, Issue 5, 1943, p. 84f.

2 Cf. Ludwig Mies van der Rohe, Galerie des 20. Jahrhunderts, design presentation portfolio (1963), Kunstbibliothek, Staatliche Museen zu Berlin, Sheet 1.

3 Telegram to Ludwig Mies van der Rohe dated September 13, 1968, signed "Your Walter and Ilse Gropius", [trans.] in: Manuscript Division, Library of Congress, Washington, D.C., MSS32847, GENERAL OFFICE FILE, 1923–1969, n. d., Container 30, Walter Gropius 1959–1969.

4 Cf. *2. Nachtrag zur Haushaltsunterlage-Bau vom 13.11.1981 für die Teilsanierung der Neuen Nationalgalerie der Stiftung Preußischer Kulturbesitz, 3. Ausfertigung*, Landesarchiv Berlin, 21.03.1983, Sign. B Rep. 014 No. 316.

5 Heinz Oeter and H. Sontag, "Das Stahldach der Neuen Nationalgalerie in Berlin", in: *Der Stahlbau*, Vol. 37, Issue. 4, 1968, p. 106–115 [trans.].

6 Ludwig Mies van der Rohe, cit.: Franz Schulze, *Mies van der Rohe. Leben und Werk*, Berlin, 1986, p. 316 [trans.].

Ashlar stone

The surfaces of the podium and its balustrade slabs consist of Striegau granite. In the early 1980s, comprehensive sealing and insulation work required these ashlar stone slabs to be dismantled and relaid. Despite the uniform stone material, the surfaces had varying structures, so that adhesions, discoloration, and traces of use also affected them. While examining the existing condition, it was impossible to ascertain which slabs were from the time of the original construction and which had been added later. A comparison between the documents and historical photographs revealed that the stone surfaces had already varied at the time of the original construction. Despite the different surfaces, the ashlar stone creates a clear overall impression.

Metal framework

Initial inspection showed that the steel structure had been retrospectively treated and remounted several times to prevent possible corrosion. At first, archives appeared to document the complete loss of the original mountings.[4] The steel structure must fulfill a wide range of demands with respect to material technology and construction. During the implementation planning, the architect stipulated that these had to be adhered to with the "utmost diligence" in order to achieve a clear appearance.[5] In this context, it is all the more surprising that the initially feared loss of original material proved unfounded. Many of the original mountings still existed, above all in the interior of the hall structure. Restoration findings and investigations also showed that the uniformity of the black paint on all steel parts, as planned at the time of the museum's construction, was only achieved by adjusting varying compositions of binders and pigments to the respective stresses.

Glazing

In addition to the steel structure, the hall's oversized glazing is a key aspect of the building concept. Mies van der Rohe believed the hall posed "considerable difficulties for exhibiting art," which however, he was unable to take into account in view of its equally "great potential."[6] Further challenges arose from the dimensions of the glass panes, with widths of up to 3.56 meters. Directly after the building was opened, the first damaged panes needed to be replaced. While such panes were initially available, the worldwide change in glass production methods meant maximum pane-widths of 3.20 meters, requiring new solutions. From then on, the hall's glazing consisted of two individual panes that were connected by a central silicon joint. At the start of refurbishing measures, only six of the hall's total of 56 panes still existed without divisions. Their individual

areas also revealed diverse color nuances. While this initially led to speculation whether the architect had intended such coloration, the tender-offer documentation proved that simple crystal plate glass had been stipulated and produced by a French manufacturer.[7] Technical testing of the existing material confirmed these findings.

Going beyond the three above-mentioned fields, renovation, addition, and adaptation measures had been carried out on the existing structure, generally in an additive or reversible process. The Neue Nationalgalerie is now preserved with a considerable amount of integrated original materials. Through its clarity and stringency, the building itself should serve as a backdrop to the defined demands of being used as a "center for the enjoyment of art." Nevertheless, the building remains a "great piece of architecture"[8] today and an exemplar of Mies van der Rohe's architectural stance.

7   Cf. Specifications: "Ausführung der Verglasungsarbeiten nach DIN 18361 für das Gebäude für repräsentative Kunstausstellungen, Berlin 30, Potsdamer Straße", published in: *Amtsblatt für Berlin*, Vol. 15, No. 18, 30.04.1965.

8   Cf. Werner Haftmann, "Nationalgalerie 1967–1974. Ein Rückblick", in: *Jahrbuch Preußischer Kulturbesitz XII*, Berlin, 1974/75, p. 33–53, here p. 36 [trans.].

1   Ludwig Mies van der Rohe designed the font for the Neue Nationalgalerie

Joachim Jäger

Museum operations

From Mondrian to Kraftwerk

Over the past five decades, the way museums are operated around the world has fundamentally changed. The history of the Neue Nationalgalerie's use also reflects that process. Analyzing it provides an important basis for planning the museum's refurbishment. This section presents a series of highly contrasting ways in which the building has been used, from its beginnings as a museum during the 1960s to exceptional events that have become a key feature of the Neue Nationalgalerie's history.

For instance in January 2015, a series of eight performances by the cult band Kraftwerk preceded the Neue Nationalgalerie's temporary closure to the public. The concerts, which were sold out within minutes, were two things at once: a celebration of radical musical aesthetics and also a homage to the architecture of Ludwig Mies van der Rohe. The Modern, serially conceived architecture provided the perfect location for the cool, technical sound of Kraftwerk. At the same time, the concerts referred to the special role of the Neue Nationalgalerie during the 1970s and 1980s. At the time, the museum was not only the most important art and exhibition venue in the walled-in West Berlin, but was also often used as a popular location for performances, theater events, and avant-garde concerts.

Naturally, the Neue Nationalgalerie has always mainly been an art museum and its spaces have been used for precisely that purpose since its opening in 1968, the way Mies had planned and designed it: the expansive basement outlined by a bright ceiling mainly presented the institution's collection. The principal artworks of the 20th century were exhibited there, joined for a long time by 19th-century pieces, such as paintings by Caspar David Friedrich and Adolph Menzel. The exhibition hall, which Mies described as a "stage," was rarely used to exhibit artworks from the collection, but was instead dedicated to temporary projects. Werner Haftmann, the museum's first Director, excelled with spectacular early exhibitions, presenting pieces by Matta (1970) and Mark Rothko (1971) on hovering walls, as well as free and, at the time, audacious contemporary installations by artists such as Bernhard Luginbühl (1972).

Beautiful photos of those early years still exist, capturing the flourishing artistic development, while also documenting how differently the museum world was still organized. For instance, one photo from the opening year reveals a view into the hall during the now famous Mondrian exhibition. In the foreground, visitors sit on Barcelona chairs in a strict geometrical arrangement (Fig. 1). The museum presents itself as a refined place of contemplation, characterized by an inherent coolness and stringency. It is no coincidence that Mies derived this furnishing concept from prestigious lobbies in American high-rise buildings. Thus, even in the Neue Nationalgalerie's early exhibitions, there was an almost grotesque opposition between Mies's notion of a museum, based on respect and distance, and the new stance of the still very young artists who attempted to break down as many boundaries between life and art as possible (Fig. 2). As a result, the strict seating groups were soon removed and the chairs arranged in a loose sequence along the windows, their backrests facing outwards.

Another photo is similarly telling in its portrayal of the staircase lobby in the basement, including a square ticket counter with a purist design that suits the minimalist overall aesthetics. Apart from tickets, it also sold catalogs and postcards (Fig. 3). A small showcase in the counter was apparently sufficient to present the publications on the building and collection. From today's perspective, such a counter would no longer be feasible since it leads to large gatherings of people on several sides. It seems that such large numbers of visitors were simply not expected at the time, while also revealing a much quieter and more elitist concept of an art museum.

Looking back on the entire period of the Neue Nationalgalerie's operation, it was above all German reunification that caused far-reaching changes. The museum became part of the extremely active tourism in the new capital city. The crowds flocking to the heavily advertised exhibitions, which not only took place in the hall, but also often in the basement, were so considerable that the museum's logistics could hardly cope. The small wooden cloakrooms in the hall had to be supplemented by temporary coat racks installed in front of the stairs leading down to the basement. Later, the situation was alleviated by converting exhibition areas into sufficient cloakroom space—a further drastic measure (Fig. 6, p. 95). There had already been experiments with gastronomic services in major 1980s exhibitions, for instance requiring chairs and tables to be set up in the foyer. There were also repeated attempts to extend the relatively small cafe in the basement into the exterior space. From 1983, the Bücherbogen bookstore took over the sale of museum merchandise in its foyer. In 1994, this led to the installation of a massive cube, which was elegantly made of glass, but nevertheless rather large (Fig. 5, p. 95).

1

2

3

1   Opening exhibition
at the Neue National-
galerie with works by Piet
Mondrian, 1968

2   Solo exhibition by
Bernhard Luginbühl, 1972

3   Ticket booth and sales
counter in the staircase
hall, designed by Ludwig
Mies van der Rohe

Work behind the scenes experienced especially radical change, reflecting all the social transformation from 1968 to the present day. Naturally, when the museum opened, all office life was completely analogue, using typewriters. Today's curatorial, preservation, and organizational work–to mention just three key aspects of museum operations–is hardly comparable with the working processes of the 1970s. A further historical photograph is helpful in this respect, showing Werner Haftmann during a meeting in his Director's office (Fig. 4). From today's perspective, not only the old-fashioned devices and utensils are striking, but also and especially the fact that the meeting was held while sitting on a lounge-like ensemble, consisting of Barcelona chairs and a table. Dieter Honisch, the museum's second Director, soon replaced this Director's "lounge" with a large meeting table.

Another completely outdated aspect from today's perspective is the way the museum's entire logistics section was organized. Every delivered artwork first had to be transported through narrow corridors, past all the offices, to the restoration department, where it was inspected and then forwarded to the collection rooms or the depot. There were neither rooms for transport packaging nor for preparing exhibitions. As the collection steadily grew, space in the depots became limited, making it impossible to ensure the artworks' professional, secure storage at all times. In individual cases, large-scale works even had to be stored in administrative auxiliary rooms. Furthermore, loaned works were sometimes examined in the museum corridors. The storage rooms for materials, furniture, pedestals, and all kinds of exhibition equipment were completely unsuitable and cramped. The museum's overloaded condition climaxed in grotesque developments such as a laundry room, which had been installed in the basement in the 1970s and 1980s, being used to wash the towels and other materials for the entire Kulturforum.

4

4 Werner Haftmann (left)
in conversation in
the Director's office, 1974

By the 1990s, the sculpture garden could only be visited "at one's own risk." The gradually rising stone slabs, which were being pushed up by the roots of the surrounding trees, created so many stumbling blocks that the garden, which is so important for the building's overall effect, had to be closed to the public around 2000. The final years before the museum's closure were characterized by mounting building-technology failures and damage to the architecture, all of which were caused by the museum's great success. Major projects such as "The 20th Century–A Century of Art in Germany" (1999/2000), "The MoMA in Berlin" (2004), and "Gerhard Richter. Panorama" (2012) had attracted millions of museum visitors over the years. The walls, the wooden elements, the carpet, and generally the surfaces of the public spaces were extremely worn, almost damaged. The refined leather covers of the Mies furniture had long become cracked and over-used. Many pieces of furniture, both in the administration and in the exhibition spaces, were no longer in use and were stacked in auxiliary rooms for the heating system. The air, above all in the basement, smelt stale towards the end, as the air conditioning system no longer managed to pump enough fresh air everywhere. In 2010, when the fire safety officers' inspection found that additional measures were required to ensure the building's safety, the Foundation was advised to close the museum in late 2014 on grounds of security. Indeed the museum did close at the end of 2014 with a final major exhibition of the collection in the basement, as well as a highly allusive installation by David Chipperfield (Fig. 1, p. 88), followed by the above-mentioned symbolic final act: the Kraftwerk concerts in January 2015.

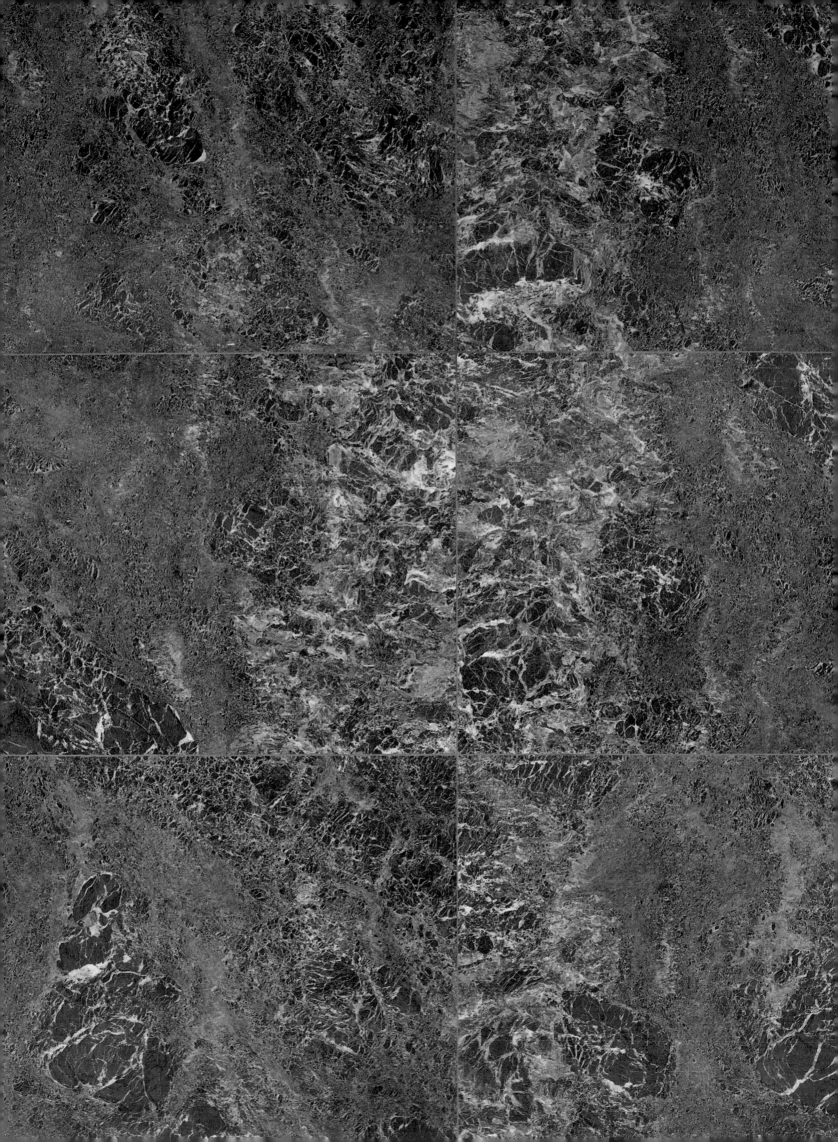

FUNDAMENTALS

Annett Miethke

Guiding principles
on the general overhaul
of an icon

The motto "As much Mies as possible" emerged as the result of many individual steps prior to the general overhaul: archive research, an examination of the existing structures, the production of an architectural datasheet for preservation purposes, design planning, the selection of the architectural office, and the insight gained at the colloquium "FORM VERSUS FUNCTION: MIES AND THE MUSEUM."

Presumably, everyone involved in the Neue Nationalgalerie project recalls their own especially vivid and personal memories. No doubt the occasions vary considerably. After three decades, I still remember one event very clearly: my first day as a Trainee at the Federal Building Authority, the predecessor of today's Federal Office for Building and Regional Planning (BBR). On that day, Barbara Jakubeit was officially inaugurated at the Neue Nationalgalerie as the first female President of the Federal Building Authority. The building provided the perfect location and backdrop, giving the event a clear, calm, dignified, and open atmosphere.

Regardless of the occasion, whether private or official, each subsequent visit to the building has always inspired me with the sense of the architecture's perfect atmosphere–be it at the grand presentation of the collection of the New York Museum of Modern Art (MoMA, 2004), the exhibitions "The Klee Universe" (2008), "Rudolf Stingel LIVE" (2010) or "Gerhard Richter. Panorama" (2012), the colloquium on the general overhaul of the Neue Nationalgalerie "FORM VERSUS FUNCTION: MIES AND THE MUSEUM" (2014), the concert by Kraftwerk (2015), project discussions, or many other opportunities. There

1

was always the impression of experiencing a space that had been specifically produced for that very event, as can only be achieved by a universal architectural concept that is open to future developments (Fig. 1).

Circumspect approach

But how does one renovate an icon without endangering the nearly 50 years of impressions that uphold it and can also be seen in the traces of its use? The answer is: with care and respect. And how does one prevent that respect from having a paralyzing effect? By systematically appropriating the details and diving into history. Looking back, if one asks how we derived an exemplary approach to heritage renovation from the task of producing an architectural datasheet, using it to record detailed spatial information on all building elements, the answer is: The driving impetus was the building's structural condition after almost half a century of intensive use, without sufficient pauses for extensive maintenance work.

In 2008, shortly after the 40th anniversary of the Neue Nationalgalerie, the Staatliche Museen zu Berlin announced that it should be fundamentally renovated in view of its structural condition and the future demands of a contemporary museum. It was proposed to examine and assess the existing structures from a heritage-preservation perspective and record the results in a digital datasheet.

It is not possible to renovate a museum ad hoc. Exhibition programs are often planned years in advance. The small matter of funding also had to be clarified. Despite the obvious

1 Installation by
Rudolf Stingel in the
exhibition hall, 2010

ongoing deterioration in the building's fabric, patience was required, also in waiting for a contemporary museum technology. Finally in March 2009, the Stiftung Preußischer Kulturbesitz gave the BBR the go ahead to begin recording the building data from a structural and heritage perspective. From the professional perspective of construction, the aim was to create an underlying basis for planning a general overhaul, even though it would be carried out some time in the future. Thus, the need for a careful, respectful and systematic approach was clear from very early on.

Perfect team

One stroke of luck for the BBR and above all for the project as a whole was the choice of Arne Maibohm as the Project Manager. He was able to contribute the ideal competences for the task: having graduated at the Bauhaus-Universität Weimar, the architect had practical experience and good networks, including professional stints in the USA, and was at the time a freshly certified assessor. He remains passionate about this project to this day. His initial step, the so-called Stage Zero of the stocktaking process, was to gather a team from the fields of heritage preservation and engineering. Then the diligent work began: detailed recording of the building's condition, researching documents from the period of its construction and seeking out people involved at the time. A very special planning consultant was found for the project in Dirk Lohan, the grandson of Mies and the original Project Manager.

Nationalgalerie
Staatliche Museen zu Berlin

FORM VERSUS FUNCTION
MIES UND DAS MUSEUM

27.
28. Nov.
2014

2

2 Invitation to the symposium "FORM VERSUS FUNCTION: MIES AND THE MUSEUM" at the Neue Nationalgalerie, 2014

In 2011, following the results of heritage-preservation and structural assessment, the BBR was instructed to plan the renovation measures for the Neue Nationalgalerie. The architectural office was selected in an EU-wide process, focusing on experience in handling heritage renovation measures. Ultimately, instead of requiring a grand design, which could not be improved upon in any case, the project needed a sensitive approach to an icon of Modernity. David Chipperfield Architects won the selection process and were contracted with the task in 2012. Further competitions in the fields of project management, expert planning, testing engineering, expertise, and consulting followed the assignment.

The team consisting of representatives from architecture, expert planning, the BBR, and the Staatliche Museen also considered experience and results from renovation projects on other Mies buildings. The research work took them on study trips to the USA and also to the Villa Tugendhat in Brno, Czechia.

The building as the starting point

At the beginning of planning for the renovation design, the project's guiding principle of retaining as much Mies as possible had not yet been specifically formulated. It required an extended learning process, involving a growing willingness to compromise for the sake of the icon. The motto was only adopted by everyone involved following deeper engagement with heritage preservation aspects and the demands of operating a contemporary museum. All participants agreed on the aim of preserving the atmosphere of the building. From that moment onward, each detailed planning decision was assessed according to the principle of "As much Mies as possible." The struggle to find the best solutions was also the subject of an international colloquium on the general overhaul in November 2014 (Fig. 2).

The same year, the first funds were approved for the relocation of artworks and furniture, as well as for external employee workplaces in preparation for the actual overhaul. Design plans were also completed. In 2015, these were approved and funding was provided for the general overhaul–seven years after it had first been announced that the building needed refurbishment. The subsequent implementation planning, initial EU-wide tender invitations, and contract awards ran parallel to the building's clearance, allowing the first dismantling measures to begin in mid-2016.

Joachim Jäger

The existing building's limits

A preliminary assessment
of requirements

The Neue Nationalgalerie's management had been aware of the need to refurbish the museum since the late 1990s. In 2010, fire-safety officials carried out an inspection and only authorized the building's public use (under specific conditions) until the end of 2014. The same year, initial user requirements were assessed for the building's potential general overhaul.

The user requirements developed in 2010 represent the first assessment of the existing situation, even before an architectural office was contracted or preliminary plans were conceived. The text printed here was continuously updated in the subsequent process together with David Chipperfield Architects, the Federal Office for Building and Regional Planning, the Construction Planning Office of the Staatliche Museen zu Berlin, and in cooperation with the Berlin Monument Authority.

Profile

1 "Sticks and Stones", exhibition by David Chipperfield, 2014

Today, the Neue Nationalgalerie is completely dedicated to international 20th-century art. The focus lies on the collection, only parts of which can be presented to the public at once due to the lack of space. It is joined by special exhibition projects in the hall, offering new perspectives on art and art history: they can be contemporary projects, but also thematic or monograph exhibitions. The architecture of Ludwig Mies van der Rohe is often a theme of its own; artists are regularly invited to present architecturally-related projects specifically for and in the Neue Nationalgalerie.

Basement exhibitions

Permanently installed exhibition architecture with fixed spatial sequences, hanging heights and lighting situations, as planned by Mies for the basement, is no longer in keeping with the times. Each collection presentation and each exhibition has its own appearance, logic, and design. Thus, each change or new presentation involves extensive modifications to the underlying architecture: New walls are erected and existing ones are changed. Showcases are installed and pedestals are set up in the rooms for standing sculptures. Wall colors and wall conditions are amended, while specific lighting situations are created. Descriptions and other texts are applied to the walls and much more. Above all from a technical perspective, the exhibition architecture in the Neue Nationalgalerie was quickly pushed to the limit:

- Air conditioning system: flexible adaptation to installations and conversions in the exhibition spaces
- Security: production of a capacitive-sensing artwork security system on the walls beneath the plaster
- Wall conditions: robust underlying condition suitable for frequent drilling, partially dismountable
- Lighting: additional, flexible illumination system, including highlighting and lighting controls for brightness and alignment, while maintaining even basic lighting for the large walls
- Ceiling suspension points: arranged in a grid with as yet undefined dimensions, for suspending artworks or video projectors
- Electrical supply sockets: on all wall sections for electrically operated artworks; data interfaces for media presentations must still be checked

Exhibitions in the hall

Special exhibitions in the hall have always been a challenge (Fig. 1). Mies originally developed his exhibition system with freely suspended walls, but it was only used for the very first exhibitions. Since the 1970s, the curators and artists tested numerous forms of presentation. Today, the clear, 50 × 50 meter space is one of the world's most in-demand exhibition venues. Every exhibition there has a high cultural-political status. Accordingly, each exhibition should look different from its predecessors, usually requiring material and technical investment with the following underlying conditions:

- Air conditioning system: flexible adaptation to installations and conversions
- Ceiling load-suspension capacity: increased load-suspension capacities and more suspension points on the ceiling for contemporary, high-quality, diverse exhibition designs
- Access: larger entrance routes into the building and walkways inside the building
- Lighting: additional, flexible, and highlighting illumination system including control of brightness and alignment

Other exhibition locations

The staircase hall in the basement was already used to present artworks when the museum was opened. To this day, the space can be regarded both as a foyer and as an exhibition area: The large wall surfaces are regularly used to hang paintings. The expansive open space in the hall is also an ideal location for sculptures. These functions require capacitive-sensing security systems for wall presentations.

The terrace is an ideal location to present sculptures. When the museum opened, sculptures by Henry Moore and Alexander Calder marked the exterior grounds. However, the terrace cannot support heavy loads on the granite slabs, making it difficult to use the space for presentations, nor can the works be secured.

The sculpture garden was inspired by a similar concept at the Museum of Modern Art in New York and represents a unique exhibition space. However, it has been impossible to use it for a long time, since it is inaccessible from the basement due to security concerns and because such access would affect the indoor air quality. In future, access should be restored to this area, taking the heritage value of the building and aspects of air conditioning into account.

2

3

4

2 Painting depot before
refurbishment, 2010

3 Showcases stored at
the heating center due to
a lack of storage space,
2010

4 Access ramp without
a separate entrance
for people, 2010

Underlying preservation conditions

For exhibitions presenting loaned artworks, the Neue Nationalgalerie must fundamentally adhere to international agreements that generally define binding climate and Lux values. Thus the standard international climate of 21 degrees Celsius (+/- 1 degree) and 50 percent relative humidity (+/- 5 percent) applies. For paper artworks, a flexible, individually adjustable lighting system with low illumination levels (generally 50 Lux) must be available.

The building's air conditioning system is unsatisfactory in many ways. Extreme conditions (due to adverse weather outdoors or enormous volumes of visitors inside) can hardly be compensated. This is for instance evident in the winter months, when large areas of the glass windows in the exhibition hall are covered in condensation. Constant climate levels with respect to the temperature and humidity must be ensured.

In future, transport routes inside the building must be barrier-free.

Depot situation

The three depots that exist at the museum (two for paintings and one for sculptures) do not provide enough space for the collection and are poorly equipped (Figs. 2, 3). The collection has grown considerably since 1968. It requires around additional 100 square meters for paintings and 50 square meters for sculptures. As elsewhere in the museum, the corridors, and transport routes must also be adapted to have dimensions that accommodate large formats.

Administration

A direct spatial connection, above all for restorers (restoration workshop) and curators to the exhibitions, as envisaged by Mies in the form of an administrative zone on the building basement, is still preferable to minimize logistical requirements. To ensure the contemporary utilization standards that are suitable for the collection and appropriate to a museum of such international standing, it should be discussed whether it is possible to create a preparation zone for exhibitions in the delivery area (Fig. 4).

Visitors

The logistics originally planned by Mies van der Rohe cannot cope with the great volume of visitors today. Problems exist with respect to capacity limits, disabled access, ticket counters, and other service facilities:

- Barrier-free access: The museum has only limited barrier-free access. The incline of the ramp on the south side of the terrace is too steep and the basement can only be accessed by one elevator, which is also the freight lift and can only be used by disabled persons under supervision.
- Museum shop: A large art museum needs appropriate space for selling publications and other items relating to the collection. In 1994, a bookstore was constructed in the staircase hall for this purpose. It was problematic both aesthetically and from the perspective of fire safety (Fig. 5).
- Cloakroom: The space provided by the two wooden cloakrooms in the exhibition halls is much too small. Cloakroom space is required for over 1,000 people visiting the museum. An additional group cloakroom for school classes and other groups is also required (Fig. 6).
- Ticket counter: Generally, the ticketing standards at the Staatliche Museen zu Berlin should be taken into account. Since the two exhibition floors are often used for different purposes and it is possible to visit only one exhibition, it is insufficient to use only the ticket counters in the exhibition hall. The concept must be able to react flexibly to different visitor capacities.
- Internet access: Retrofitted in the Director's offices. WiFi is preferable because it is important for exhibition information and educational projects.
- Cafe: One indoor area was sensibly furbished as a cafe to provide gastronomic services. Such services should continue to be provided, whereby the cafe's dimensions and facilities should be discussed (Fig. 7).

5

6

7

5   Bookstore in
the staircase hall, 2010

6   Temporary conversion
of an exhibition area for
use as a cloakroom, 2010

7   View into the café,
2010

Ralf Nitschke

Mediating between
different user interests

Museum operations
with contrasting demands

The requirements of managing a contemporary museum have changed considerably since the 1960s. This also applies to the Neue Nationalgalerie. It is the task of the Construction Planning Office at the General Directorate of the Staatliche Museen zu Berlin to act as the user's representative, gathering the fundamental demands of the different collections, departments, and sections for a general overhaul or a new construction project.

Different stakeholders at the Staatliche Museen zu Berlin do not always initially have the same demands with respect to a construction project. Thus the Construction Planning Office must coordinate the sometimes divergent interests through internal negotiation, before forwarding them all together to the building administration representing the client, the Stiftung Preußischer Kulturbesitz. In the subsequent planning and construction process, the unit consults with the building administration, architects, expert planners, and public bodies involved, such as heritage preservation authorities, to ensure the ideal conditions for the exhibits, the general public, and the employees, if necessary negotiating compromises between the different interests.

The project "General Overhaul of the Neue Nationalgalerie" is the first of its kind, since it has attempted to assess the damaging effects of the interior materials used on a large scale in combination with the air quality of the respective spaces. The aim was to guarantee perfect conditions for artworks and thereby fulfill the museum's preservation task, as well as minimizing possible damage risks, without limiting the choice of materials too

1 New ticket counter in the basement, 2021

much. The Oddy Test is a long-established method for testing showcases, but it sets very narrow limits and is only partially applicable to the building sector. Certification for building materials, such as the Blue Angel, indicates how environmentally friendly and sustainable they are, as well as focusing on their potential risk to human health. In the case of the Neue Nationalgalerie, all participants found themselves in uncharted territory following an instruction by the Construction Planning Office to test material compatibility, including the examination of carpets, wall paints and curtains, to assess their potential damage risks. Since there is hardly any relevant past experience to draw on, the BEMMA assessment process[1] served as the basis, while taking air exchange rates in the exhibition spaces into account. Since no binding threshold values have yet been defined in this field, alternative materials were compared and samples with the lowest damage risk were selected.

In addition to buildings, the Construction Planning Office's main focus lies on the general public and employees, especially people with disabilities. Thus, barrier-freedom and inclusion are key elements of user requirements for the Staatliche Museen zu Berlin. It is the office's task to ensure that these demands are fully taken into account during the planning and building process. This could lead to situations where special requirements, for example wheelchair-accessible and lowered counters at the ticket office (Fig. 1) and cloakroom, would need the originally conceived high, closed cubes to be redesigned.

One underlying condition of successful project implementation, to which the Construction Planning Office can contribute, is good communication between all participants. This not only applies to the Neue Nationalgalerie, which will reopen in the summer of 2021 and thereby return a major international public attraction to the Kulturforum. The office will also contribute to the planned extension to the Neue Nationalgalerie, dedicated to 20th-century art, which will be situated on the large, central open space along Potsdamer Strasse and will complete an area that had been left unfinished for decades. The Kulturforum will then join the Museum Island as the second important location of the Stiftung Preußischer Kulturbesitz and the Staatliche Museen zu Berlin in the heart of the capital.

1   A process to assess emissions from materials for museum equipment (Bewertung von Emissionen aus Materialien für Museumsausstattungen, BEMMA).

Uwe Heuer

Climate requirements

Ideal conditions
to protect the collection

**One of the core tasks of museums is to preserve objects in their collections. That includes protecting them from damaging environmental influences. The Neue Nationalgalerie's air-conditioning system is aimed at ensuring such preservation and shielding the objects from influences that could change their condition.
But it can also affect how comfortable people feel in the building.**

Each piece of art reacts differently to changes in its environment. These reactions can lead to artworks being damaged or destroyed. Some environmental factors have a direct influence on their condition, for instance temperature, air humidity, drafts, light, vibrations, contaminants, and dust.

During World War II, museums were able to gather experience with different storage conditions as they protected their pieces from air raids, by storing part of their collections in mine shafts. It quickly became apparent that the climatic conditions there, with stable temperatures, but almost 100 percent relative humidity, damaged the stored objects. Makeshift heating solutions in the mine shafts helped to reduce the humidity to levels around 50 percent, thereby minimizing the spread of damage to the objects.

In the 1960s, the first museum buildings were equipped with air conditioning, including the Neue Nationalgalerie. Systems technology made it possible to maintain an almost constant climate in the collection rooms. But an air-conditioning system alone is not enough to create a "museum climate." One decisive factor in the room climate is the regulating technology, which measures the actual air in the room, compares it to the required levels and, if necessary, adjusts the systems technology to the necessary temperature and humidity.

Generally, when it comes to finding the ideal conditions for art collections, higher temperatures accelerate the biological and chemical processes of aging and decay. It has been discovered that frequent temperature jumps are detrimental to objects consisting of more than one material, such as oil paintings on wooden panels. The changes lead to internal tensions since the warmth cannot spread evenly through the material. By contrast, slow temperature changes are acceptable to a certain degree, since they have little or no effects on the objects.

It is similar with the humidity, although objects react much more sensitively to such changes. Sustained high humidity can exacerbate chemical transformation processes and also biological growth such as mold. Frequent fluctuations in a short period of time can lead to material tension due to volume changes, or internal tensions similar to those caused by temperature jumps.

The temperature and relative humidity are thermodynamically connected. A change in one factor always results in a change in the other. The stability of temperature and humidity levels in the room's air is therefore very important for museum air conditioning, although the frequency and gradient of the changes are even more relevant.

At the same time, both aims of air conditioning in a museum must be harmonized: preserving the collection and maintaining the comfort of the museum visitors and employees.[1] Temperatures between 18 and 24 degrees Celsius are beneficial for objects and people alike, while a relative humidity between 40 and 60 percent is also experienced as pleasant.

Two aspects had to be taken into account with respect to air conditioning for the collection rooms at the Neue Nationalgalerie: the collection's own exhibits, consisting of different materials, and regular demands arising from loan contracts with other institutions. A relatively narrow corridor was defined, ranging between 19 and 21 degrees Celsius (+/- 1 Kelvin) and 50 percent relative humidity (+/- 5 percent), whereby the target temperature is 19 degrees Celsius in the winter and 21 degrees Celsius in the summer. The regulations also stipulate that the gradient of the temperature and humidity changes per hour may not exceed 0.5 Kelvin and 0.5 percent relative humidity respectively. These narrow margins ensure that international loans can be exhibited all year round at the Neue Nationalgalerie, while also protecting its own collection from damage.

1 → Moammer, "Flow simulations", p. 222–227.

Arne Maibohm

Stage 0

Project development
for the general overhaul of an icon

The early stage of a project project–before the actual planning begins–is one of the key fields, if not the most decisive factor in the success of the overall project. Ideally, it involves the client outlining a clear framework, defining the structure and setting targets, not only with respect to costs and timetables, but also and especially in terms of quality.

1 Planning instruction to the BBR on March 9, 2009.

In the case of the general overhaul of the Neue Nationalgalerie, the early development stage was highly influential for the subsequent planning and implementation process. The goals and guidelines defined at the outset continue to apply at the conclusion of work around twelve years later.

Underlying investigation

In September 2009, the Federal Office for Building and Regional Planning (BBR) faced the tasks of assessing the existing building's condition and producing an architectural datasheet for the Neue Nationalgalerie.[1] Its structure and technical condition were very poor. Together with the building's user, the Staatliche Museen zu Berlin (SMB), the BBR prepared a clear framework for the urgently needed restoration by means of a targeted examination of the existing building. The assessment particularly focused on the deficits and security risks, rather than purely on aspects of monument preservation.

Under the auspices of the BBR, the team of experts from the fields of monument preservation, fire-safety, toxin, and load-bearing planning, structural physics, and surveying, as well as specialists from the fields of technical building equipment, spent nine months to produce a comprehensive report. The Berlin Monument Office and the SMB supervised the report's development. Already at that stage, long before the beginning of planning for the general overhaul, the BBR established contact with Dirk Lohan, the former Project Manager of the Neue Nationalgalerie's original construction and the grandson of Ludwig Mies van der Rohe. Fritz Neumeyer, an architectural theorist and Mies expert, was also brought on board as a consultant in producing the report.

At the start of the examination, each field viewed and sampled the building's fabric on site, while documents on the existing structures were also researched. Over 40 on-site meetings, building-element openings, and samples of materials and paints were carried out without interfering with ongoing museum operations. An important element was also the assessment of its current use, in order to report on deficits at an early stage and thereby create a basis of the subsequent requirement brief.

The technical reports' assessment of the condition was unambiguous, naming findings (Figs. 1–3) that demanded urgent action (excerpt):

- Compromised public safety in the vicinity of the glass facades due to the quality of the glass and deficits in the steel and glass structure
- Danger to the fabric of the steel structure due to corrosion
- Cracks with moisture intrusion in the reinforced concrete structure
- Compromised fire safety and danger to public safety due to high load stresses on the suspended ceilings, among others
- Lack of smoke-extraction systems for inner rooms
- Numerous fire-safety inadequacies, including the deficient or flawed fire-proof production of load-bearing building elements (ventilation center, basement) and insufficient shielding in fire-proof ceilings and walls
- Roof insulation and water drainage partially dysfunctional
- Missing rainwater drainage system and drinking water installation
- Extensive toxic substances, including asbestos, artificial mineral fibers, polychlorides, biphenyls, polychloride aromatic hydrocarbons, phenols, formaldehyde, and lead oxides in or on building elements
- Missing ventilation ducts
- Critical condition of the entire electricity supply, including deficient high- and medium-voltage systems, emergency power generators, and low-voltage switch gears without fire-safety detachment

The technical systems had exceeded twice their lifespan and the construction was in an extremely critical maintenance condition. As a result, the rooms could no longer be used without endangering the people inside them. There was also a risk of losing valuable building fabric and damage to objects. While the technical report was extremely critical,

1

2

3

1 Condition of the steel
and glass structure
after dismantling the
retaining rails,
2010

2 Damage to the granite
terrace floor, 2010

3 Aquiferous cracks
in the reinforced concrete
on the ceiling of the
medium voltage center,
2010

it was diametrically opposed to the monument-preservation assessment. It found an extremely high amount of preserved materials and confirmed that the Neue Nationalgalerie has the highest authenticity level of any building by Mies van der Rohe worldwide. Three-stage, interdisciplinary workshops were held while producing the report. The aim was to examine interdependencies between the different fields. Beside the assessment of the building's condition, which forms the basis of a comprehensive general overhaul, measures were also recommended to prevent the museum from closing immediately. At the same time, experts worked with the Berlin Monument Authority in determining the underlying conditions in a binding plan, thereby defining an initial restoration strategy.

One key element of the assessment in preparation for the general overhaul was document research, initially in the archives in Berlin. In a second step, documents were viewed at the Museum of Modern Art (MoMA) in New York and the Library of Congress in Washington, D.C. The Mies van der Rohe Archive at the MoMA preserves all documents belonging to the former Chicago office. The Library of Congress stores Mies van der Rohe's personal correspondence. The documents in the USA had not been fully recorded and cataloged, so experts did not know the full extent and content of the archive sources before traveling there. After arriving in New York, the three experts were overwhelmed by the quality and especially the huge quantity of the files. For instance, the MoMA stores most of the correspondence on the construction of the Neue Nationalgalerie, as well as working drawings and assembly plans with precise annotation by Mies van der Rohe. Within three days, more than 1,000 photos of all relevant documents had been taken for assessment in Berlin.

The report based on this examination and research concluded that museum operations could only continue until the end of 2014 due to concerns of public and fire safety, even if temporary security measures were carried out. The BBR therefore recommended immediately preparing for a comprehensive general overhaul to prevent a long vacancy period. The restoration aim developed by the BBR, at the time still without a conclusively formulated spatial brief from the SMB, stipulated remaining "within the boundaries of the existing structures" and thereby developing exceptional solutions in an iterative process, which would fulfill the artistic, functional and economic demands of a modern museum standard, while preserving "as much Mies as possible."[2]

2 Draft resolution of the BBR on February 25, 2011 for the planning task of the AG-Bau to establish the EW-Bau for the general overhaul.

3 The AG-Bau is a deci-
sion-making and work-
ing body for building measures within the Stiftung
Preußischer Kulturbe-
sitz (SPK), consisting of
the Ministries of Finance,
Building and Culture,
which are represented in
the Supervisory Founda-
tion Board.

4 → Chipperfield,
p. 116–119.

Team-building

On March 21, 2011, the working group known as AG-Bau[3] assigned the BBR to carry out the general overhaul. At the same time, this triggered the development of a project team. A large part of the team, consisting of the Director of the Neue Nationalgalerie, Joachim Jäger, representing the user, Norbert Heuler from the Berlin Monument Office, Fritz Neumeyer and Dirk Lohan as consultant experts, and myself as the client's representative, were able to continue working on the early stages of the project. In addition to his consulting work, Lohan ensured the necessary planning assurance as a representative of the joint heirs, the family of Mies van der Rohe. The next task was to find the right planners in all fields for this important task. In addition to professional expertise, teamwork skills, and especially an openness to moderation were required, in order to unite all participants in solving conflicting aims with respect to use, monument preservation, and technical requirements.

Normally, an architectural office would be found in an open competition process with a concrete spatial brief. However, the planned restoration demanded working closely on the existing structures, without significant adaptations and without a concluded spatial brief, so the program for a competition did not exist. An office had to be found that placed itself firmly behind Mies, while working as a designer, engineer, and moderator of the planning process, thereby making itself almost invisible, which is no mean feat. The BBR announced that the contract for architectural services would be awarded in a two-stage EU-wide negotiation process. 24 applications were submitted. Following an initial selection stage involving the participation of the Neue Nationalgalerie and consultants, this list was shortened to five qualifying applicants. The BBR carried out two discussions with each of these five offices: one formal interview without a larger committee, and a second discussion with representatives from the SPK, the SMB, the Neue Nationalgalerie, the Berlin Monument Office, the consultants Dirk Lohan and Fritz Neumeyer, and the BBR, with the support of two independent architects as expert advisers. Based on spontaneous designs by the applicants on two specific aspects of the general overhaul, the architects' proposed solutions were discussed to simulate the subsequent planning process. The team from David Chipperfield Architects excelled through its recognition of the key challenges of an "invisible architect",[4] and above all through its open approach to finding a solution. Following consultation and discussion within the committee, the BBR made its decision in March 2012. The joint selection process ensured widespread acceptance. This provided planning security for the subsequent process. The selection of around ten additional offices involved in planning measures, including landscape planning, structural physics consulting, acoustic consulting, and lighting planning, was carried out together with the architectural office. The planning team began its work in mid-2012.

Planning begins

The first stage consisted of research, the transfer of information from the BBR to the planning team and the completion of the already extensive underlying research. One special challenge was the study of the enormous volumes of material, starting with the monument-preservation report on the existing structure and moving on to the archive documents. The MoMA archive and the Library of Congress alone provided over 1,000 data files–these were documents on the existing structure in the form of plans and texts. In total, around 4,900 data files had to be viewed and assessed.[5]

To form a common basis for implementation and communicate already known sources, the BBR made it a priority for the team to come together and develop a joint project idea. Thus, the first months were accompanied by specialist lectures from the fields of architecture and monument preservation with respect to post-war Modernity.[6]

David Chipperfield Architects structured the preliminary planning with workshops involving the user, in order to analyze and organize the building, as well as considering existing and intended uses.[7] At the same time, the planning team further consolidated research based on the already produced technical reports. In late 2012, the functional spatial brief was reorganized in an interim stage of preliminary planning. The project team traveled to the USA with the interim results, in order to view constructed buildings by Mies van der Rohe and integrate the insight gained into the ongoing process of reflection and planning. Above all, the buildings in Chicago and New York display many analogies with the design and use of different materials for the Neue Nationalgalerie. A comparative study of these buildings was crucial for the continuing planning process (Figs. 4, 5). In Chicago, the team presented the preliminary plans to Dirk Lohan and discussed the decisions that had been made until then (Fig. 6). Viewing visits were made to the IIT campus and Farnsworth House together with Gunny Harboe, an architect who had refurbished numerous IIT buildings,[8] and Dirk Lohan. This extensive trip had an immeasurable value for the further planning and shaped the joint underlying understanding of the restoration's aim.

5 → Akay, "Archive research", p. 109–113.

6 See, among others, Christine Hoh-Slodczyk, "Das Haus Schminke in Löbau: ein offenes Haus", in: *erhalten & gestalten*, Vol. 5, Augsburg, undated, p. 8–9; Britta Bommert, "Direktiven für die Direktion. Das unterschätzte Untergeschoss der Neuen Nationalgalerie von Ludwig Mies van der Rohe", in: Astrid Lang, Julian Jachmann (eds.), *Aufmaß und Diskurs*, Berlin, 2013, p. 278–294; Carsten Krohn, *Mies van der Rohe. Das gebaute Werk*, Basel, 2014.

7 → Reichert, "Spatial reorganization", p. 131–139.

8 → Harboe, p. 66–73.

4

5

6

4 At the Federal
Center by Mies van der
Rohe in Chicago, 2012

5 Steel stairs at the
Arts Club by Mies van der
Rohe, Chicago, 1948–1951

6 Exchanging ideas
with Dirk Lohan on
a project trip to the IIT
Campus in Chicago, 2012

Dirk Lohan frequently visited Berlin to accompany the progress until the design plans had been completed in mid-2014. Regular workshops and events were held to provide space for the exchange of ideas and allow the discussions required to make specific decisions. For instance in June 2013, the planning team visited Tugendhat House in Brno, Czechia (Fig. 7), which had just been refurbished. Before the museum was closed to the public at the end of 2014, an expert colloquium was held at the Neue Nationalgalerie, where the project team presented its plans to the public.[9]

On January 7, 2015, the SPK and the BBR held a joint press conference to announce the successful approval of budget funds for the measure. Following the concerts by the band Kraftwerk in the exhibition hall, the stage was set for the building measures to begin in spring 2015.

9 Lectures at the expert colloquium held by David Chipperfield, Dirk Lohan, Joachim Jäger and Martin Reichert can be viewed on the YouTube channel of the Staatliche Museen zu Berlin: https://www.youtube.com/smb (accessed on January 15, 2021).

7

7 Project trip to Villa Tugendhat in Brno, 2013, left to right: Arne Maibohm, Alexander Schwarz, Martin Reichert, Dirk Lohan

Marianne Akay

Archive research

The foundation of
refurbishment measures

Comprehensive archive research was an important precondition of preparing and planning the general overhaul of the Neue Nationalgalerie, while conforming to heritage preservation demands. The almost completely preserved original project-related documentation produced in Chicago by the architectural office of Ludwig Mies van der Rohe, as well as construction plans by the implementing companies, paint a detailed picture of the Berlin museum's building and planning history.

1 Büro für Architektur, Denkmalpflege und Bauforschung Ewerien und Obermann: *Bestandserfassung des Hauses Neue Nationalgalerie*, Berlin, 2011.

2 Museum of Modern Art: *The Mies van der Rohe Archive*, New York, 1968.

3 Franz Schulze, George E. Danforth (eds.), *New National Gallery, Martin Luther King Jr. Memorial Library, and Other Buildings and Projects*, Garland Architectura, Vol. 19, New York, London, 1993.

During a heritage-preservation survey[1] contracted by the Federal Office for Building and Regional Planning, the archives and archive documents were initially examined on a superficial level for preliminary expert assessment. Based on this, the aim of in-depth archive research by David Chipperfield Architects was the systematic, comprehensive evaluation of documents in all known archives, to gain insight into the existing material structures of the Neue Nationalgalerie, understand the process leading to its construction, and perceive it in the context of architectural history. The insight gained enabled an assessment of the existing structures and the identification of changes due to intensive use, building maintenance, and the operations of a transforming art and exhibition institution. A detailed record of the facility's inventory and condition was produced according to building elements and museum sections.

During archive research, the documents found in *The Mies van der Rohe Archive*[2] at the Museum of Modern Art in New York provided crucial information. Not only the 116 cataloged and published original plans from the construction period were of interest.[3]

The 383 previously unstudied loose sheets known as the "Blueprints",[4] as well as 610 written documents containing the correspondence between the office in Chicago and the builders involved in Berlin,[5] were read, sorted chronologically, and recorded in finding aids, including key words and analysis. Filtering by theme provided insight on planning procedures and the content with respect to individual trades. It confirmed Ludwig Mies van der Rohe's final word in design decisions, verified the planning stages, and conveyed an impression of the planning and construction conditions at the time. A comparison with the archived documents in Berlin[6] and the Library of Congress, Washington D.C.[7] revealed many unique documents, especially the construction plans and correspondence. The documents also confirmed the planners, builders, and users involved. Individual on-site witnesses from the period of construction were able to reflect on the results of the analysis, explain findings, and make the construction period come alive. The Berlin archives mainly contained image material that visually supplemented the correspondence and planning documents. Only few post-war monuments of Modernity have such a detailed archival record. This is largely due to the fortunate circumstance that the office archive was handed over immediately after the death of Mies van der Rohe. By contrast, the documents stored by the Stiftung Preußischer Kulturbesitz and the Berlin Senate are almost entirely lost.

The batch of architectural plans to build the Neue Nationalgalerie contains a total of only 43 items (A-Batch II 1965–1968). The architect's planning was not oriented by the standard planning stages used in Germany and was instead implemented according to the American system, as Dirk Lohan, the Project Manager at the time, has stated. This is reflected in the architectural plans on the project in the American and German archives. The Schematic Design from 1962 to 1963 comprised studies and concepts for the museum, as well as a presentation portfolio. In the Design Development of 1964, A-Batch I (A2–A21) was labeled "Preliminary." In the Contract Administration from 1965 onward, the entire project was recorded in A-Batch II (A1–A43), providing a binding foundation for all further measures (Fig. 1).

Mies's design intention was reflected by the construction plans required by the contracted companies in all trades, before being examined in detail and authorized by the Project Manager, Dirk Lohan. The construction plans for the "Glass facade, upper hall" produced by the company Rieth & Sohn, Stahlfensterbau Berlin on November 22, 1965 to a scale of 1:100 / 1:33 ⅓ / 1:2, show the stamp of the architectural office of Mies van der Rohe, dated February 8, 1966, with "APPROVED AS NOTED" hand-written by Dirk Lohan in red ink, and the additional comment "MUST BE RESUBMITTED FOR FINAL APPROVE" (Fig. 2). Approved plans received an "APPROVED" stamp, while rejected plans were "NOT APPROVED."

4 The "Blueprints" included blueprints, whiteprints, and copies. Kathleen Fluegel (ed.), *Inventory of the Documents of the Mies van der Rohe Archive*, Project 6204, New York, 1978.

5 Correspondence: Job 6204, *The Mies van der Rohe Archive*, Chicago, Berlin, 1962–1973.

6 Berlin archives: Kunstbibliothek, Neue Nationalgalerie and Institut für Museumsforschung of the Staatliche Museen zu Berlin; Federal Office for Building and Regional Planning, Planning Archive, Berlin; Berlin State Archive; Berlin Monument Authority; Berlinische Galerie, Berlin.

7 Private correspondence, Mies van der Rohe 1921–1969.

1 Architectural plan A 18, "Column with details", dated July 20,1965 (Index 0)

2 Construction documentation by Rieth & Sohn, Stahlfensterbau Berlin with inspection notes by the architectural office of Mies van der Rohe, 1966, blueprint, Mies van der Rohe Archive, gift of the architect, Acc. no. MR6204

1

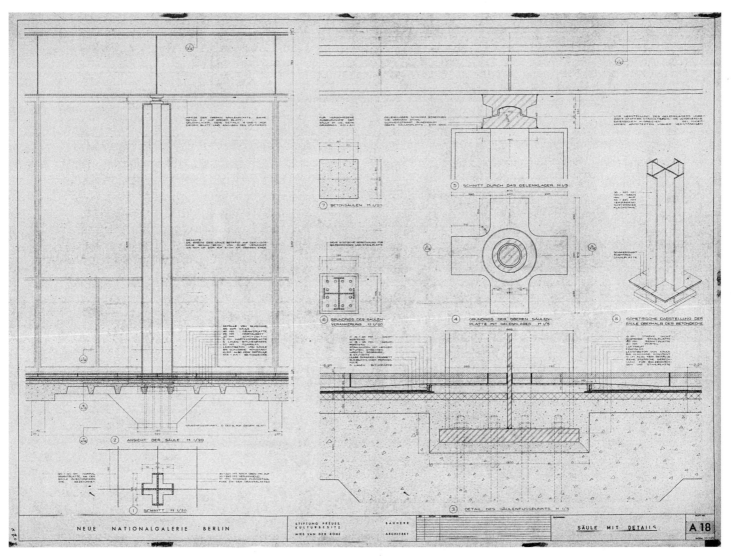

NEUE NATIONALGALERIE BERLIN | STIFTUNG PREUSS. KULTURBESITZ — MIES VAN DER ROHE | BAUHERR — ARCHITEKT | SÄULE MIT DETAILS | A 18

2

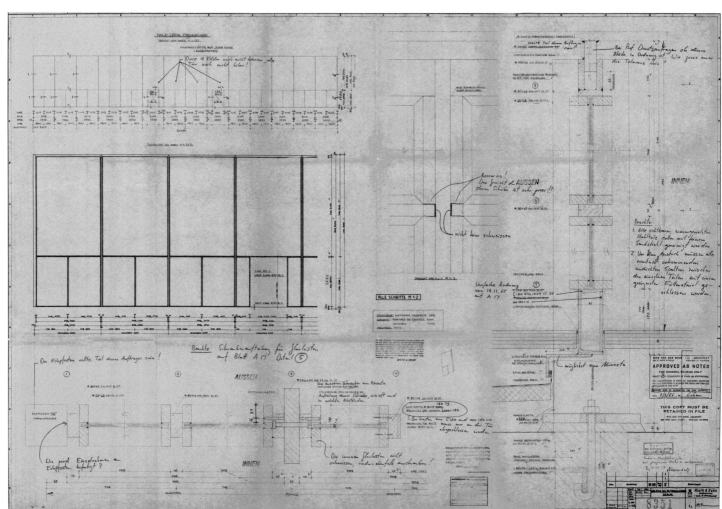

Dirk Lohan traveled regularly to Berlin to attend construction meetings and inspect the progress of building work. In 1965, the Berlin planning team went on a study trip to visit buildings by Mies van der Rohe in the USA, attending an exceptional meeting at the Chicago offices, at which Mies was also present.

The Berlin archives contained photographs and slides of views into the large exhibition space on the collection floor during the construction period and after its completion in 1968, which were compared with sketches and written documents from the *Mies van der Rohe Archive* at the Museum of Modern Art (Figs. 3, 4).

Heinz Oeter, the Project Manager of the steel construction company Krupp-Druckenmüller, photographed the entire process of the roof construction, including the delivery and welding of steel elements at the building site, and the elevation of the completed roof in a "lift-slab" process on April 5, 1967 (Figs. 5, 6).

The research process and visits to buildings by Mies during a study trip to the USA provided detailed insight into all structural elements and background information on the design (Fig. 4, p. 36). Furthermore, they enabled a holistic underlying grasp of the building with respect to its construction at the time, changes caused by its use as a museum, and its importance within the œuvre of Mies. This formed the basis for further planning and decision-making processes with respect to the architectural monument.

3

4

3 Grand exhibition hall during the construction period, 1967

4 A column shortly after the museum's construction, 1968

5 Delivery and storage of a steel column at the building site, 1967

6 The roof shortly before its elevation, 1967

5

6

CONCEPTION

David Chipperfield

"God is in the details"

But what happens
if the details don't work?

The project to repair and restore Ludwig Mies van der Rohe's Neue Nationalgalerie was not initiated by any particular failure or trauma, rather it was decided that it was time to address the gradual and cumulative degradation of 50 years in service.

While the building had been spared of any significant modifications or interventions, it had suffered continuous adaption and was showing the results of age and wear. Most critically, the iconic glass and steel facade was designed without proper consideration of its thermal performance, and from the beginning, this had caused significant problems regarding the running, maintenance and appearance of the building. Many other operational and technical issues had accumulated over time, so it was finally seen necessary to renovate the building. This visionary and innovative building, this monument of modernism, was tired. Tiredness expresses itself on a steel and glass building of the 20th century differently than it records itself on a masonry building of the 18th or 19th centuries. A building that brandishes modernity and technology as its identity has a different tolerance to patina and age. This consideration, as well as the importance of the building in the canon of modern architecture, and its symbolic importance in post-war West-Berlin, informed our approach to this delicate and in some ways unenviable task. After decades of continuous use, the museum was closed in December 2014, and it was emptied of all its contents so the work could begin.

Our approach to the building's restoration was based on a process of research, diagnosis and evaluation of its history, the design and construction ideas and intentions, while also taking into consideration the current state of the building, its operations and materials, and its overall technical performance. Drawing these matters together, we concluded that the refurbishment should accept the traces of aging and repair as long as the aesthetic appearance is not significantly affected, nor the functionality compromised. Over this period of analysis and planning, our considerations were not only informed by extensive research into the documentation available to us in various archives both in the US and Berlin, but also through visiting other buildings by Mies that had undergone restoration. Visits to buildings in New York, Chicago, Houston, and Toronto revealed consistent issues, particularly concerning the building envelope and thermal performance. Considering its status as an architectural masterpiece of the second half of the 20th century, the strictest considerations of heritage restoration had to be adopted despite its relatively young age. The project's planning phase was focused on the building fabric, especially in relation to structural fire safety and protection against corrosion, involving the full replacement of insulation and waterproofing for the building. Of equal priority was the complete replacement of the building service systems. However, in dealing with these aspects, consequential works inevitably extended throughout the building structure and all surfaces. About 35,000 elements and construction parts were removed from the building, restored, and reassembled in executing these actions.

As part of the planning, various operational and organizational problems were addressed too. Most of these issues concerned visitor services such as cloakrooms, the ticket counter and a museum shop. It was also necessary to reconsider some of the back of house areas, particularly for exhibition preparation, workshops and storage. The reason for replanning these functions was the desire to remove the interim cloakroom and the museum shop from the public circulation areas and thereby re-establish Mies's original plan. It was a unique consideration of the project that the clarity of the plan was an artistic achievement in itself, and that any modifications would, of course, be finally experienced physically, but also abstractly through the graphic medium of the plan itself. The beauty and order of the plan was part of our context. Moving functions around allowed us to restore some order to the spaces on the lower level that had been compromised by operational modifications. This required us to extend the lower-level spaces underneath the building's front podium, allowing new locations in previous storage areas for both the new museum shop and cloakroom. In the end, these are the most noticeable interventions to the building.

When it came to the restoration of the actual building fabric, the most explicit and complex element of this process concerned the more exposed and identifiable elements of the building: the elegant and iconic glazing frames and windows that enclosed Mies's temple. Our further work on the building would reveal many more issues and failings, especially in relation to the concrete construction on the lower levels, but it was the failure of the window glazing that was at first the most visible. Soon after its construction, it became clear that Mies's detail for the glazing enclosure–the element that defined the building–was not going to withstand the Berlin climate. Designed using simple rolled, mild steel profiles without any thermal break, Mies reduced the architectural facade to an elegant and minimal composition of steel sections and large plates of glass–a facade reduced to the tensest composition of pure elements. This intense reduction exemplifies Mies's mantra that "God is in the details." The failure of these details was, therefore, the most demanding aspect of the restoration. While the structural steelwork of the building has performed and survived well, the steelwork of the facade itself, subject to extensive condensation due to a lack of thermal isolation, has been continuously rusting and inhibiting necessary expansion in the facade, which resulted in the persistent breaking of the large glass panels and a constant maintenance problem. While we might concede that, in this case, perhaps God is not in the details, we could not avoid the fact that the spirit of the building, and indeed the philosophy and aesthetic vision of the great architect, was indeed in these details. To redesign them would be to undermine not only the design of a window but also the very idea of the building itself.

Beyond repair to the building fabric and technical systems, some of the most complicated reflections involved the restoration of internal surfaces and finishes. The materials and detailing presented many challenges, especially regarding those surfaces that we might call time-bound elements. For instance, the ceilings and the carpet floor for the exhibition rooms in the lower level stimulated discussions regarding aesthetics and taste, given their particular character and what we might even describe as their unfashionable appearance. These particular surfaces raised most intensely the temptation to improve or update materials that would probably not be chosen for a contemporary exhibition space and yet lacked the authority of materials of another epoch. In these cases, the proximity in terms of time gave legitimacy to the possibility of substitution. In both cases, the decision to stay faithful to the original was upheld.

The apparently simple task that we were entrusted with was, of course, something of a poisoned chalice. It is a significant responsibility to repair, protect and restore a building that is regarded as one of the greatest monuments of the Modern Movement, and one of the most important works by the great architect Ludwig Mies van der Rohe. The building needed no interpretation or reconsideration, only to be put back into a good condition seemingly untouched. The building, however, was constructed in a period of limited resources and experience in the isolated half of a divided city recovering from war, a city struggling with its identity. The Neue Nationalgalerie, along with the other great monuments of the Kulturforum by the architect Hans Scharoun, carried the responsibility, beyond those defined by their own functions, to symbolize the vision of rebuilding the city, an unfair burden to be carried by these buildings and one that tested the resources and technology available at the time.

The dismantling of the building over the past years has revealed this struggle in the mismatch between the manner by which it was constructed as an expression of modernism, not only through its radical composition but also through its ambitious embrace of technology. Because of this, our work has involved a realignment of building technology and material with the poetic vision and aspiration that was not reliably possible in the original construction. The depth of this misalignment only revealed its real dimensions as we carefully removed broken and failing surfaces, only to find more failing layers of construction.

Restoration projects depend–rather like archaeological excavations–on a common agreement about the building's significance, and on the common understanding of its cultural worth and its physical qualities. Despite its relative youth, radical form, and complicated history, it is a testament to the architect that this building is held in such high regard, not just by historians and architects, but by the people of Berlin. Although regarded with a certain skepticism when first built, it has become deeply connected to the city, its history, and with the city's sense of itself. Because of this history and its significance, it has been possible to elevate consideration on the restoration of a 1960s modernist building to a level of consideration normally reserved for buildings of other epochs. Only through this common respect could our work be regarded with the importance it has been given. Only with this attitude could the decisions be taken so seriously and the task elevated so rewardingly above the practical and technical, restoring not only its substance but protecting its spirit.

Martin Reichert

Monument preservation and renewal concept

The outstanding importance of the Neue Nationalgalerie, representing the climax and conclusion of late Modernity, and its almost undisturbed material and visual preservation, placed high demands on monument-preservation compatibility of the building measures. The perfection of the "temple of Modernity" affords hardly any leeway and is unforgiving.

The building measures focused on the general overhaul of the structure, including the removal of toxins and achieving contemporary technical and energy-related standards– in so far as this was compatible with the demands of the monument. The client's defined goal, "As much Mies as possible," as well as the building's given limits and potential, left little room to maneuver. Firmly in the spirit of the task, our team at David Chipperfield Architects regarded ourselves as "invisible architects," who planned and implemented the required adaptations and measures in the service of and with a responsibility toward the original designer, Ludwig Mies van der Rohe, thereby refraining from incorporating our own personal preferences.

The general overhaul had the aim of giving the building a new lease of life of around 40 to 50 years, in its original and future function as an art museum and venue for special exhibitions. During that time, appropriate building maintenance should suffice to ensure the building's operations, without making fundamental or structural changes necessary. Often, the desired sustainability of the general overhaul conflicted with efforts to retain as much of the original material structure as possible, while only using minimal measures.

1   View inside the freight elevator, 2016

The starting point for our planning considerations was the actually built structure, having aged and partially changed on its journey through the decades. The approach to the
monument was subject to the familiar questions, criteria, and methods that are generally applied to high-ranking monuments elsewhere. We saw the value of the monument
in the following main aspects:

1 → Akay, "Archive research", p. 109–113.

- The existing material
- The building's original appearance and its visual integrity
- The geometry of the floor plan and elevation,
  as well as the modular system
- Use as a self-sufficient "Museum of the 20th Century" by preserving
  all of its functions and functional areas (continuity of use and location)
- Continuity of the respective uses at the original locations
  within the building
- The "aura" of the building
- The traces of time, especially the "patina" of
  the visible material surfaces
- The unity of the building and equipment (fitted and moveable),
  as well as "artworks bound to the building" (Henry Moore
  and Alexander Calder)
- The unity of the building and exterior grounds,
  as well as its integration into the urban landscape of the Kulturforum

During archive research work lasting over a year, we gathered, viewed, systematized,
indexed, and analyzed thousands of documents.[1] The extremely large volume of diverse,
preserved original sources painted a virtually complete picture of the planning and
building history. The archive documents were saved in a database and supplemented
with a report on the existing structures and the condition of the relevant building elements and sections, pooling the findings in the "Monument Preservation Guideline" in
April 2014. In the following years, this guideline formed a solid basis for our planning
decisions. With respect to the value of the spaces, the project team quickly agreed
on "preservation zones" with a staggered priority of 1 to 3, which were consistently
adhered to in subsequent planning (Figs. 2, 3).

Mies's design for the Neue Nationalgalerie and its structural implementation are defined
by principles and typical characteristics. The underlying motif of the temple hall upon a
podium is "timelessly Modern," as are the exterior appearance's high degree of abstraction, the modular design principle, refraining from an ostensible functionality for the
exhibition hall, as well as the use of natural stone (granite and marble), brown oak, steel,
bronze, and glass. By contrast, the aesthetic expression of the original period can be
seen in the modular suspended ceilings in the basement, the illumination of the spaces
using down lights and wall washers, the warm tone of the artificial light, the design of

2 Heritage preservation
   plans, upper level,
   2014

   Priority 1 heritage
   preservation areas
   Preservation of the spatial
   structure and the spatially
   formative fittings,
   including fixed and
   moveable equipment

   Historical utilization
   forms part of
   the heritage value

   Priority 2 heritage
   preservation areas

   Priority 3 heritage
   preservation areas

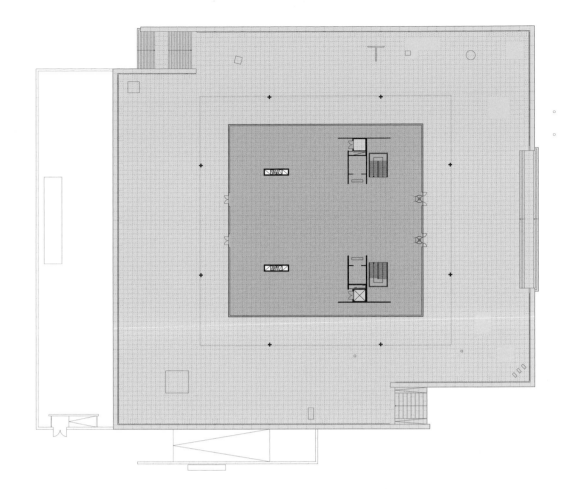

3 Heritage preservation
   plans, lower level,
   2014

   Priority 1 heritage
   preservation areas
   Preservation of the spatial
   structure and the spatially
   formative fittings,
   including fixed and
   moveable equipment

   Historical utilization
   forms part of
   the heritage value

   Priority 2 heritage
   preservation areas

   Priority 3 heritage
   preservation areas

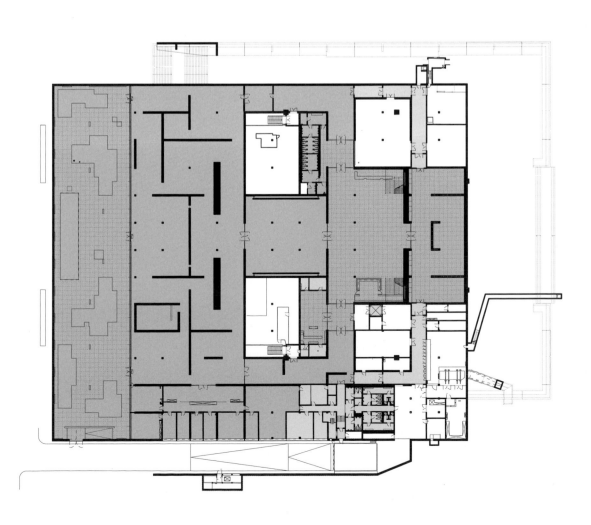

the sanitary rooms, the woodchip wallpaper together with the fitted carpet flooring in the collection rooms, the use of curtains, and the floor-flex tiles in the back-of-house area. We regarded both aspects as equally important, while preserving and replacing them wherever they were missing.[2]

2 → Freytag, Betzold, "Interior finishing", p. 260–265.

3 → Sommer, Fritzsch, "Restoration planning", p. 200–203.

While implementing the general overhaul, we deliberately refrained from visually "refreshing" the monument or reinterpreting it by "updating" colors, materials or details according to our contemporary tastes. It is common practice when handling Modern or post-war Modern buildings to restore them to an "untarnished," original condition. This underlying international stance (a late consequence of Modernity's promise of "eternal youth") contradicts otherwise standard monument-preservation practice. The removal of traces of age "de-historicizes" the monument and alienates it from the time of its construction. We accepted the traces of use and ageing on the natural stone, on the original metal mounts in the interior and on all wooden building elements, repairing damage in accordance with standard restoration methods. Additions that would otherwise stand out were visually integrated through reserved retouching.

Theoretically, the building equipment has an equal status with the rest of the monument. In view of today's demands, there was no chance that we could pursue that aim everywhere. In a building's high-performance use as a museum, its technology is an ephemeral, transient layer that would only have been preservable by turning the building into the museum of a museum and extensively using the technology. However, we did preserve elements of the technical equipment if its continued use was possible with or without technical adaptation (such as the supply-air grilles and lights) or when their preservation was feasible even though they no longer fulfilled their function (wall telephones, security-inspection key-switches, and others) (Fig. 4). The freight elevator and the curtain technology in the exhibition hall were materially preserved as technical heritage, retaining their original function (Fig. 1).

The almost complete renewal of the technical building equipment and the necessity to refurbish virtually all the in-situ cast concrete shell construction required large-scale, far-reaching measures. All wall shafts and flooring ducts had to be opened to dismantle the existing building technology and install the new systems. Likewise, all flooring and suspended ceilings had to be lifted or demolished. The renewal of the insulation for the building envelope required all the granite slabs to be removed on the exterior grounds.[3]

The depth of measures, combined with the removal of toxic substances, resulted in a considerable loss of original building fabric–albeit fortunately in a non-visible area. Following the general overhaul, the "skin," i.e. the original surfaces, and the "bones," i.e. the shell construction, are the most important carriers of material heritage. Large volumes of the "meat" were lost: screed, plaster, wire-plaster ceilings, porous concrete facing formwork, as well as heat and other insulation could only be retained as evidence in preservation zones. Some of the historical building elements, such as sheet steel doors in non-public areas or technical installations, such as control cabinets, could no longer

4

be used as originally intended or had to be moved to a different location. Wherever possible, instead of disposing of them, we kept them despite their lack of function or installed them in a different place.

Despite the necessary optimization and re-qualification to fulfill technical standards, to improve safety standards for people and objects, to enhance the convenience of use, or reduce running expenses, we did not remove all defects or imperfections (from today's perspective) no matter the consequences–for instance at the cost of losing a substantial amount of the building fabric. In some cases, we merely alleviated the situation to a tolerable level, for example the condensation. Such aspects, which are typical for buildings from the construction period, form a significant element of the building's character and are a genuine part of the historical evidence that we wished to preserve as far as possible.

The monument preservation concept and the individual measures were developed and implemented in close collaboration with the Berlin Monument Authority. We particularly wish to thank Norbert Heuler and Prof. Dr. Jörg Haspel, as well as the State Monument Council.

4 Parts of the original
fittings after dismantling,
2016

Daniel Wendler

Planning

General introduction

The planning focus for the general overhaul of the Neue National-galerie consisted of an intensive research on the considerable archive source material and the existing building. The design work involved studying and organizing the document-based findings to derive approaches to solutions and develop concepts that could ideally be implemented directly. The planning methods of this project were consistent with those of comparable restoration measures.

1 → Maibohm, "Stage 0", p. 101–108.

2 → Waninger, "Fire-safety concept", p. 146–149.

As is customary today for complex building measures, the planning process was shaped and accompanied by a large team of specialist planners and other experts. Many approaches to solutions developed in this integrated planning process cannot be ascribed to a single author or discipline, since they were shaped into a concept in a process of countless iterative steps. The planning of the steel and glass facade, for example, was developed in close collaboration between the structural planners, facade planners, and the architect.

Due to the importance of the building measure, the planning process was extensively prepared and very closely accompanied by the Federal Office for Building and Regional Planning, the Neue Nationalgalerie, the Berlin Monument Authority, external experts, and Dirk Lohan, representing the joint heirs of Mies van der Rohe.[1] Most issues could be decided upon unanimously. However, some questions, such as access to the sculpture garden, the fitted carpet in the basement exhibition areas, and the interpretation of the exhibition hall as a gathering space,[2] were controversially discussed. Generally, the ultimate decisions were made in favor of the monument.

1 View of the refurbished exhibition spaces, 2021

The key themes of the general overhaul were the reorganization of use,[3] the comprehensive renovation of the building envelope, the removal of damage to and deficiencies in the building structure,[4] and the renewal of the building technology.[5] Since the approved use as a museum and exhibition building continues to apply and was only partially amended without being fundamentally changed, the measure is defined as modernization according to building law.

Even at the onset of planning work, the reports on the existing structures had made it clear that the depth of measures to the building fabric would be considerable, since the shell construction needed to be laid bare to renovate the building envelope. The planning process this entailed, involving the dismantling, storage, and relaying of building elements, can be described as a project within a project. Above all the dismantling work, including the removal of contaminant substances[6] and the storage of the protected building parts and artworks,[7] had to be organized in terms of planning and logistics.

Regarding the especially critical themes of preservation-compatible solutions for aspects such as the steel and glass facade, the natural stone cladding, the doors, and barrier-freedom, the preliminary planning already developed detailed sub-concepts, which were consolidated further in the subsequent design and implementation planning. These sub-concepts were repeatedly checked using samples and tests, to gain insight and ensure planning security (Fig. 2).

3 → Reichert, "Spatial reorganization", p. 131–139.

4 → Chapter "Steel and glass facade", p. 204–221; Chapter "Natural stone", p. 236–249.

5 → Domann, Moritz, "Building technology", p. 140–145.

6 → Heide, "Contaminant removal", p. 188–191.

7 → Matthes, Rüth, "Relocating the collection", p. 178–182.

8 → Dechant, Trembowski, "Concrete refurbishing", p. 196–199.

9 → Reichert, "Preservation concept", p. 120–125.

2

2 Planning meeting, 2016, left to right: Dirk Lohan, Norbert Heuler, Arne Maibohm, Daniel Wendler

3 Revealed concrete surfaces in the basement, view from the staircase hall through the exhibition spaces towards the sculpture garden, 2017

3

One key question arose as implementation planning began, namely regarding the development of a procurement concept: Should the dismantling process be separated from the relaying process or should the tasks be contracted together? An argument against separating them was the loss of important information gained during the dismantling process that could benefit the relaying work, since responsibility for the building elements would be transferred from the dismantling firm to the relaying company. Contracting the tasks separately had the advantage of being able to start building work even during the implementation planning stage, applying insight from the removed building elements as part of simultaneous planning and building work. In the end, it was generally decided to split the tasks. The dismantling work was comprehensively documented and reflected upon in further planning measures. Overall, it can be said that the dismantling and relaying processes worked very well, with hardly any loss of the original building fabric.

One theme that could not be fully clarified at the beginning of the measure was the concrete refurbishing.[8] The problem in planning was connected to the fact that the concrete surfaces were almost completely covered and it was impossible to accurately estimate the scope of required work. Thus, while the building was still operational, spot checks were performed by opening building elements. Refurbishing measures and their scope could be derived from the insight gained in these tests. Above all, the extent of the required measures was not assessed correctly (Fig. 3). This led to considerable delays in the planning and building processes, since their planning had to be constantly adjusted. The entire building was categorized into preservation zones,[9] including smaller building elements that contributed to the monument's value, such as doors and installations in the technical areas, which had a virtually equal status to the exposed spaces and the

CONCEPTION

building parts. Some elements could be preserved relatively easily due to fortunate circumstances. For instance Schneider Spezialbau repaired the guiding rails and motors of the approximately eight-meter high curtains in the exhibition hall. The same company had delivered the original system when the Neue Nationalgalerie had been built.

The process has shown that integrative planning and concerted efforts by the many different professional fields and contracted companies enabled solutions to challenges that had initially appeared to be difficult to solve when measures began.

Martin Reichert

Spatial program

Reorganization
improves use

The Neue Nationalgalerie is a temple of art, but like all modern art museums, it is also a high-performance machine. At the time of its construction, it was probably the most modern art museum in Central Europe, with innovative solutions in the fields of room typologies, air conditioning, and artificial light.

1 → Chapter "Fundamentals", p. 84–113.

The technical demands for exhibition spaces have hardly changed in recent decades. By contrast, operating such a building has undergone a fundamental transformation. The original two-part division, with the collection presented in the basement and the special exhibitions in the hall, has made way for a dynamic sequence of temporary exhibitions with growing numbers of visitors. This requires different logistics and has knock-on effects on the public infrastructure, as well as the organization and nature of the back-of-house areas.

Project participants

The spatial program, the restructured use, and the building's adaptation to a more contemporary museum standard were developed in an iterative process with the project participants during preliminary and design planning.[1] Under the auspices of David Chipperfield Architects, the coordination was carried out on equal terms between the Staatliche Museen zu Berlin as the building's user, the Stiftung Preußischer Kulturbesitz as

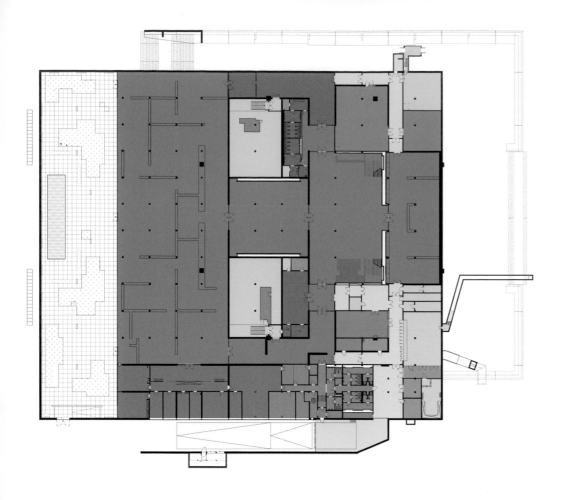

1   Basement level
with the identified
incorrect placement
and multiple uses,
condition in 2013

- Exhibition area
- Visitor infrastructure
- Personnel areas
- Director's offices
- Depot
- Storage
- Technical areas
- Mobility

2   Basement level with the
identified incorrect placement and multiple uses,
condition in 2013

- Incorrect placement
- Multiple use

3   Basement level with new
     uses outside the boundaries
     of the existing structure

[ ] Technical areas
[■] Depot

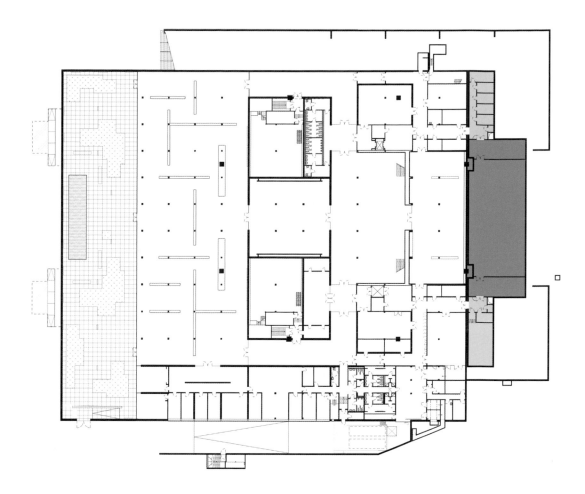

4   Basement level
     after restructuring
     the uses

[■] Exhibition area
[■] Visitor infrastructure
[■] Personnel areas
[■] Director's offices
[■] Depot
[■] Storages
[ ] Technical areas
[ ] Mobility

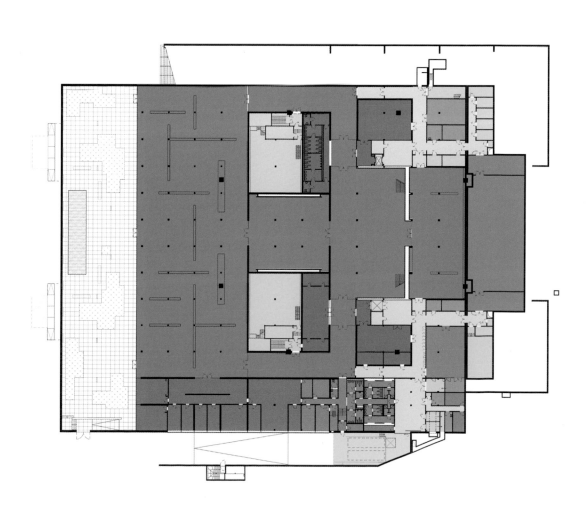

the client, the Federal Office for Building and Regional Planning as the client's expert representative, the Berlin Monument Authority as the responsible preservation authority, and the participating expert planners. They were accompanied on an advisory basis by Dirk Lohan, the grandson of Mies van der Rohe, and the architectural historian and Mies expert Fritz Neumeyer. Structural measures and amendments to the building had to be kept to a minimum.

2 → Reichert, "Preservation concept", p. 120–125.

Status quo assessment

In a first stage in 2013, we investigated the current utilization and identified extensive misuse and multiple uses (Fig. 1). We defined misuse as a different use compared to original utilization plans, such as reassigning the northern museum corridor as an interim cloakroom and a makeshift art depot; multiple uses are unplanned overlapping utilization, such as technical rooms and halls used for art or furniture storage.

The most striking deficits were identified during workshops
with the different user groups:

- Undersized visitor infrastructure in unsuitable locations,
  especially the cloakrooms and museum shop
- Undersized back-of-house areas such as social rooms,
  workshops, and diverse storage areas
- No exhibition-preparation spaces
  and poor transport routes for the artworks
- Severe deficits with respect to barrier-freedom

Reorganizing the spatial program

We then began organizing the uses in the basement in complete accordance with the "Binding monument-preservation plans,"[2] including the reintroduction of the ideal plan for the public spaces at the time of the original construction, by moving the interim cloakroom from the northern museum corridor and the bookstore out of the basement foyer (Fig. 2). The café remains at its established location. The original place for food and drinks dispensers, which were removed in the 1970s, is restored according to the 1960s plans, while being reinterpreted. As before, the self-service cafe with 56 seats keeps to the building's opening hours and can be accessed without an entrance ticket. In future, the historical cafe will be supplemented by a wider choice of gastronomic services offered in the extension building by Herzog & de Meuron.

The visitor toilets remain at their original location and have only been modified in specific places: the barrier-free WCs have been accommodated in two auxiliary rooms, while the baby's changing tables are available in the front rooms.

The new main cloakroom and museum shop were relocated in the former painting and sculpture depot, while the displaced depots are now accommodated in a new underground structure in the area of the terrace that formerly had no basement (Fig. 9).

The reallocation and conversion of the majority of the former technical rooms provided space for a modern-day exhibition-preparation space, as well as additional storage rooms for furniture, showcases, lights, and other operative equipment. The technical rooms were moved to the new depot extension (Figs. 3, 4). The Director's offices and the adjoining social rooms remain almost unchanged, since we only enhanced the employee entrance and separated it from the delivery zone (Fig. 5).

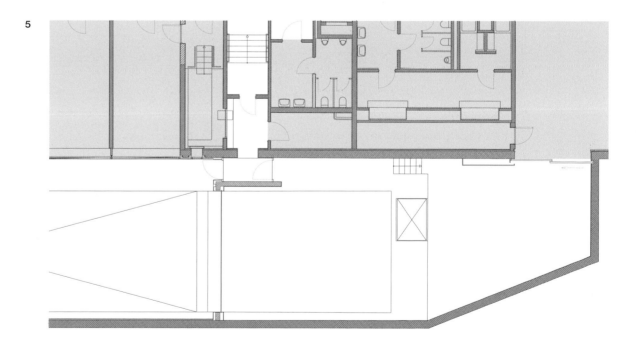

5 Floor plan detail, basement level with separate personnel entrance via the door at delivery entrance, scale 1:200

6

Barrier-free accessibility

In an iterative process, the substantial barrier-freedom requirements were defined and assessed in terms of their feasibility, before being specified in more detail during the ongoing planning process. Improving barrier-freedom for a wide range of needs and user groups was the highest priority (Figs. 7, 8). A new ramp on the podium's southeastern stairs made the large terrace and the main entrance wheelchair-accessible for the first time (Fig. 6). Opposite the existing freight elevator, in the former cleaning room of the northern cloakroom facility, a new elevator was added to serve the lobby of the new cloakroom area on the basement, directly adjoining the foyer. Exhibition spaces and service facilities are now connected by open doors and a spatial continuum.

These and many more measures, such as the guidance system for blind and visually impaired people, were conceptually coordinated and discussed in detail with the responsible specialist Senate department.

6 Barrier-free ramp at the southeast podium stairs after refurbishment, 2021

7 Barrier-free measures,
upper level

● Accessible elevator with
acoustic announcement

○ Tactile information on handrails

● Step-markings,
first and last steps

● Step-markings,
every step

i Info-point

Ⓗ Bus stop, public transport

iBo Door/ gate opened
during business

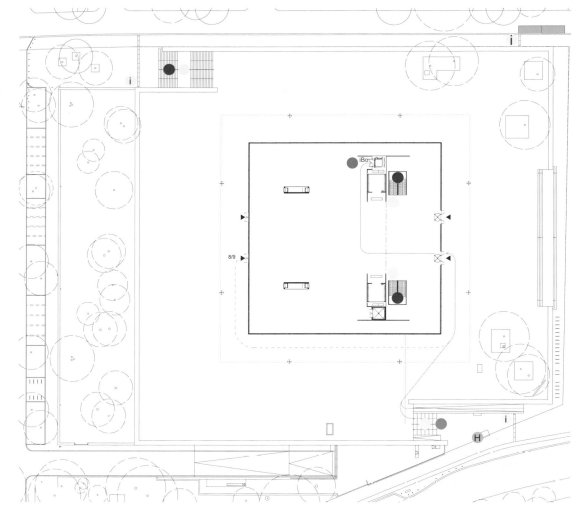

8 Barrier-free measures,
lower level

● Accessible restroom

● Accessible elevator with
acoustic announcement

○ Tactile information on handrails

● Tactile floor plan basement

● Tactile WC information

ⓘ Accessible cash/
information desk with
acoustic amplifier

● Low counter,
accessible for wheelchairs

● Step-markings,
first and last steps

● Step-markings,
every step

iBo Door/ gate opened
during business

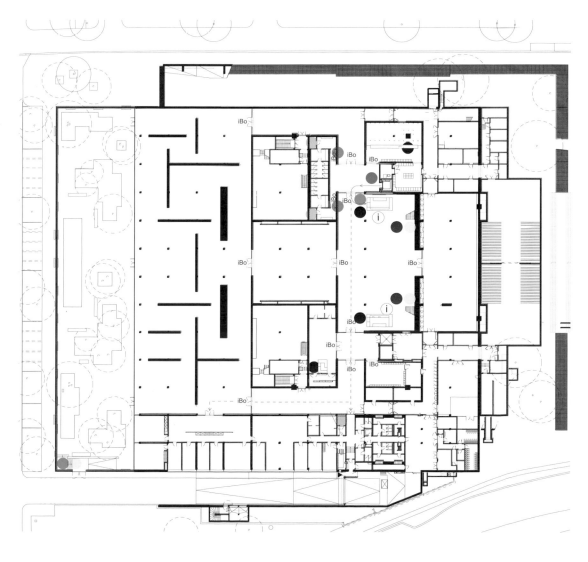

Technical improvements

In addition to the use improvements resulting from the technical overhaul, we implemented a series of additional enhancements in the exhibition areas: These focused on the exhibition climate,[3] the building's security, and the artificial light,[4] as well as the modular ceiling [5] over the basement area for the collection.

Conceptually, the historical modular ceiling was designed for flexibility. The modular suspended ceiling needed to be able to adapt to changing exhibition constellations by switching the 60 × 60 centimeter ceiling tiles. In practice, as a result of its very simple finishing, the ceiling system was unable to cope with actual requirements. For reasons of fire safety and due to the existence of toxic substances, the historical suspended-ceiling material had to be renewed during the general overhaul. The new modular ceiling is a system solution tailored to the Neue Nationalgalerie that allows simple handling, while discreetly integrating the power rails required by the curators, fitted flush with the ceiling.

Unlike the exhibition hall, uncompromising climate conditions were required in the basement, thereby conforming to international loan standards. While retaining the location of the air inflow and outflow, as well as the fitted ceiling grilles, it was possible to optimize the swirl ventilation outlet and controls to achieve a high degree of vertical and horizontal homogeneity, as well as adhering to the prescribed climatic levels.

To reduce the transmission of daylight, curtains towards the sculpture garden were installed with the quality of sunblinds. Behind the curtains, there are new suspended shading elements for temporary use if required. The exhibition hall is also equipped with fittings for temporary curtains in front of the glass facades.

Limits of monument preservation

However, not all demands and requests could be taken into account in the planning. The idea of "upgrading" the hall into an official crowd-gathering venue for event culture and marketing it to third parties was dropped due to the structural consequences, such as the perforation of the roof for smoke-extraction apertures.[6] The considerable additional expense, as well as visual and technical implications, also prevented the desired large aperture in the facade for large-scale exhibits. Instead, simple fittings are used to remove one of the upper panes. The use requirements continued to be updated until the production of the "Building Design Document," whenever new insight during the planning measures made this necessary.

3 → Heuer, "Climate requirements", p. 99–100.

4 → Chapter "Light", p. 250–259.

5 → Freytag, Schwarzbach, "Modular ceiling", p. 266–269.

6 → Waninger, "Fire-safety concept", p. 146–149.

9

It is generally believed that Mies implemented his vision at the expense of functional aspects. In fact, the building has proved to be surprisingly functional in the approximately 50 years or so of its operations. Despite the challenging underlying conditions, the hall remains to this day one of the most in-demand exhibition spaces in the world. The collection rooms in the basement and the hall apply contrasting means to serve complementary aspects of contemporary exhibition and museum operations. During the general overhaul, we enhanced the qualities of both fields with resolute, yet gentle measures.

9 New structure for
depot and technical areas
beneath the terrace,
shell construction, 2018

Stefan Domann, Michael Moritz

Building technology

Essential inner workings

The design of an exhibition hall without any walls, planned by Ludwig Mies van der Rohe for the Neue Nationalgalerie, raises one key question: Where can the technology be installed? Both at the time of its original construction and during its general overhaul, solutions were sought to make systems such as the underfloor heating and air conditioning as invisible as possible.

While planning the new technical facilities, the increased requirements compared to the existing building constructed in 1968 posed a particular challenge. It involved modified specifications in adhering to climate parameters, higher energy-saving standards–for instance the European Ecodesign guideline–as well as current fire-safety regulations. Secondly, further safety measures had to be carried out in the existing spatial conditions, using the building envelope and suspended ceilings, wall cladding, and shafts. Compensation measures to take the demands of monument preservation into account also represented a considerable challenge in planning the technical systems and their interaction. These challenges included the retained single glazing in the exhibition hall and limited means of structurally enhancing the heat insulation in accordance with today's energy standards. Despite a number of compromises, good collaboration between all participating planners ensured that the technical systems' renewal was successful.

1 New screed with underfloor heating in the exhibition hall, 2020

Underfloor heating

The exhibition hall of the Neue Nationalgalerie was already equipped with underfloor heating beneath the natural stone surface when it opened in 1968. That was unusual at the time, since underfloor heating only slowly became prevalent in Germany during the course of the 1970s. Thus, it was highly innovative, since planning for the Neue Nationalgalerie had begun as early as 1962. It is likely that the idea to build a highly efficient heating system that requires relatively low heating temperatures had not been the key aspect in the original decision to install it. Instead, the challenge faced by the architect Ludwig Mies van der Rohe was to heat a transparent exhibition hall with a volume of 25,000 cubic meters and room-high, uninsulated glazing–without visible radiators.

However, during the building's construction period between 1965 and 1968, there was insufficient experience concerning the compatibility and durability of various materials with respect to underfloor heating. One result was that the steel tubing laid in the screed was very quickly damaged by corrosion, leaked, and had to be taken out of service not long afterwards. After the breakdown of the original underfloor heating, radiators were provisionally installed in auxiliary rooms in the basement, as well as in the Director's offices.

The new planning for the general overhaul included the complete reconstruction of the underfloor heating (Fig. 1). The new system benefits from the latest insight and experience with heating and cooling technology, including using the floor to cool the spaces, since the system can be operated with cold water in the summer. The floor's considerable thermal storage mass, with active heating or active cooling as required, makes an essential contribution to stabilizing the spatial climate. The compensating effect was proven using thermal simulation calculations.

One special challenge in replanning the underfloor heating was considering the potential heavy movement loads caused by weighty artworks–during transportation or installation–combined with the low installation height of the flooring as a result of the flooring in the original structure (Fig. 2). The collaborating fields of building planning, structural physics, and building-technology planning, as well as experts and installation companies, combined to harmonize the resulting technical and normative requirements for the underfloor heating. Even during construction, the fittings had to be adapted to the installation heights of the existing situations, leading to the installation of four different underfloor heating and cooling systems in the entire building. Furthermore, the necessary technical modernization measures had to fulfill monument-preservation specifications.

In principle, the active loading and unloading of the thermally effective storage mass in the floor is a key element of the building-climate control system, acting together with the ventilation system to stabilize the temperature level. This effectively reduces thermal peaks in both directions.

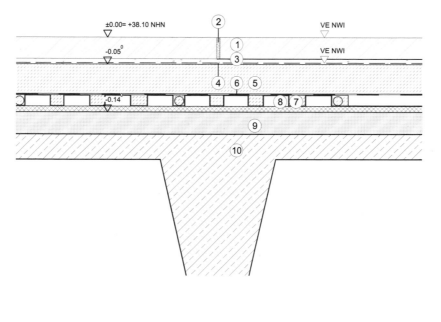

1 Remounting, natural stone slabs,
existing structure
l/b/t = 1200 × 1200 x 40 mm

2 Joints, 6 mm, closed with
cement-bound joint mortar

3 Synthetically enhanced ready-mixed
mortar based on trass cement with
crushed limestone sand

4 Double-layered epoxy-resin
to seal the screed

5 Calcium sulfate floating screed as a
heated screed in accordance with
DIN 18560 CAF - F7 - S55 (VE EST)

6 PE foil as slide bearings, double-layered

7 Fast-drying cement floating screed
between the studs/heating conduits

8 Stud plates with integrated PE-Xc
heating conduits, d = 17 mm and
integrated system insulation for underfloor heating in accordance with
DIN EN 1264-4, λ ≤ 0,035 W/(m K)

9 Leveling filler, cement-based

10 Reinforced concrete ribbed ceiling,
existing structure, d = 80/220mm

2 Detail of the
floor structure in the
exhibition hall

With the reconstructed underfloor heating, we have come full circle and returned to the building's original configuration (Fig. 3). It recreates the original design, as envisaged by Mies, even in detail. At the same time, it fulfills more stringent preservation requirements.

Room ventilation systems

During the original planning for the Neue Nationalgalerie around 60 years ago, preservation demands were already made with respect to the relative humidity and temperature in the exhibition rooms. Although the concrete values on which they were based are not known, the actually implemented air volumes and performance allows us to deduce that they were similar to today.

The air was originally cooled using local compression refrigerators that were only replaced in the 1990s by long-distance cooling from Potsdamer Platz (Fig. 4). Since the museum opened, the heating supply has been provided by the public long-distance heating network. Exterior air was induced into the interior by means of an induction ventilator building situated to the south of the main building. Since the exhaust air was transported away through underground channels, it appeared unfeasible at the time to install a heat recovery system. It would also have been uneconomical, because energy costs were far lower than they are now, while the available heat exchangers, as well as the long channel distances, would have produced a very poor level of effectiveness. However, for the new plans, it could be shown that despite the great distance between the pumping station and the newly developed exhaust air units, the use of a highly efficient combined circulatory system would significantly reduce performance demand. Furthermore, it is economically viable despite the considerable structural work involved.

In the meantime, it has even transpired that the newly planned heat recovery plays a key role in the summer months in achieving the required cooling performance for the building, since the capacity of the central cooling supply from Potsdamer Platz is limited for the entire Kulturforum.

Compared to the original planning for the Neue Nationalgalerie, the thermal envelope of the building could hardly be improved, especially in the area of the large-scale glazing in the exhibition hall and the collection rooms in the basement. At the same time, the preservation demands for the interior climate and the summer temperatures on which their interpretation is based have increased. Thus, according to today's plans, higher connection supply levels are required for the cooling system.

To ensure the high levels of cooling and heating performance in the exhibition areas, which the underfloor heating cannot fully compensate, the air conditioning system still has to move very large volumes of air in the building. In the 1960s, it was perfectly normal to move these air volumes using high-pressure ventilation systems. These moved the conditioned air at high speed (20 to 25 meters per second) through the channels and only decelerated it at the end, just before the air vents, in sound-insulating expansion boxes. This required channel cross-sections to be only 20 percent of their size today, allowing good integration into the highly reduced architecture of the cuboid building at the time of its construction. The energy crisis in the 1970s saw the onset of new approaches to air-conditioning technology, with a shift toward low-pressure systems with much lower air speeds. Today, the amendments to energy-saving law and most recently to building-energy law stipulate maximum pressure losses in a building's ventilation systems, so that only a fraction of the air speeds originally planned at the time of construction is now permitted. As a result, unlike the original plans, the structural design for the required channel cross-sections and their installation in the existing building posed one of the greatest planning and structural challenges for the general overhaul measures (Figs. 5, 6).

3

4

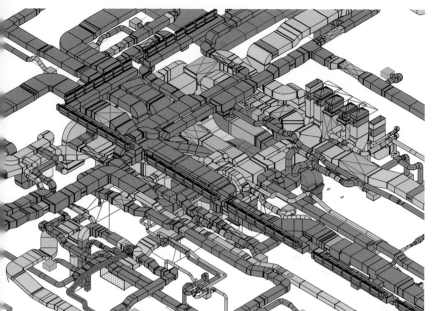 

1 → Schanze,
"Facade ventilation
outlets", p. 228–231.

By contrast, the underlying principles of air inflow into the exhibition areas have remained largely unchanged–not only for reasons of monument preservation, but also because these were ideally chosen during original planning to suit the building and its technical requirements. Due to the dimensions of the spaces–and because the principle of displacement ventilation had been largely unknown in the 1960s–swirl diffusers were mainly used for the ventilation (Fig. 4, p. 191). Only their acoustics had to be slightly enhanced through aerodynamic optimization in the new plans.

The air outlets on the facades of the exhibition hall had to be significantly improved to fulfill their task.[1] Originally, the facade inlets in the hall were only intended to counteract cold-air downdrafts. Due to high preservation demands–maintaining the relative humidity of around 55 percent at a temperature of around 20 degrees Celsius, while still retaining the uninsulated glass facade–they also had to be used to reduce condensation on the facade. Optimized aerodynamics for the outlet slots, combined with an inlet air-temperature of 50 degrees Celsius, should keep the glass facade condensation-free almost all year round.

3 New installation of the underfloor heating in the exhibition hall before laying the screed, 2020

4 Original local compression refrigeration machines before dismantling in the basement, 2016

5 Three-dimensional collision planning of the ventilation installation in the basement, 2015

6 Ventilation installation in the staircase hall with implementation pattern on the ceiling and ventilation outlet, 2019

CONCEPTION

Till Waninger

Fire-safety concept

A tailored solution
to ensure protection

Developing the fire-safety concept for the Neue Nationalgalerie was a particular challenge: especially because Ludwig Mies van der Rohe's design for the Berlin museum is characterized by spaciousness and openness in the visitor areas.

The museum's spacious quality made it difficult to implement standard fire-safety measures for a building, for instance by creating fire compartments or separate fire-escape routes. Another problem was that the existing structure had not even fulfilled all requirements of the building permit at the time of its construction, and that structural changes in subsequent decades had further undermined fire safety. Solutions were required during the general overhaul. Expert fire-safety planners, architects, planning participants, and the Federal Office for Building and Regional Planning jointly developed a concept that represents a decidedly tailored solution, preserving the original character of the Neue Nationalgalerie. Three example aspects are described in detail below.

Basement foyer

The central space in the basement provides access to all museum functions and is mainly open to them, or connected by glass doors with wooden frames. At the same time, it is a key element of the emergency exit system. In the building permit of 1966, zero fire loading and at least smoke-proof, self-closing doors were required for the neighboring

1

1 → Meier, Gaede,
"Wooden doors",
p. 275–279.

rooms. By the time the bookstore was installed, if not before, zero fire loading no longer existed. Furthermore, the glass doors with wooden frames, which were so important to Mies's design, had not even fulfilled fire-safety regulations at the time of the building's construction. Wherever possible, these and other existing limitations to structural fire safety were compensated with complex staffing measures. Zero fire loading in the foyer would have prevented using the area to present exhibits, provide visitor information, or hold events there. Thus, the concept defined tolerable fire loading for the staircase hall (25 KWh/m²), which did not endanger fire-escape routes in the concrete spatial situation. Furthermore, the new museum shop is now adjacent to the foyer in a separate room.

One challenge was proofing the wood and glass doors without major effects on the original aesthetics (Fig. 1).[1] The doors should prevent the influx of smoke and close automatically in the case of a fire. This was achieved in dialogue with the expert fire-safety planner through the addition of brush sealing, the use of fireproof glass and the integration of a catch system that is activated in the event of a fire.

Fire-escape corridors and fire-fighting methods

1 Wood and glass doors
in the basement
after strengthening, 2021

Secure fire-escape routes for all people in the building represent the most important element of fire safety. Ideally, from the perspective of fire safety, these routes should be corridors and spaces with low fire loading, which are also secured by technical systems, since they can allow people to escape and also aid the work of the fire services.

CONCEPTION

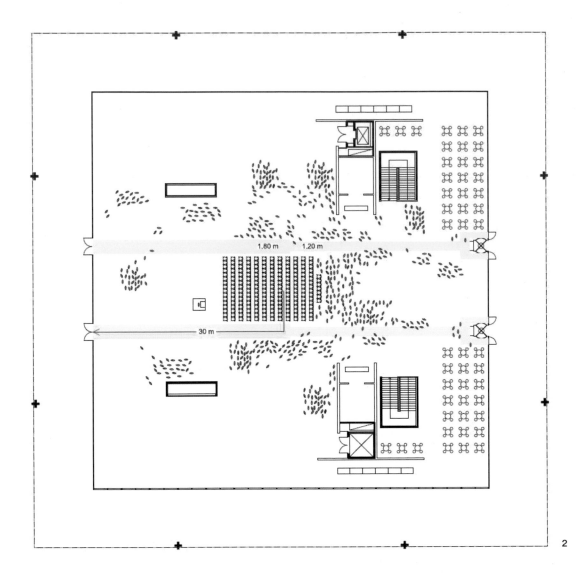

1,80 m   1,20 m

30 m

2

However, the entire Neue Nationalgalerie has no continuous corridors to use as fire-protected escape routes to the emergency exits. The new fire-safety concept involves mechanically smoke-extracted corridors that connect the key functional areas and thereby make several emergency exits indirectly accessible. This also allows the fire services to fight any fire from a safe position.

Events

Like most museums, the Neue Nationalgalerie desires maximum flexibility with respect to the nature of events and the number of participants. The exhibition hall offers a wide range of possibilities that have frequently been used in the past. From the perspective of fire safety, it is decisive whether a building must be treated as a crowd-gathering venue with according building regulations concerning fire safety. Fundamentally, the underlying regulations for crowd-gathering venues do not apply to museums. According to the regulations, events with a museum character, such as an exhibition opening in the usual

2 Event concept for
the exhibition hall,
max. 200 seats and 1,000
guests with catering,
fire-safety certificate
HHP West, 2015

environment or a lecture situation, do not require special fire precautions. The Neue Nationalgalerie also intends to host events with catering services.

Since the qualities of the existing fire-safety installations in the building had to be taken into account to a significant degree, definitions were made from a safety-oriented perspective, i.e. relating to the capacity of the emergency exit routes and the risk of fire emergence, in limiting the number of people permitted in the exhibition hall (up to 1,000 people, Fig. 2) and the simultaneous number of people in the foyer (up to 200 people) during events without catering. Events with catering services are limited to 200 people. Event formats going beyond these limits are not impossible, but require an individual concept with an authorization process.

In addition to proofing the building's structural elements, the following technical systems are key parts of the described solutions and integral to the overall concept:
- Fire alarm system (full protection)
- Self-closing doors and gates in the case of a fire
- Emergency lights (with emergency exit signs)
- Mechanical smoke extraction (in a few sub-sections)
- Building radio system for the fire services

All planning participants jointly developed the fire-safety system, which preserves the historical appearance of the Neue Nationalgalerie. It was possible to rectify deficits from the original construction period and significantly improve the level of protection. The fire-safety improvements to individual building elements and the deliberately minimized retrofitting of technical systems during the general overhaul combine with organizational measures to ensure that people can escape safely and fire-fighting operations can be implemented smoothly.

Scaffolding to dismantle the glazing, 2017

Toxin removal in the grand exhibition hall, 2016

Lifting and coding the granite slabs in the sculpture garden, 2016

Shell construction work for the new visitor elevator at the future cloakroom, 2017

Excavation pit for the newly constructed depot, 2017

Grand exhibition hall before the start of concrete refurbishing, 2017

Large-scale scaffolding in the exhibition hall for refurbishing work on the hall ceiling, 2018

New construction of the floor channels beneath the floor plate in the basement, 2018

View with crane for work on the new depot, 2018

Relaying the granite slabs on the terrace, 2019

Northwest steps, shell construction, 2020

Retouching work on the original ceiling-girder attachments, 2020

Remounting the substructure of the cloakrooms in the exhibition hall, 2020

Remounting the original granite slabs in the exhibition hall, 2020

Installing the building technology in the grand exhibition hall, 2019

Producing the wire-plaster ceilings in the basement library, 2020

Installing the painting surveillance in the exhibition walls of the grand exhibition hall, 2020

Installing the modular ceiling in the grand exhibition hall, 2020

IMPLEMENTATION

Arne Maibohm

Three-stage model

Implementing
the general overhaul

**The period between the last notes of the Kraftwerk concerts marking
the Neue Nationalgalerie's temporary closure, and the exhibition
on Alexander Calder on its reopening, represents years of mediating
between preservation and development. The excellent collaboration within the entire team enabled it to successfully manage both
the ambitious demands and the inevitable setbacks.**

In January 2015, approval of the design documents (known as "EW-Bau") provided an
ideal basis for the general overhaul of the Neue Nationalgalerie. Museum operations
ceased as planned after the concerts by Kraftwerk, allowing building work to begin. As
is the case for every construction project, key parameters affected the success of the
general overhaul, although the project itself was characterized by its special approach
to the restoration work.
Implementation was divided into three key stages, each focusing on a different aspect.

Stage 1: Clearance operations and dismantling

A first step, before the actual building work began, involved responsibly managing the
complete relocation of the world-famous, extremely valuable, and sometimes highly
fragile collection of the Neue Nationalgalerie, comprising 1,441 artworks.[1] This task was
followed by carefully removing or protecting the original surfaces.[2] Six construction

1 → Matthes, Rüth, "Relocating the collection", p. 178–182.

2 → Figaschewsky, "Dismantling natural stone", p. 183–187.

3 → Heide, "Contaminant removal", p. 188–191.

4 → Chapter "Reinforced concrete", p. 192–199; Hurtienne, "Steel and glass facade restoration", p. 210–217.

5   The highest expected groundwater level is the maximum level that can be caused by weather conditions such as periods of extreme precipitation, if the groundwater level in the surrounding area has neither been raised nor lowered by artificial means.

companies dismantled around 35,000 building elements over the period of six months: lights, natural stone slabs made of Striegau, Epprechtstein, and Labrador granite, Tinos marble, wooden parts made of brown oak, steel railings, and emergency-exit signs. All these elements were coded using a 16-digit system, packaged, and stored in separately rented spaces (Fig. 1). The dismantling work was documented with exceeding precision and in great detail, to ensure that the later reassembly work could be carried out without losses and, wherever possible, in the same position, potentially by a different team, like a complex, three-dimensional puzzle. Other parts, including most of the Tinos marble and a few granite slabs on the ground, were protected in situ to prevent damage throughout the construction period. This process was followed by painstaking contaminant removal, which laid the shell construction bare for the first time, thereby allowing it to be refurbished.[3]

Stage 2: Refurbishing the shell construction

At this stage, the planning and construction teams could fully inspect and assess the gutted building for the first time (Fig. 2). Despite the intensive advance checks, surprises were unavoidable. As the stripped shell construction revealed, it had been right for preliminary plans to prepare for a fundamental refurbishment of the concrete, as well as in-depth renovation of the steel structure of the facades, which required the removal of all surfaces. However, the actually required scope of the refurbishing work proved to be much greater than the planners had dared to calculate. The scheduling consequences were considerable, changing the project situation and forcing the client's representative to make appropriate adjustments (Fig. 3).[4] However, the greatest of all surprises followed when the ventilation channels in the floor were laid bare directly below the 2,400 square-meter exhibition space, which are situated beneath the expected highest groundwater level.[5] While the existing channels in the inspected reinforced concrete sections had been in a good condition, the unexpected quality of the structure beneath the floor plate, consisting of simple brickwork, was very poor and leaky after a period of 50 years, which could not have been expected. Not repairing it would have been irresponsible, but any changes had far-reaching consequences for the entire scheduled process. A fast, but feasible solution had to be developed by the planners and the client's representative. The direct and early involvement of those implementing the measures also made them extremely effective and therefore considerably shorter. The section's complete demolition and new construction in waterproof reinforced concrete was achieved as a sub-project within the overall project. While elsewhere, technical installation was already underway, it was impossible to walk in the rooms over the floor channels for around nine months. This significantly delayed progress in that area compared to the rest of the building.

3

1

2

1 16-digit code on
the dismantled wooden
building elements to
locate them for later re-
assembly, 2017

2 Grand exhibition hall
after the completion
of toxin removal, 2017

3 Revealed steel struc-
ture after the removal of
the existing glazing and
partial incisions in the
steel structure to install
expansion bars on the
sculpture-garden facade,
2018

6 → Freytag, Betzold, "Interior finishing", p. 260–265.

7 → Chapter "Light", p. 250–259.

8 → Stieb, "Project steering", p. 175–177.

9 → Bergande, Kauls, "Exterior grounds", p. 288–295.

10 → Chapter "Furniture", p. 280–287.

Stage 3: Finishing and restoring the surfaces

Returning finishing work to the same level of progress everywhere required measures to catch up in the exhibition area. Everyone involved worked to realign all areas to the planned level of the overall schedule. The actual finishing stage already began immediately after the dismantling work and was carried out in parallel to the structural measures, while the original building elements were being restored in the workshops of the carpenters, electricians, metalworkers, and natural-stone masons, or directly in the storage areas of the Federal Office for Building and Regional Planning (BBR). In addition to the original elements, some parts no longer existed or could not be reused following restoration measures. For instance the existing power sockets did not conform to today's standards and could not be retrofitted. The existing floor plates in the corridor areas, the so-called floor-flex tiles, contained asbestos and had to be professionally discarded. WC tiles and asphalt floor plates were so badly worn that they had to be replaced.[6] In such cases, suitable manufacturers and the right production processes had to be found for duplicate parts. The search entailed considerable planning, sampling, and contracting work. The results, which are as similar to the originals as possible, were only achieved because the manufacturers also identified with the project and showed outstanding commitment.[7] Integrating these procurement processes into the building-site schedule was one of the project management's greatest challenges.

The actual technical finishing would have been the only comparable stage to a normal (new) construction project, had it not been necessary to adapt to the existing cubature. In addition to handling the painstakingly retrofitted existing building elements, the work was above all characterized by the very small fitting tolerances for the technical installations. The BBR reacted with micro-targets and principles of lean construction to support the building managers, the teams carrying out the work, and their coordination.[8]

Work on the exterior grounds to plant trees formed the conclusion of the building measures (Fig. 4).[9] The final sub-project of the overall measure before the museum's reopening was to install the original, restored furniture by Mies van der Rohe.[10]

Throughout the restoration work, in addition to the cooperation between the teams of the implementing companies, planners, and the BBR, the exchange of knowledge and communication to sensitize one another on aspects of handling the historical fabric was especially important–all the way from the funding to the artisans carrying out the work. Each company and every single artisan received sufficient information on the significance of the building before they began their work. It is above all the achievement of David Chipperfield Architects that everyone working on the site was fully aware of the cultural heritage of Ludwig Mies van der Rohe and the planning precision its handling required.

4

The BBR and the planning team paid particular attention to identity-boosting measures with continuous, active public relations work by all participants, in addition to countless public building-site tours and content-related press work. They were supported by some special and artistic projects among others by Rosa Barba, Veronika Kellndorfer, and Michael Wesely, that also inspired and motivated those working on the building. Together, all of these joint efforts helped the project over the finish line–despite a very tense market situation in the building sector, with around 30 percent increases in building prices during the construction period and the resulting shortage of specialists, not to mention the Covid-19 pandemic and its far-reaching limitations.

4   Large-scale planting
of silver maple trees
on the terrace, 2020

Mathias Stieb

Project steering

Tools and momentum

The extensive overhaul, which included stripping the building down to its shell construction, as well as removing and relaying around 35,000 parts, required meticulous planning. This section presents a number of project-steering methods for the Neue Nationalgalerie.

The general overhaul of the Neue Nationalgalerie began with the planning process in 2012 and ended in 2021 with the resumption of operations and the museum's reopening. The process therefore took no less than nine years. The construction period alone was almost five years long. How did the team manage to work consistently on its goals and tasks throughout this long period to ensure the project's success? What momentum can project steering (also) generate in public, classically organized construction projects? Appropriate methods include micro-targets, a collaborative production planning, and a steering system consisting of Lean Management principles, as well as autonomous commissioning management.

Micro-targets

Using this method, we formulated, coordinated, and defined written agreements between construction companies and the building management on tangible, achievable, and short-term milestones. At the same time, managers were integrated into the procedure at both ends, thereby stabilizing the processes and focusing on the key themes.

1

Lean construction

Due to the building fabric's condition, there were repeated interruptions to the planned construction process. For instance the schedule had to be delayed by nine months to renew the ventilation channels beneath the large collection room in the basement. Due to the extent of the refurbishing work, special measures were required that also involved the use of the Last Planner system, which is a Lean Construction tool. The project participants used weekly, sometimes daily stand-up meetings at a planning board to discuss the work and timetable. The teams carrying out the work made concrete assurances on a daily basis, thereby creating a personal network of binding targets. These assurances and target achievements were measured and made visible. At times, the meetings were held directly at the building site in the affected area (Fig. 1) to facilitate the necessary coordination and decision-making. For this purpose, the client, planning team, and the implementing personnel were continuously trained by the project steering with the help of simulations. As a result, it was possible to completely compensate the delay caused by the unexpected measure.

Commissioning management

A museum requires a large number of technical systems that work together in a complex arrangement to ensure the required climate quality and the security of art and the museum visitors. These facilities were gradually completed, commissioned and coordinated to achieve their harmonious interaction. For the Neue Nationalgalerie, project

1 Lean Board to visualize the schedule detailed work processes and unresolved themes to accelerate work in the grand exhibition hall, 2019

steering actively shaped the process of overriding commissioning management, allowing the systems to be gradually activated in parallel with the construction work's completion, as well as finding the right system settings. The result closely interwove the processes, shortening the time until the building could be handed over to the user.

During the process, it became clear that there is no golden method to steer such a demanding building task. However, there are many ways with which one can constantly react to individual challenges, using fresh ideas and concepts to find professional solutions. Such innovative approaches were successful in overcoming the three challenging cases mentioned above.

Gertrud Matthes, Cornelia Rüth

An empty museum

Relocating artworks
and stocktaking

**Before the actual refurbishment could begin, a rather unusual task–
at least for a building administration–had to be accomplished:
the relocation of an entire collection and numerous original pieces of
furniture. Handling the priceless artworks was a project in itself.**

During the general overhaul, the task of completely vacating the museum proved to be
extremely laborious (Fig. 1). Since Ludwig Mies van der Rohe had also designed the fittings for the Neue Nationalgalerie, the furniture belongs to the monument and had to
be retained wherever possible. Thus, the art and the furniture had to be relocated to an
appropriate place, while employees required alternative offices. Unlike standard procedure, the building was presented to the Federal Office for Building and Regional Planning
both including the artworks stored there and in a fully furnished state.

The different sizes and material components of the 967 paintings and 459 sculptures in
the three depots of the Neue Nationalgalerie required contrasting storage conditions.
24 sculptures also had to be removed from the terrace and garden for storage, as well as
numerous pieces of furniture from the exhibition rooms and the Director's offices.

Search for appropriate storage spaces

The planning team consisted of one restorer for the sculptures and paintings, one
restorer for the outdoor sculptures and one Project Manager. The initial focus was to

seek existing spaces owned by the Staatliche Museen zu Berlin that were appropriate for storing the artworks. Eventually, the shed building of the Scharf-Gerstenberg Collection, situated in the Museumshöfe at the Kupfergraben, and the external warehouse in Hohenschönhausen provided 210 square meters of non-air-conditioned space for the interior and 300 square meters for the exterior pieces. Thus, around half of the required storage space was found internally.

Storage requirements were coordinated to facilitate the search for additional depots. The first step was to examine the various storage options. While everyone agreed that the sculptures should be packed for storage, there were a number of options for the paintings:

- Storage in crates
- Purchasing and assembling half the sliding-wall system that would later be required in the Neue Nationalgalerie, while storing the remaining paintings in crates
- Purchasing and assembling the entire sliding-wall system
- Relocating the existing sliding-wall system

Since it was the most economic measure, the entire sliding-wall system that would later be needed for the museum was already acquired before refurbishing work began and assembled in the rented depot. This solution entailed renting around 300 square meters of storage space for the paintings—the lowest amount of all the considered options (Fig. 2).

1 Recording and packing
artworks in the
collection rooms, 2015

After a number of inspection visits, two providers were selected that fulfilled requirements, including retrofitting some climate and security systems, by offering one depot for storing painting and sculptures with high climate demands, as well as two further depots with a constant climate for storing sculptures and historical furniture respectively.

2

3

New workplaces at the Hamburger Bahnhof

In addition to the relocation of artworks, another major challenge was to find interim accommodation for the seven employees with permanent workplaces at the Neue Nationalgalerie. It was ultimately decided to provide workplaces for them at the Hamburger Bahnhof–Museum für Gegenwart. Four suitable rooms were found, converted, and equipped with furniture from the Neue Nationalgalerie that did not need to be restored, as well as pieces from the library and other equipment (Fig. 3).

Preparatory measures for transporting the artworks

Between mid-October 2014 and early December 2015, the three external restoration teams worked with the planners to supervise preparatory work on the paintings, as well as the indoor and outdoor sculptures, including packaging, transport, and storage at the five intended depot locations. Prior to their relocation, the contracted restorers examined the preservation condition of all artworks in detail. They produced a protocol of the condition of each painting and sculpture, including drawings and photographs of their overall appearance and details. The following measures were carried out to prevent damage during transportation:

- Surface cleaning
- Preservation measures to loose paint layers and frame mountings
- Improved frames to protect against rabbet abrasion
- Removal of old hangers and application of new hangers
- Vibration protection
- Protection for the paintings' rear sides
- Double frames for rear-side protection
- Re-rolling of large-format paintings onto archive-compatible rolls
- Unframed paintings mounted onto cardboard
- Assembly of a hanging system for storage on the sliding-wall system

2 Sliding-wall system in the interim depot for the temporary storage of paintings during the construction period, 2015

3 The reference library in the Neue Nationalgalerie before its relocation, 2013

The dismounting and relocation of the outdoor sculptures to the warehouse in Hohenschönhausen proved to be a special challenge. For instance the heaviest sculpture, "Berlin Block for Charlie Chaplin" by Richard Serra, weighs around 60 tons. To position the heavy-duty cranes, it was necessary to temporarily close Sigismundstrasse and the nameless street directly by the sculpture garden. Articulated trucks transported the sculptures to the external warehouse, where another heavy-duty crane was required to unload the sculptures.

Some of the sculptures on the terrace, such as "Têtes et Queue" by Alexander Calder and "Vier Vierecke im Geviert" by George Rickey, were dismantled into individual parts before being transported and mounted onto specially produced transport frames.[1] The measure to move the sculpture "Granit Bleu de Vire" by Ulrich Rückriem on the lawn along Reichpietschufer required the prior removal of earth all around it. A team that had originally supervised the sculpture's installation also assumed the complicated task of dismantling the sculpture's many parts. Five granite blocks were stored in a dismantled condition in Hohenschönhausen. Special casing prevented any weather damage during the storage period. Three fountain sculptures by Bernhard Heiliger in the sculpture garden were also stored in specially tailored casing to protect them from weathering.

1 → Lucker, "Sculpture restoration", p. 296–301.

Last but not least: the furniture

The surfaces of the office and exhibition furniture designed by Mies van der Rohe, as well as additional historical fittings, were cleaned before their relocation. Three historical carpets measuring 6 × 10 meters were rolled onto protective archive-compatible rolls. A total of 925 individual pieces of historical furniture and fittings were packed, transported, and placed in storage (Fig. 4). Thus, the Neue Nationalgalerie was fully vacated in time for the start of the general overhaul's construction work.

4

4 Storing the original furniture in an interim warehouse before its restoration and reuse, 2015

Manuela Figaschewsky

Laid bare

Preservation-compatible dismantling of natural stone slabs

Before the actual refurbishment of the shell construction and the building's technical systems, it was necessary to dismantle all the natural stone elements, since this was the only way to refurbish or renew the Neue Nationalgalerie's load-bearing structure and technical facilities, such as the underfloor heating.

The task of dismantling the natural stone was a mammoth effort, since around 14,000 slabs–or around 800 cubic meters–mainly consisting of Striegau and Epprechtstein granite, had to be moved. The individual parts have varying sizes and weigh between 1 kilogram and 3.5 tons. Only a few block steps could remain in situ.
The dismantling measures included:

- Outdoor natural stone slabs and drainage stones, laid on a grit bed, 120 × 120 centimeters
- Interior natural stone flooring slabs and plinths, laid on a grout bed, 120 × 120 centimeters
- Block steps and solid ramp slabs
- Solid seating balustrades and benches on the terrace and in the sculpture garden, with an individual size of up to 360 × 120 × 32 centimeters
- Exterior wall slabs up to approximately 155 × 120 centimeters
- Tinos-marble wall cladding in the interior, 163 × 91 centimeters per slab

1   2

The great challenge consisted of dismantling all pieces without any damage, marking them uniquely according to their position and alignment, and finally charting and cataloging them. All recognizable damage such as cracks, breaks, and missing pieces were charted in the work plans before the dismantling measures. The stones were then stored in a way that allowed them to be re-installed exactly in their original positions following the general overhaul, up to four years later.

Controlled dismantling

Before the dismantling work began, a 3D-scan of all natural stone surfaces was ordered by the Federal Office for Building and Regional Planning to document the existing structures down to the millimeter compared to the grid system in the original plans by Ludwig Mies van der Rohe (7,200 × 7,200 millimeters). The precision with which the slab size was integrated into the remarkable grid and the overall proportions is evident in the size of the granite slabs stipulated by Mies: the edge length is only 119.40 centimeters, allowing the joint to lie precisely in the middle of the 120-centimeter grid. Measurements were integrated into the work plans to check the position of individual slabs with respect to the grid system and each natural stone element was marked with a unique identification number that conformed to the client's guidelines: Construction task/Room or level/Building element/Grid section/Element number (Fig. 1).

In masonry work, it is standard practice for masons to chisel a mark onto a stone as a personal signature. However, in the case of the Neue Nationalgalerie, this was impossible due to monument-preservation regulations, since the measure would have meant the loss of a considerable amount of original material. Ultimately, it was decided to apply UV-resistant plastic signs on which the identification numbers were engraved, black on white.

1 Storing the dismantled and coded natural stone slabs to prevent damage, 2016

2 Vacuum lifting device to dismantle the natural stone slabs in the basement, 2016

3 Dismantling the Tinos marble slabs on the supply shafts in the exhibition hall, 2016

Testing on samples

Before the work on the actual stones was carried out, the method was tested on sample surfaces to ensure that the stones could be dismantled without any damage. Lifting the large granite slabs from the composite cement proved especially challenging. A master mason had to produce a special tool to carry out the task. Using vacuum excavation tools (Fig. 2), stone tongs, small, electrically controlled chain hoists (Fig. 3), gantry and mobile cranes (Fig. 4), and other specially produced tools, the experienced team of masons and restorers managed to dismantle the natural stone slabs undamaged.

The stones were then stored in a way that was compatible with the material, on specially produced palettes. To prevent transport damage, the palette size was chosen to ensure that the slabs did not project beyond the edges. All slabs were packed standing upright, while solid elements including the balustrade benches were stored individually on squared timber. When planning the palettes, both the technology to lower the heavy slabs onto the stands, and the palettes' transportation were considered all the way until storage. For sustainability reasons, plastic sheeting was not used as packaging material. T-shaped placeholders made of a recycled plastic between the individual slabs allowed each slab to be ventilated from all sides. This prevented them from discoloring as a result of moisture build-ups and sweating (Fig. 5).

3

Systematic storage

The natural stone elements were stored on a 100 × 200 meter, fenced-in and guarded concrete area outside Berlin. Each building element had its own space, on which the palettes were arranged in two directions as in a coordinate system, using numbers and letters. The arrangement of all the elements on their palettes was recorded in a digital dismantling list that connected the original position of each piece of natural stone from the Neue Nationalgalerie to the coordinates in the temporary storage.

The relocation process required over 100 transports in 24-ton articulated trucks to move over 1,600 palettes of different sizes and the solid balustrade seating, before unloading and sorting them at the storage location. The measure fulfilled the preconditions for their successful re-installation at a later date.

4 Dismantling the Striegau granite on the terrace using a vacuum lifting device, 2016

5 Storing the valuable Tinos marble after being dismantled from the supply shafts of the exhibition hall, 2016

Tobias Heide

Contaminant removal

Professional disposal
of toxic substances

Despite extensive inspections prior to the refurbishing work, the team working on dismantling the "skin layers" of the Neue Nationalgalerie experienced numerous surprises. One of them was the extent of the contaminated and therefore potentially hazardous building parts on the upper and lower levels. Contaminant removal was a key milestone on the way to reopening the museum.

After removing the wooden, steel, and stone surfaces and materials that needed preserving from a heritage perspective, the focus shifted to the remaining building elements, such as plaster, concrete, tiles, carpets, technical systems, and wooden substructures. These were treated in a completely different way compared to the dismantling measures: The preservation aim shifted from preventing damaged building elements to the people working in the building. When the museum had been originally constructed, a number of materials were used that were only later discovered to be damaging to human health. Instead of requiring restoration information, expertise was required from the field of engineering, for instance on hazardous-substance law, health and safety measures at the workplace in contaminated areas, and recycling law.

Since it was a preparatory measure for the later finishing and conversion work, and despite the great care and detailed planning processes involved, the museum's restoration and repair work had to be a tightly scheduled procedure to avoid delaying the overall project's timetable and ensure a smooth transition to subsequent professions. Around 4,600 tons of non-hazardous demolition materials such as concrete and screed,

1 Removal of the
PCB-contaminated wall
cladding on the basement
exhibition walls, 2016

as well over 580 tons of hazardous waste, including asbestos, artificial mineral fibers, and materials contaminated with PAHs[1] and PCBs,[2] were removed and disposed of correctly (Fig. 1). Despite the extensive preliminary planning using all available documents and plans on the existing structure, as well as prior studies to investigate the constituents and composition of the structure's building elements, the actual extent of contaminants and the nature of their use often only became apparent when the surfaces were laid bare in order to work on them.

The screed in the exhibition hall, which lay hidden beneath the natural stone slabs for around 50 years, is an ideal example of this situation. The documents on the existing structure indicated a cement screed with underfloor heating on cork insulation and a sealant containing PAHs on the reinforced concrete coffered ceiling. To preserve the existing building fabric, it had been intended to dismantle the flooring by hand. However, this had to be interrupted shortly after work began, since the screed had been reinforced with steel mats. In close coordination with the contracted company, a method was developed to dismantle the screed in grids using large electric cutting devices with a previously defined cutting depth, to create extractable blocks. The screed could be removed block by block including the cast underfloor heating, ensuring its proper disposal (Fig. 2). On the upper level, around 12 kilometers of incisions were made in this way, while the basement required no less than 34 kilometers of joint-cutting.

The bands of tarred cork beneath this layer presented a further challenge. Decades of pressure had worn down the mats, which had become firmly merged with the layer beneath them. Once again, the demolition plans had to be amended. The solution was to remove the contaminated tarred cork adhesion using large-scale high-pressure sand-blasting by personnel in protective coveralls. In coordination with the responsible authority for health and safety at the workplace, the blasted sand had to be contained to prevent it contaminating the vicinity. So the blasting work was carried out inside tent constructions with a fresh-air supply, which caused considerable additional work. Ultimately however, the insight gained proved very valuable for work on the much larger areas of the basement, where the removal of the old flooring involved far fewer surprises. To remove the contaminants in the inner roof area of the exhibition hall, "solid" spatial

1   PAHs are polycyclic aromatic hydrocarbons. The 2015 contaminant report for the Neue Nationalgalerie found low levels of PAHs, which meant that already built parts posed no significant health risks to humans. See Michael Hermann, Henrick Demankowski, IUP Ingenieure, "NNG Rückbau- u. Entsorgungskonzept schadstoffhaltige Baustoffe", Berlin, 14.07.2015.

2   PCBs are polychlorinated biphenyls. PCBs are also considered to be carcinogenic. Building materials containing PCBs were used in the museum. There is no transmission from PCBs to natural stone, so, after removing the affected elements, no risk to human health remained. See Michael Hermann, Henrick Demankowski, IUP Ingenieure, "NNG Rückbau- u. Entsorgungskonzept schadstoffhaltige Baustoffe", Berlin, 14.07.2015.

2

3

4

5

scaffolding was installed over the entire area of 50 × 50 meters. At a height of 6.50 meters, on a plateau measuring 2,500 square meters, old ventilation shafts and various other building elements were removed (Figs. 3, 4). Access was provided by two interior stairs and a transport platform. This made it possible to work continuously inside the steel girders of the roof's load-bearing structure using simple scaffolding and ladders at low working heights.

Once the dismantling work and contaminant removal had been completed, the Neue Nationalgalerie only consisted of a raw concrete and steel skeleton (Fig. 5) and was ready for stage Stage 2 of the general overhaul–refurbishing the shell construction.

2   Removal of the PAH-
contaminated cork
insulation beneath the
existing screed in
the exhibition hall, 2016

3   Construction of a
plateau scaffold with a
working height of 6.5
meters, around 2 meters
beneath the ceiling of
the exhibition hall, 2017

4   Original ventilation
channels before disman-
tling from the ceiling
of the exhibition hall, 2017

5   Storage of contamina-
ted blasting material
after the completion of
toxin removal, 2017

Marc Gutermann

Ceiling load-bearing test

Structural capacity for fluent spaces

It is often necessary to take unusual steps when preserving monuments. During the general overhaul, the existing reinforced-concrete coffered ceilings could only be saved from demolition on the basis of experimental testing, thereby preserving them as part of the monument.

Ludwig Mies van der Rohe was able to implement his concept of a fluent space in the Neue Nationalgalerie by choosing biaxially suspended reinforced-concrete coffered ceilings. Making ideal use of the building-part heights and a moderate dead weight, he created load-bearing structures over the basement with a maximum spatial flexibility, architectural quality, and load-bearing capacity. This plays a decisive role in using the hall and terrace as exhibition spaces, for instance to present sculptures. The structure's load-bearing capacity is key to the building's continued use.

Controlled test loads

During the general overhaul, samples taken from the ceiling showed that the reinforcement hoops had not been installed in accordance with the relevant standard. The concrete covering was therefore partially missing and the upper, bent-open hoop-ends were exposed outside the surface plates. Since the hoops were too deep, the thrust evidence near the bearing could neither be modeled nor derived, because the load transfer could

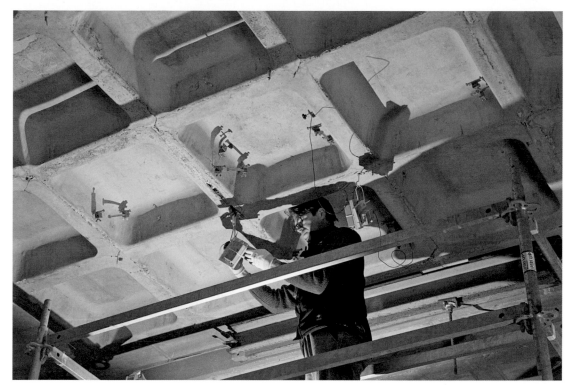

1   Installation of noise-
emission measuring
devices to determine
micro-fissures in the
case of additional loads
underneath the exhibi-
tion-hall ceiling, 2017

2   Steel structure to
apply loads in the area of
the test ceiling sections,
2017

3   Connection and
activation of the hydrau-
lic presses on the steel
structure, 2017

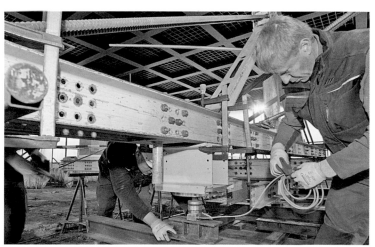

not be calculated. A lack of proof of the load-bearing capacity would have had far-reaching consequences to the building measures on the ceilings, including strengthening measures, dismantling, and new construction. In 2015, to receive dependable information, test loads were applied to selected areas in accordance with the guideline for load testing by the German Committee for Reinforced Concrete (DAfStB). Mobile steel frames, anchored beneath the edges of the plates, were installed on the floor of the hall. Hydraulic presses stressed the plates at specific points that had been previously derived in comparative calculations. Extensive measuring equipment allowed the team to simultaneously analyze the structural reactions, allowing them to stop the experiment immediately in the case of any critical events. Neither the building's usability nor the durability of the building parts could be undermined. Due to the risk of a sudden failure in the thrust range, acoustic emission monitoring was also installed in addition to the obligatory warpage and extension measurements. During the load experiments, it monitored the inside of the concrete with the aim of detecting specific events at an early stage, such as crack growth or crack border friction. The loads were cyclically increased in increments up to the experiment's target load, to achieve the nominal stress including all the safety sub-factors in the load-bearing structures. Since no critical criterion was exceeded, the desired load capacity (5.0 kN/m²) could be proven, making strengthening or demolition measures and new construction unnecessary for the ceilings.

Sustainable results

The result was immediately available after the tests and remain valid until regular structural analysis suggests the necessity of further load-capacity testing–as for any new building. Experimental methods are an economic alternative when extensive calculation analysis delivers unsatisfactory results. They make an important contribution to upholding building culture.

4 Measuring units
for sagging and extension
measurements on
the basement floor, 2017

5 Assessment center
for the measured data in a
tent inside the exhibition
hall, 2017

4

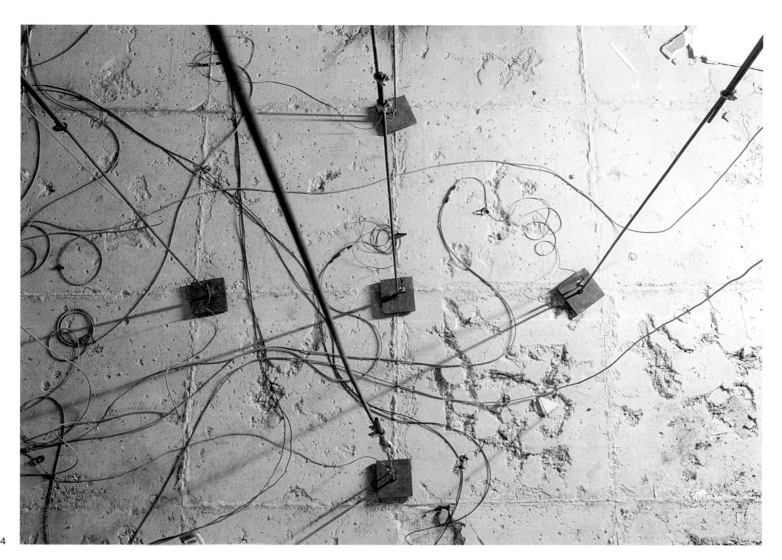

5

Peter Dechant, Marek Trembowski

Concrete

Refurbishment and restoration
of the building core

The work carried out on the shell construction involved earth and shoring work, demolition and disposal, masonry work, concrete and reinforced concrete work, steel and metal work, sealing and insulation, screed work, coating, technical facilities, and concrete repair. Of those tasks, the latter proved to be the greatest challenge.

The procured services for concrete refurbishment were based on analysis of the existing structure during preliminary and design planning. Since not all building elements could be inspected during running operations, assumptions were made based on the visible elements. However, especially the demolition work, which was relevant to the load-bearing structure, revealed far greater damage to the concrete than had been assumed. For instance the coffered ceilings, which had been produced with the then standard prefabricated formwork elements made of pulpwood, were significantly cracked and spalled. Some of these flaws appear to have already been present during the original shell construction, but were considered "not relevant" and hidden behind the ceiling cladding. However, most of the damaged sections were caused by the building's use and were probably the result of installations that were documented during the damage protocol. The damage protocol was produced in advance, but after removing the natural stone cladding from the exterior walls, it was discovered that much of the revealed concrete was damaged more seriously than expected. Unfortunately the phenomenon is common among reinforced-concrete buildings constructed in the 1960s and 1970s, since the concrete coverings at the time were not adapted to the relevant environmental influences.

1

This was especially the case for exterior building parts in the sculpture garden and additional retaining walls.

Fig. 1 demonstrates the corrosion damage to the reinforcements, which had been exposed to increased environmental burdens in recent years due to the insufficient concrete cover. The occurrence was not detected since the walls had been covered by the natural stone cladding.

Comprehensive damage recording

While recording the damage, a total of around 7,150 square meters of walls and 14,600 square meters of ceilings were inspected in the basement, lower level, and the exterior grounds to detect hollows, exposures, cracks, and other damage. Every square meter of concrete surface was inspected in the process–from the ceiling, which required considerable scaffolding, down to the smallest ventilation shaft, which sometimes needed particular agility.

All refurbishment was carried out in strict accordance to the applicable guidelines and standards at the time of its implementation, as well as being supervised and carefully documented. The overhaul was carried out in individual steps according to the defined underlying principles:

- Lateral chipping off of damaged concrete to a depth of 15 millimeters around the corroded reinforcement
- Local exposure of the reinforcement rod, also behind the rod

1 Concrete damaged by corrosion to the steel concrete reinforcement of the wall in the sculpture garden before refurbishment, 2017

2

- Rust removal of exposed reinforcements
  with solid blasting material to the defined degree of cleaning
- Removal of dust and other layers on the concrete surface
  that undermine adhesion, as well as at least prior moistening
  before applying mortar or concrete
- Insulation of discovered cracks and grouting
  using high-pressure injection
- Filling missing sections, depending on the chiseling depth and
  the location of the surfaces with concrete, shotcrete,
  cast concrete, or PCC mortar

Structural refurbishment in the basement

The original fair-faced concrete surfaces of the coffered ceilings were reconstructed according to the design by David Chipperfield Architects to convert the former depot rooms into a cloakroom (Fig. 2) and a museum shop. The first stage involved structural refurbishment, which was limited to the actual damaged elements, to ensure that as much of the original building fabric as possible remained preserved. One important step was applying the materials of the structural strengthening measures with a slight recess, to allow the later two-to-three millimeter surface coating to be applied flush with the adjoining existing layer. Damage that was not structurally relevant, such as sporadic edge chipping, small holes, or fine cracks, were left untouched as traces of aging and use.

2 Restored concrete surface of the former painting depot before its conversion into a cloakroom, 2020

The next stage consisted of carefully cleaning the fair-faced concrete surfaces of the walls, supports, and coffered ceiling. The latter task needed to retain the individual formwork and formwork system of the dome-shaped coffers, ceiling ribs with formwork joints, and joists with board formwork. One measure proved to be especially work-intensive, namely to cover the exposed iron parts. The main aim was to create a uniform and even overall effect without patches, which was achieved by the concluding application of a transparent varnish.

It was not economically viable to repair the concrete on all existing building elements. In the case of the walls surrounding the sculpture garden, the Federal Office for Building and Regional Planning, in agreement with the heritage-preservation authority, decided to demolish it and build new walls. The existing walls were sawn down into sections and dismantled, before being replaced by new in-situ cast, reinforced concrete walls with drilled joint reinforcements.

During the almost three-year construction period, between 50 and 100 employees worked to restore and refurbish the concrete (Fig. 3). Almost every day, the planning and implementation work provided new insight on the preservation-listed building. The good, constructive cooperation ensured a new lease of life for the museum in the coming decades.

3

3 Applying shotcrete onto the outer walls after refurbishing the steel concrete reinforcement, 2018

1

Roland Sommer, Anke Fritzsch

Restoration planning

Strategic approach
to a monument

"For buildings such as the Neue Nationalgalerie, which are restored as monuments, it is decisive that they remain themselves and are not replaced by something that is identical to them." [1] **The intention is deceptively simple, especially since the material diversity of this icon of Modernity is manageable and the overhaul tasks could initially be described as fundamental craftsmanship.**

1 → Schwarz, "Preserve the aura or regain an image? Considerations on the restoration of the Neue Nationalgalerie", p. 52.

It quickly became apparent that detailed restoration planning was essential to find solutions that would fulfill preservation demands, future user requirements, and contemporary technical standards. A planning process was therefore begun to combine the aesthetic and preservation competence of David Chipperfield Architects, the analyses of the existing structures and conditions, and the development of detailed restoration solutions by ProDenkmal.

Restoration goals

In a first step, the restoration aims were analyzed and defined together with the Berlin Monument Authority and the project consultant Fritz Neumeyer with respect to materials and aesthetics, as well as being documented in a restoration strategy. In doing so, it was agreed that to restore and supplement the surfaces, all measures must be implemented with a high degree of craftsmanship, great empathy, and personal modesty. Technical

1 Restored wooden panels ready for reinstallation, 2020

means were to be exploited to the full to find the best way of integrating amendments to the existing structure. The aim was to ensure a refined appearance, while retaining as much of the original building fabric as possible. Thus the goal was to get as close to the original appearance of the building, while allowing the traces of 50 years of use to be subtly visible, thereby upholding the building's authenticity.

2 → Matthes, Rüth, "Relocating the collection", p. 178–182.

Restoration measures

Three main groups had to be considered with respect to the materiality: wooden building elements (not fitted), natural stone, and fittings on different carrier materials (metal, wood, concrete, plaster, wallpaper). These material groups were studied from the perspective of restoration, science, and structure, while the respective preservation conditions were documented and possible treatment methods were experimented on using initial samples and tests. Based on the insight they provided, the required measures were compiled in a concept catalog.

In addition to questions concerning the surfaces, the second major theme was to plan the almost complete dismantling and reassembly of the cladding, fittings, and coatings: the main themes of the general overhaul lay beneath the surface. The task of strengthening the structural building parts, for instance to refurbish the concrete, required the removal of the natural stone curtain facade and the natural stone slabs on the terrace. The modernization of the building's technical equipment, such as the renewal of the underfloor heating and the replacement of the underground piping and risers, required considerable preparatory measures: the cloakroom in the hall, the free-standing exhibition walls in the basement, and all the wood veneer had to be dismantled, while the majority of the flooring had to be lifted. The well-documented details of working methods at the time of the original construction were meticulously analyzed to ensure that the process of dismantling, storage, and reassembly was carried out with as little damage or loss as possible. The structure of the flooring and fitted elements was studied in depth, while dismantling and lifting techniques were tested on the existing structures. Furthermore, a coding system was developed for the individual parts, along with diverse packaging, transportation, storage, and reassembly concepts.[2]

Like the planning stages of architecture and engineering offices, this concept and design stage was followed by implementation planning for the restoration measures. Continued sampling and tests provided answers to the sometimes very specific questions. For measures on the natural stone, techniques were defined for cleaning, tiebar anchoring, and bonding the broken slabs; clear boundaries were set between supplementing the stone with mortar, grafting or slab replacement. The resilience of the existing slabs relaid on a new bed was tested and methods were developed to adapt the surface of older supplementary slabs to the original condition at the time of the building's construction. A new

3 → Chapter
"Natural stone",
p. 236–249.

4 → von zur Mühlen,
"Steel paint", p. 218–221.

5 → Dambacher,
"Brown oak surface",
p. 270–274.

replacement material was also determined and the mortar for joints was differentiated according to the type of stone and its level of exposure, while tests were carried out on the original slabs' treatment after being relaid.[3]

With respect to the fittings, sampling focused on restoring and remounting the matte black coating on the metal[4] in the indoor and outdoor areas, as well as on the wood in the interior. For the wooden building elements, a solution also had to be found to adapt the tone of the brown oak veneer of the cloakroom surfaces in the upper hall, which had faded considerably in some parts, to the much darker inner surfaces.[5] Supplementary laboratory support and on-site diagnosis accompanied the sampling and tests.

The concept catalogs were continuously updated in parallel to the sampling. The data on working methods and the preservation condition, including reference charts, were supplemented to include a detailed description of the resulting restoration measures. For instance, these catalogs comprised information for the carpenters including the measures on the above-mentioned cloakrooms in the exhibition hall, as well as all veneer wooden doors including their frames, exhibition walls, skirting boards, modular ceilings, fitted cabinets, and shelves. The catalog for the fitted metal building elements included a large number of metal doors and windows, as well as the grilles on the coffered ceiling in the exhibition hall, a control cabinet, numerous ventilation grilles, balustrades, and the two flagpoles. The natural stone catalog was similarly extensive, including the outdoor ground surfaces (terrace, sculpture garden), the interior (hall, foyer in the basement, graphics cabinet), the facade and balustrade cladding, and the Tinos-marble cladding for the two installation shafts in the hall. Dismantling and reassembly work also required removal and packaging catalogs for the wooden and metal building parts, as well as the exterior and interior natural stone elements. These catalogs, with all their detailed descriptions of measures, formed the basis to develop service specifications and also to define requirement profiles for the respective contracted services.

The task of quality assurance during the restoration measures involved not only close supervision of implementation samples from the contracted companies, but also the examination of work plans, expert building management for contracts with restoration services, and reviewing all produced documents.

Work on the Neue Nationalgalerie showed that restoration planning for a Modern monument requires the close consideration of all material elements in the context of the overall artwork–in the same way as for classic monuments. It is the only way to recognize and implement a reference back to the original building's expression at the time of its construction, in the spirit of the architect who designed it.

Daniel Wendler, Torsten Glitsch, Jochen Schindel, Ingo Weiss

Form versus function

Planning the steel and glass facade

The exhibition hall of the Neue Nationalgalerie gains its transparency and lightness through the combination of the self-supporting steel coffered roof and large-scale glazing. A number of structural measures were required to preserve the architectural beauty.

To a certain extent, the challenges that needed overcoming in relation to the steel and glass facade were already part of the design by Ludwig Mies van der Rohe. The architect paid greater attention to the design's impression and proportions than to its usability. Even at the time of its construction, the steel and glass facade had not conformed to contemporary technical standards. One reason lay in the choice of sharp-edged solid steel profiles–which Mies insisted on–and the single glazing. Although the office inquired at different manufacturers about double glazing between 1963 and 1965, the desired size could not be produced, so Mies decided in favor of single glazing and the proportions it offered.

Flaws in the building structure caused the facade to remain in a critical condition throughout its lifespan. Eventually, the safety of people inside the building was undermined. This was the result of the statically undersized glazing and broken glass caused by tension in the structure, as well as steel-glass contact corrosion, to mention just the most significant deficits and damage. The facade structure was therefore investigated in detail at the start of the general overhaul and during the planning process: using charting, assessment of the archive documents, material analyses, opening of the building parts, and measuring programs.

1

2

3

1　The blade and sheath
structure at the top of
the facade allows the roof
to move without stress,
2017

2　Broken glass due to
temperature changes,
wind stress, snow loads
and corrosion, 2013

3　Condensation on the
exhibition hall glazing,
2013

Causes of glass breakage

Various calculations were made in 1967 concerning deformation as a result of snow, wind, and temperature stress.[1] On that basis, further FEM (Finite Element Method) calculations and re-calculations were carried out to forecast the movement of the roof. At the same time, an extensive measuring program[2] was implemented, which also took temperature fluctuation into account by means of climate measurements. The deformations could be clearly estimated using the simplified temperature approach in the FEM. One key finding of the studies was: At the time of the original planning and construction, the influence of the steel coffered roof on the facade structure was not sufficiently taken into account. Although vertical expansion was permitted through the blade-and-sheath construction at the head end of the facade (Fig. 1), the corner posts of the original facades were nevertheless connected to the roof. The large-scale girder-grid roof with a span of 64.80 meters is supported by 8 columns and projects 7.20 meters beyond the facade. In both building elements, the facade and the roof, divergent horizontal movements are created due to thermal deformation and also wind and snow burdens. These deformations were wrongly transferred via the facade corner posts to the facade sections, leading to glass breakage (Fig. 2). Furthermore, the posts and bars of the facade structure were welded without expansion joints over a length of 50 meters. As a result, the total expansion of building elements due to temperature fluctuations in the summer and winter at each facade corner amounted to 26 millimeters. Thus the enormous constrictions led to a distorted facade geometry and consequently to glass breakage.

The steel structure, which is neither thermally separated nor air-tight, in combination with the single glazing, caused a high level of condensation–especially when there was a normal interior exhibition climate, with a humidity of 50 percent and a temperature of 20 degrees Celsius, combined with exterior temperatures of below 5 degrees Celsius (Fig. 3). Due to the constant condensation on the steel, the steel profiles corroded (Fig. 1, p. 103), especially in the steel rebates that could not be seen, leading to an increased volume (oxide jacking). The resulting steel and glass contact led to further glass breakage and cracks. By the time the Neue Nationalgalerie was closed in 2014, only 4 of the 56 original glass panes had survived on the upper facade sections.

Choice of new glazing

When Mies had scaled the pane formats for the Neue Nationalgalerie, he had operated at the limit of what was possible at the time: when the museum was constructed, it used glass produced by the Libbey Owens process, which could deliver widths of up to 3.60 meters. However, by the late 1980s, the last tank for this process had been decommissioned. From then on, only float glass was produced up to a maximum width of 3.21 meters.

1 Certified calculation, p. 1–317, by the office Prof. Dr. Ing. Dienst und Richter, and certified calculation dated 10.05.1967 by Prof. Dr. Ing. Karlheinz Roik, also: Report on the influence of solar radiation on the temperature conditions in the roof structure dated 07.04.1966 by Prof. Dr. Ing. K. Krebs.

2 Final Report 2 (exterior) by Ruth & Zech on measurements of weather-induced deformation to the roof and facade at over 30° C, dated 30.07.2013.

3 → Moammer, "Flow simulations", p. 222–227; Schanze, "Facade ventilation outlets", p. 228–231.

Only one French manufacturer was able to supply the pulled glazing in sufficient sizes as original equipment. Later replacement glazing had to be produced as two panes of float glass with a central butt joint, which could only use bearings on three sides.

In the past, the formation of condensation had caused many problems and had to be prevented as far as possible in future. When preliminary planning began, the use of double-glazed insulating glass was investigated in a detailed feasibility study. The respective arguments were assessed from the perspectives of monument preservation and technical concerns. The Federal Office for Building and Regional Planning, the Neue Nationalgalerie, and the Berlin Monument Authority jointly decided against insulating glass. Thus, single glazing was again planned and implemented since it was most appropriate in preserving the original appearance of the exhibition hall (Fig. 4). Aside from the even greater production difficulties involved with insulating glass in such sizes, it would also have had entailed further preservation implications such as a different glass tone, reduced transparency, a changed color, and double the amount of reflection. Furthermore, using a solution with contemporary insulating glass would also have meant the loss of the entire facade profile structures and resulted in a significant change to the profile dimensions.

In parallel with planning for the facade, aspects of climate technology were considered to reduce the condensation despite the use of single glazing.[3] Nevertheless, the decision in favor of single glazing meant that the Neue Nationalgalerie, as the building's user, would have to continue to put up with condensation, albeit to a lesser extent.

Due to its proven load-bearing capacity and increased burglar protection, while ensuring maximum transparency, a composite safety glass with a thickness of 2 × 12 millimeters, consisting of partially tempered glass, was selected. The intermediate layers of foil to produce the composite glass had to be rammed and bonded at the center due to the oversized formats of the panes, because no foil on the market could be supplied in the required width. The new total glass thickness of 27 millimeters exceeds the thickness of the original mono-glass by 12 millimeters. To preserve the contour of the facade, the glass holding rail was shortened on both sides.

The initial search for European and international suppliers who could produce the required glass for the general overhaul yielded no results. Eventually, the oversized glass formats were provided by the manufacturer JinJing from Zibo in the Chinese province of Shandong, before being processed further by the Chinese glass refiner NorthGlass in Tianjin to create the tempered composite safety glass.

Improvements in the facade structure

Planning envisaged modifying the facade to allow a sufficient degree of unconstrained movement to avoid damage in the future. To that aim, the neighboring glazing sections around the corners had to be strengthened as bracing panes to stabilize the facade

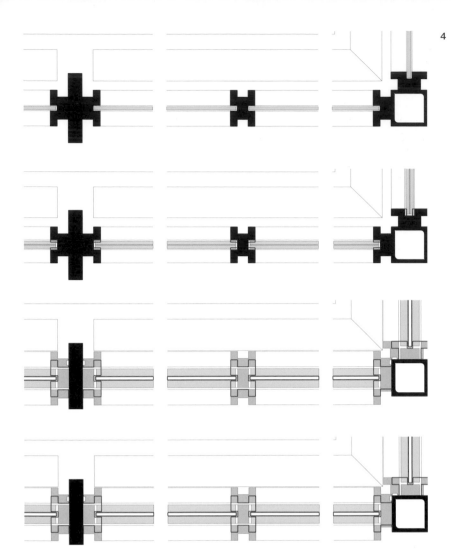

4

Existing structure
(single-glazed structure
without thermal separation)

Selected planning version
(single-glazed composite
safety glass structure without
thermal separation)

Rejected planning version
(partially separated structure
with insulating glass)

Rejected planning version
(insulating glass structure
with thermal separation)

5

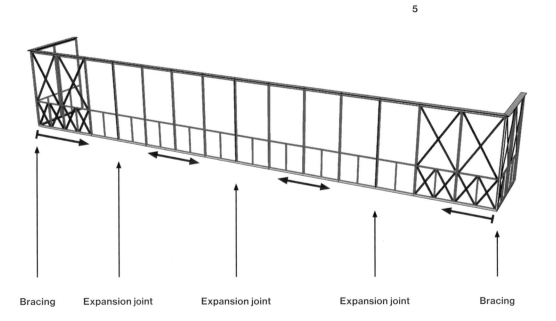

Bracing   Expansion joint   Expansion joint   Expansion joint   Bracing

4 Facade structure
versions (adaptations and
additions in red)

5 Structural measures
to allow the facade's
stress-free expansion
(bracing through glass
adhesion in the
corners, installation
of three expansion posts)

6 Horizontal section
of a facade post
with integrated expansion
joint, scale 1:2

corner posts that were no longer connected to the roof (Fig. 5). On each facade side, three so-called expansion posts were introduced that invisibly absorb the movement in the inner corner of the post profile by means of an expansion joint (Fig. 6). The structure is constructed to be airtight and vapor-proof to prevent corrosion within the profile joints and cavities. Furthermore, small suspension packages are integrated into the complex geometry, enabling the planned mobility and later retraction. A 3D-CNC milling machine was used to mill and drill the two halves of the posts from one solid steel element. Despite the high demands, the team applied these exceptional, almost invisible technical solutions to "heal" the structural deficits of the unique facade without damaging the existing structure.

6   1 Exterior selective milling as vapor pressure apertures
     2 6 × 6 mm in accordance with DIN 18545, insulation class E
     3 Interior 3 × 3 mm phase with polyurethane joint
     4 Glass rail embedded in polyurethane joint material

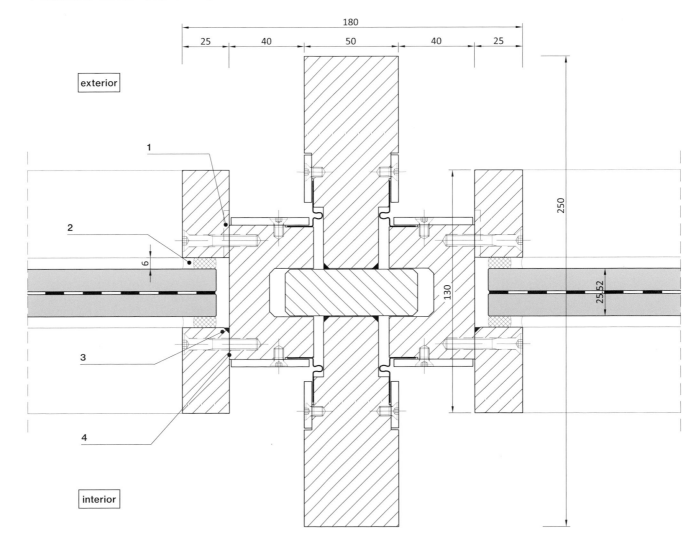

Martin Hurtienne

Restoring
the steel and glass facade

Working report

The steel structure of the Neue Nationalgalerie defines the museum's appearance. Thus a key task of the general overhaul was to renovate the steel and glass facades of the exhibition hall, the collection floor facing the sculpture garden, and the window band of the Director's offices.

Work on the steel and glass facades comprised the refurbishment and technical conversion of the steel structure, anti-corrosion measures, the restoration of the original coats of paint and new coating, the acquisition and assembly of new glazing, and the renovation of the door systems. The following descriptions of the refurbishing measures only apply to the exhibition hall. However, they are also generally applicable to the other two facades in the area of the Director's offices and the sculpture garden.

One characteristic element of the steel and glass facades of the Neue Nationalgalerie are the almost sharp edges of the chosen profiles, nearly all of which were cold-drawn. The use of these profiles with an edge radius approaching zero is part of the overall architectural concept, to create exact, hard-edged building elements in "mechanical engineering" quality. Thus, steel elements were used in the structure that had excellent visual qualities, but were not all suitable for welding, which posed a great challenge to the refurbishment. The profile edges, with radii of between 0.50 and 0.25 millimeters, had to be respected and could not be changed on principle due to preservation considerations (Fig. 1). The existing steel, which had been shown by laboratory analysis to be unsuitable for welding, was strengthened for such purposes or accepted with reduced strength values.

1

2

1 Sharp-edged existing
profile after blasting
and priming, 2018

2 Expansion post
installed on the sculp-
ture-garden facade, 2019

3 Expansion posts
on the facade of the exhibition hall, already
installed, before coat-
ing, 2018

3

Above-average sized glass elements up to a construction width of 3.60 meters were used with defined visual qualities for transparency, color, degree of reflection, and evenness. High tolerances in the existing steel facade structure required the use of customized panes in some parts.

1 → Wendler et al., "Steel and glass facade planning", p. 204–209.

2 Cf. GSI – Gesellschaft für Schweißtechnik International mbH Niederlassung SLV Berlin-Brandenburg, GSI SLV Mecklenburg-Vorpommern: Prüfbericht Nr. PB210-180710-01 REV 0, Bestimmung der chemischen Zusammensetzung am Bestandsmaterial, 07/2018.

Exhibition hall steel structure: Technical conversion

The following technical measures were carried out to mount the facade onto the steel roof without constriction:[1] dismantling three main posts per facade and inserting expansion posts (Fig. 2), decoupling the facade corners from the roof structure by freely projecting the web plate over 3.60 meters on the four facade corners, bracing twelve glass elements per facade corner to transfer pressure forces by means of unit blocking, dismantling the continuous blade structure (100 × 40 millimeters) at the roof section, four facades each 50 meters long, and replacing them with shorter elements with gliding bearings (100 × 35 millimeters, length 300 millimeters), adapting the glass rails to accommodate the new glass thickness (old: 15 millimeters, new: 27 millimeters, requiring glass rails to be milled down from previously 55 × 25 millimeters to 45 × 25 millimeter in cross-section).

The new expansion posts were specially developed for the project using the building material known as S355 J2G3 (Fig. 3). The underlying requirements for the new posts were retaining the original external geometry, the ability to absorb the longitudinal movements of the facade sections, and ensuring the demands of structural physics with respect to vapor, water, and wind proofing.

A number of preparatory measures were necessary before technical implementation could begin. These included determining the steel parameters through chemical analysis, as well as assessing the mechanical qualities and welding suitability of the existing steel elements. Furthermore, some of the joint-welding carried out at the time of the original construction did not conform to proper standards. These findings formed the basis of an appropriate refurbishing concept.

Determining steel parameters: Chemical analysis and test welding

Preliminary studies were already carried out in 2013 to determine the building materials' welding compatibility.[2] Some of the building materials proved to be unsuitable for welding, for instance due to the untreated effervescence during the original steel casting. In steel construction, "effervescence" is an effect when the steel is permeated with small, unwanted bubbles because the residual oxygen in the material bonds with carbon to produce carbon monoxide, making the steel appear to "boil." Segregation zones typically

3 Re. the process to retrospectively treat steel, see "Seigerungen und Desoxidation", http://www.isa.fh-trier.de/home/Projekte/Kreutz/html/58.html (accessed on January 13, 2021).

4 Cf. Martin Hurtienne et al: *So viel Mies wie möglich. Instandsetzung, Restaurierung und technischer Umbau der Stahl-Glas-Fassaden der Neuen Nationalgalerie Berlin. Ein Werkbericht*, no date or location, p. 6.

5 Cf. GSI SLV Mecklenburg-Vorpommern: Prüfbericht Nr. PB210-180712-01 REV 0 bis Prüfbericht Nr. PB210-180712-12 REV 0, Materialuntersuchungen zur Bestimmung der mechanischen Eigenschaften und der Schweißeignung, 07/2018.

6 Cf. GSI SLV Mecklenburg-Vorpommern: Prüfbericht Nr. PB210-180612-01 REV 1, Materialuntersuchungen zur Bestimmung der mechanischen Eigenschaften und der Schweißeignung am Mittelriegel 40 × 80 mm, 06/2018.

7 Implemented by the company Mika Schweißtechnik GmbH.

8 Cf. Mika Schweißtechnik GmbH, Wärmebehandlung der Mittelriegel 80 × 40 mm, Abschlussbericht, 07/2018.

appear inside such steel. These are deposits and accumulations of damaging elements such as sulfur and phosphor,[3] as was the case with samples from the facade steel structure. The damaging substances in the segregation zones have a negative effect on the rigidity of the steel and can lead to hot and warm cracking. However, looking exclusively at the chemical values, extensive analysis of samples from the hall facades found that the steel structures were suitable for welding.[4]

Checks on the mechanical qualities and welding suitability showed that the steel rigidity conformed to required level with a value of S235, but the elongation at break was too low for this quality at 18 percent. The steel therefore showed no significant yield strength. The results of the tensile tests in accordance with DIN EN ISO 6892-1 indicated aging, as well as embrittlement and strain-hardening processes. In the absence of resilience reserves (impact energy: 4 joule), welding measures were out of the question.[5]

The solution to weld the new expansion post was to produce new short bolting elements that were attached to the existing bolts using single-bevel welding. To improve the rigidity (impact value) of the remaining original bars, the company Gesellschaft für Schweißtechnik International mbH SLV Mecklenburg-Vorpommern (GSI) recommended heat treatment.[6] Two methods were tested: heat treatment at 1,000 degrees Celsius for 45 minutes in a laboratory furnace, and heat treatment using the Pro Net mobile system from the company Miller (inductive annealing). The ideal parameters for the applied measures were calculated to be 850 degrees Celsius for a period of 45 minutes. In a sample on the central girder, the elongation at break during a tensile test could thereby be more than doubled from 18 to 39 percent, while the impact energy was increased from 4 to 69 joule. The on-site heat treatment work was electronically recorded, saved, and documented.[7] Depending on the process, the temperature was monitored by up to four thermo-elements.[8] The subsequent welding work was carried out in full following process testing.

Refurbishing the welded joints

The layer on the corroded particles was removed by means of sand-blasting, along with the substantial filler material. It was a complete surprise to discover that most of the existing welded joints on the nodes had not been properly implemented. Numerous samples were taken from building parts that had already been dismantled, according to the schedule, and would subsequently be discarded. A total of 22 nodes were examined. They revealed that in many samples, only a very limited connection existed, or even none at all.[9] Some joints revealed cracks, slag inclusions, and porosity; another curious finding was the extremely coarse grain of most parts.

After extensive expert dialogue between the Federal Office for Building and Regional Planning, David Chipperfield Architects, Wetzel von Seht, and flz I Stahl- und Metallbau

Lauterbach GmbH, it was determined that all existing welded joints should be recorded and refurbished in accordance with preservation requirements and with the aim of retaining the original substance. The required cross-sections of the welded joints to transfer the node loads were calculated on the basis of a simplified measuring process for welded joints in accordance with DIN EN 1993-1-8. Manual arc welding using basic-coated electrodes was chosen as the welding method and certified in process tests.[10] The auxiliary welding materials were electrodes in accordance with DIN EN ISO 2560-A-E 42 3 b12 H10 (KB SE Kestra, Thyssen). The preheating temperature was at least 100 degrees Celsius, while the interpass temperature was 150 degrees Celsius (Fig. 4).

Corrosion protection

To determine the existing coating and corrosion on the steel structure, extensive studies were carried out before the refurbishing work began.

For the new coating, the project was classified in the corrosiveness category C4 "Heavy" in accordance with DIN EN 12944-2, which also applies to interior areas such as chemical facilities and swimming pools, as well as exterior areas such as industrial locations and coastal regions with moderate salt levels. A coating system provided the protective level "High" (H) for 15 years in accordance with DIN EN ISO 12944-1. Various initial conditions had to be expected for the uncoated (hidden) and the coated (visible) areas. To at least reduce future corrosion damage, the facade received a vapor-proof finish.

Existing and new surfaces: New coating in an old guise

It was stipulated that the new coating on the steel and glass facade had to conform to the original intention. That meant that in addition to the deep black tone, the matte quality and also the paint-brush technique had to be recreated. The brushwork on the original building in the 1960s was probably performed as simple craftsmanship, but it posed a real challenge to today's coating companies, which they mastered successfully:

9 Cf. GSI SLV Mecklenburg-Vorpommern: Prüfbericht Nr. PB210-180727-01 REV 0, Untersuchungen von Bestandsschweißnähten (Teil 1), Prüfbericht Nr. PB210-180831-01 REV 0, Untersuchungen von Bestandschweißnähten (Teil 2), 06/2018.

10 Cf. GSI SLV Mecklenburg-Vorpommern: Prüfbericht Nr. PB210-181016-03 REV 0, Verfahrensprüfung nach DIN EN ISO 15613 für das Lichtbogenhandschweißen von Bestandsstahl/Ausstellungshalle, 10/2018 and GSI SLV Mecklenburg-Vorpommern: Prüfbericht Nr. PB210-181018-10 REV 0, Verfahrensprüfung nach DIN EN ISO 15613 für das Lichtbogenhandschweißen von Bestandsstahl/Ausstellungshalle, 09/2018.

4

5

11 GU: gloss unit

12 → von zur Mühlen, "Steel paint", p. 218–221.

13 Cf. individual approval in accordance with §§ 20 and 21 BauO Bln Nr. 231/2017 on July 12, 2017 and individual approval in accordance with §§ 20 and 21 BauO Bln Nr. 230/2017 on September 28, 2017.

Following the primer and protection for the edges, an interim coat was applied in two stages (Stage 1: interim coat between 80 and 120 micrometers; Stage 2: interim coat with 40 micrometers). Brushstrokes were added to the latter to recreate the effect of the original paintbrush technique (Fig. 5). A specific paintbrush with a defined hardness and brush quality was drawn through the wet coating. Thus the "brush-traces" were reproduced and retained. The final coat was applied using an air-spray process, whereby the gloss level had to lie between 1 and 3 GU.[11]

The thicknesses of the individual coat layers were chosen within a very low tolerance range. "Training units" were required for this purpose because in many coating systems, significantly higher tolerances are state of the art compared to the applied system. In the area of the exhibition hall, frame structures covering 1,900 square meters of the glass facade and 4,000 meters of glass rails were treated in this way.

The visible original coat

Not only the new coating had to conform to the original intention. The restoration of the existing surfaces, for instance the facade of the exhibition hall and the inner side of the facades up to the central lateral girder, had to preserve "as much Mies as possible." The aim was the permanent presentation of the revealed original coat as the visible layer. The several-stage restoration process required a sensitive approach, since the paint applied at the time of the building's construction could not be damaged by the removal of the upper layers of paint, while the brushstrokes and the even matte gloss-level had to be retained.[12]

Glass elements

The glass panes of the exhibition hall were reinstalled without divisions for the first time since the museum's opening in 1968. In addition to its anti-burglary qualities, the Class-P613 composite safety glass in accordance with DIN EN 356 also has a bracing function for the facade. All glazing was contractually required to have the same color and visual qualities, especially with respect to the color- and light-reflection.

Out of the 193 panes of glass installed during the project, 120 are made of customized glass. The glass manufacturing was monitored according to strict parameters at the production site, for which the participating firms were contractually licensed and two approvals were provided by the Senate Administration and the City of Berlin.[13] North-Glass in Tianjin, China, supplied the glass panes in the highest quality with a width of 3.60 meters. The glass was shipped from China to Hamburg in sea containers with a maximum weight of 17.50 tons. From there, special transportation via interim storage

4 Refurbishing the existing welding joints after sandblasting the steel structure, 2018

5 Visible paintbrush technique on the intermediate layer, 2021

IMPLEMENTATION | STEEL AND GLASS FACADE

in Lauterbach on the island of Rügen brought the glass to Berlin. Rotating and pivoted glass suckers placed the elements onto elastomer-stainless steel bearings, while some bracing areas were additionally "rammed" (Figs. 6, 7).

Transparency of the exhibition hall

Mies van der Rohe developed a form of architecture that is regarded as the expression of structural logic and spatial freedom. In doing so, he created Modern load-bearing structures made of steel, which enabled a high degree of variability for the usable space and allowed the facades to be glazed on a large scale. The steel and glass facades were restored, refurbished, and converted to achieve unconstrained mounting onto the roof structure, while adhering to the strict regulations of the monument preservation authority. The necessary welding work was prepared using material studies and welding-technique developments, while the existing steel was strengthened. Following the installation of the new glazing, all the large-scale panes of glass can be seen without divisions for the first time since the building's opening in 1968, allowing the transparency of the support-free hall to achieve its full effect.

6 Fitting the glass on the terrace using a crane and vacuum lifter, 2019

7 Transportation to the installation site on the exhibition-hall facade using a crane runway fixed to the roof, 2019

6

7

Konstanze von zur Mühlen

Black is not always the same as black

Restoring paint on steel

To ensure proper presentation of the steel and glass facade as a visible finish in the interior of the exhibition hall, the original coat of paint on the lower section of the facade was restored. Above the first horizontal bar, the posts and framework profiles received a new coat of paint.

1 Revealed original first coat of paint on the anti-corrosion layer of the steel profiles for the exhibition hall, 2019

In addition to the technical demands of revealing and restoring the original coat, the task mainly focused on aesthetic aspects. The right tone and matte value had to be found for the retouched interior flawed sections and for the transitions to the new coat. One special challenge was to achieve adequate protection against corrosion without exceeding the maximum paint thicknesses defined by the original structure. The ungalvanized steel frames of the window fronts were originally painted in a matte black tone. First, an extremely thin, matte coat had been painted on an orange corrosion-protection paint containing lead oxide (Fig. 1). On top of this, two further coats of paint had been applied during subsequent renovation measures. During the preparatory work, great attention was paid to preventing damage to the original layer. The secondary coats of paint were removed using paint stripper and subsequent cleaning with polar solvents. Corrosion products on very small areas were removed by hand using a rotary grinder to a cleaning degree in accordance with DIN EN ISO 12944-4: P St 3. The cleaned areas were then patched up with two coats of a dual-component epoxy-resin glimmer primer. Flawed areas, and consequently where the required coating was not thick enough, were additionally patched up with an epoxy-resin-based binder to achieve an even underlying layer (Figs. 2, 3).

Finding the right tone

The special challenge to the refurbishing measures lay in recreating the warm black tone of the original structure with varying gloss levels in the restored sections. Retouching the flawed elements was carried out in several coats and applied to very small areas at a time (Fig. 4). The measures used a single-component acrylic resin combination, the forge paint, in a color that conformed to the original, at various dilution levels. The demanding task was achieved using special paintbrushes and subsequent treatment of the retouched areas in an almost hardened condition by partially polishing them. Good timing was especially important because the reaction time of the paint changes with external influences such as temperature and humidity.

At the lower end of the upper section of the steel and glass facade, the transition from the revealed and restored original paint layer to the newly applied coat proved difficult. The key aspect was not only to find the right tone and matte level, but also to adapt the thinner existing coat to the more prominent new coating due to the defined thickness requirements. These areas were first patched in order to create a tactile transition. In a second step, the paint was applied by spraying as a continuous, very thin mist layer.

In its restored condition, the paint on the steel and glass facade has a homogeneous appearance. Only on closer inspection can a trained eye detect the difference between the new and old materials.

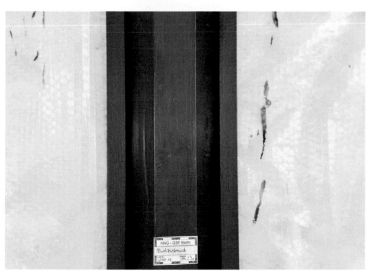

2   Revealed corrosion
damage before
retouching, 2019

3   Restored surface
in completed condition,
2020

4   Retouching small-
scale damaged areas in
several layers, 2020

4

IMPLEMENTATION | STEEL AND GLASS FACADE

Mark Moammer

Air-conditioning for the exhibition hall

Replanning based on simulations

From a technical perspective, a building with solid, thick walls and small window apertures would be the ideal place to fulfill preservation demands with respect to the interior climate. However, Ludwig Mies van der Rohe's Neue Nationalgalerie is exactly the opposite, thereby posing considerable air-conditioning challenges both to the engineers at the time of the building's construction and their contemporary counterparts.

Sudden temperature changes make many materials alter their volumes, which in turn causes internal tension that can damage an object. The same risk occurs with changes in humidity. Thus, the aim of air-conditioning in a museum is to create suitable environmental conditions to protect the objects in a collection. Firstly, the indoor climate is subject to preservation requirements that define strict limits on the temperature and humidity in a room, as well as the maximum speed of their changes. Secondly, an agreeable room temperature is a subordinate goal of air-conditioning: The room climate in the exhibition space can only be adapted to the requirements of the general public and employees in a way that still adheres to the climate conditions stipulated for preserving the objects in the collection.

However, the exhibition hall of the Neue Nationalgalerie has an enormous spatial volume of around 25,000 cubic meters, with dimensions of around 50 × 50 meters and a height of around 10 meters, including the hollow space behind the ceiling. Furthermore, the

1 Newly installed facade air outflow in the ceiling area of the basement on the facade facing the sculpture garden, 2020

exterior walls consist of steel and glass, materials with extremely poor heat-insulation qualities. Thus, there is no wall structure that can absorb heat and humidity, creating high thermal loads due to sunshine exposure in the summer and considerable heat loss in the winter. These aspects significantly hamper precise adherence to specific room-air conditions. In these underlying circumstances, the challenge consisted of achieving a constant exhibition climate and also reducing the condensation on the facades as much as possible.

1 → Domann, Moritz, "Building technology", p. 140–145.

In a first stage of preliminary planning, the office Arup Deutschland produced thermal building and flow simulations to examine the existing system's effectiveness and gain insight for a new concept (Fig. 2). The original air-conditioning concept was also analyzed. One especially important aspect was the correct incident air flow on the glass facades with respect to its speed, temperature, and humidity, to minimize the condensation on the glass facades when outdoor temperatures fall below 5 degrees Celsius. The aim was to develop solutions to determine the dimensions of the air-conditioning systems,[1] forming the planning basis for all further measures. Four systems are used to air-condition the exhibition hall, of which two produce the room climate in the interior and two are used to create the right incident air flow on the steel and glass facade.

Concept for the air-conditioning system

The Neue Nationalgalerie is divided into a total of eight different climate zones in which the room air is conditioned by the system according to defined levels. Depending on the respective spatial zone, the priority lies on achieving suitable environmental conditions for the objects in the collection, or creating a room-air temperature that makes people feel comfortable. In the exhibition zone, a variable program of set values is planned to control the air-conditioning system. Room-air temperatures are set between 19 and 21 degrees Celsius, according to the season, while the relative indoor humidity remains constant at 50 percent. The set values are adapted to each season and depend on the differences between the interior and exterior temperatures. The solution made it possible to optimize system sizes, thereby also reducing energy consumption. The climate requirements must be maintained at a specific room height defined by the level at which the pictures are hung. In the exhibition hall, this specified area lies between a height of 20 centimeters and 4 meters, at a distance of 2 meters from the facade.

In a first stage, the induced outdoor air is conditioned centrally. The conditioned outdoor air-flow of 55,000 m³/h is fed into the concrete channel of the existing ventilation center. Depending on the climate zone's requirements, further air conditioning is carried out by subsequent central systems to achieve the desired quality. In several steps, the air is filtered, heated, humidified, cooled, and dried, as well as transported and distributed. The system comprises a total of 21 central air-conditioning devices with different levels of air treatment (Fig. 3). A heat recovery system in the combined circulation system ensures efficient energy consumption. In the winter, it preheats the air, while in the summer, it acts to cool the induced outdoor air. Underfloor heating is also planned, which can be switched to cold-water operation in the summer to lower the temperature, while also supporting the removal of thermal loads in the room.

Air supply for the exhibition hall

Simulation results confirmed the original concept of blowing air into the hall by means of ceiling inlets. The planned air-conditioning system for the hall has supply and exhaust volumes of 43,000 m³/h. The air is supplied by two central air-conditioning systems. The hall's ventilation inlets are arranged in a ceiling grid over the open coffered ceiling. Adjustable outlets for summer and winter operation improved the flow behavior. Depending on the thermal load, the conditioned air inflow can be supplied to the exhibition hall through adjustable inlets set either horizontally (for cooling) or vertically (for heating). The exhaust air continues to be drawn away via grilles in the column area near the floor.

2

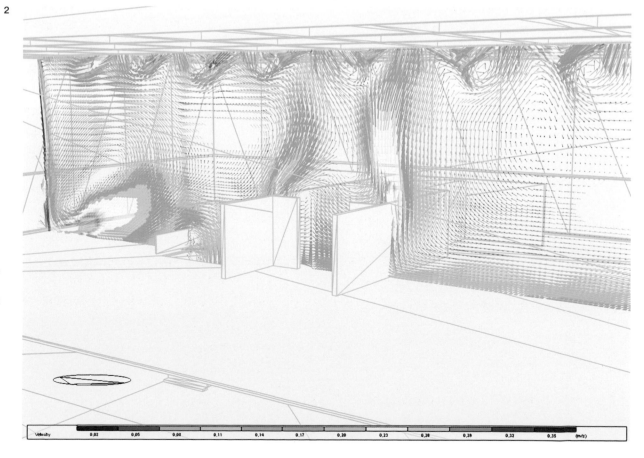

2 Graphic flow simulation, Arup planning documentation, presenting tests on the created air speeds, 2013

Incident air flow on the glass facades

2 → Schanze, "Facade ventilation outlets", p. 228–231.

The facade ventilation system represents a separate project within the project and was planned and conceived in parallel with the air-conditioning systems for the exhibition area. The concept basically follows the original construction, which already planned an air-conditioning system with surrounding air inlets to act as curtaining for the facade (Figs. 4, 5). Extensive thermo-dynamic studies enabled significant improvements during the replanning measures. The aim of the planning was to use a stable flow of incident air that remains attached to the entire height of the facade and thereby reduces condensation to a minimum. Another objective was to prevent the facade ventilation system from having any influence on the interior climate, since this would have affected the conditions in areas where art was displayed.

Thermal building simulations produced specifications for the required condition of the supply air at the glass facade. Depending on the outdoor temperature, set values for the supply air temperature, inflow volume, room humidity, and inflow speed were defined. The air supply inflow of the facade ventilation system is provided by two central air-conditioning devices that heat, cool, and dry the air in various air-conditioning stages. The exhaust air is drawn out at the edges of the ceiling. In the code case, the supply air volume flow is 42,000 m³/h for the facade inflow. Depending on the outdoor temperature, the supply air temperature is between 16 and 50 degrees Celsius. The slot outlets are situated beneath the grille structure from the time of the building's construction, which was refurbished in accordance with preservation standards. The manufacturer SLT Schanze Lufttechnik developed special slot outlets based on the simulations.[2] In future, they will ensure that the entire facade height will receive the airflow, with air streams remaining close to the facade. The measure successfully shields the facade from the interior space, enabling constant climate conditions in areas where the art is presented, while keeping the facade as free from condensation as possible.

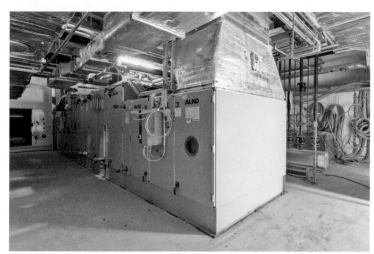

4

5

3 Central air-conditioning system in the technical area of the basement, 2019

4 Ventilation channels integrated into the floor structure to supply the airflow to the exhibition-hall facade, 2019

5 Shafts clad in Tinos marble conceal the entire technical media cabling up to the ceiling of the exhibition hall, 2019

Jochen Schanze

Ventilation outlets
on the facades

A breath of fresh air
to reduce condensation

On the preservation-listed facade of the exhibition hall, condensation forms in winter when there are large differences between the outdoor and indoor temperatures. To prevent this problem or at least reduce it, the ventilation system had to be optimized–by developing suitable ventilation outlets and induction nozzles to blow air onto the facades.

The exhibition hall of the Neue Nationalgalerie gains its transparent lightness through a combination of a modern steel load-bearing structure and large-scale facade glazing. However, condensation on the room-high windows was already a known problem at the time of the building's construction. Furthermore, all the technical innovation required to alleviate such flaws during the general overhaul had to be assessed from the perspective of its aesthetic effects and adapted accordingly. One special challenge was the hall's surrounding facade glazing, with a height of over eight meters. It required particular attention in conceiving the ventilation systems with closely connected outlets.

The measures began with an examination of the existing air-conditioning situation during an on-site inspection. Mobile equipment was used to experiment with an air-flow on the glass facade. A projecting transom on the glass at a height of around three meters made it necessary to carry out additional theoretical simulation. Based on the architectural plans, a 3D-model of the sample area was produced including the supply and exhaust air components. A computer-supported simulation was used to verify calculations on the proposed measures. It showed that the air not only flows over a distance exceeding 8 meters, but also flows over the projecting facade structure, without leaving the glass

1 Smoke simulation of the facade outlet to test the airflow's adhesion using different outflows, planning stage, 2015

IMPLEMENTATION | ENGINEERING

panes. The results of the simulation calculations, as well as the user's intention to enable the installation of curtains when the museum is reopened, made it necessary to carry out a further air-flow experiment to a scale of 1:1. A cooling cell measuring 8 × 2 × 1 meters was specially produced for this purpose in the company's own laboratory using appropriate technical equipment, in order to generate temperatures on the glazing down to minus 20 degrees Celsius (Figs. 2, 3). This made it possible to simulate the different conditions relating to the air-flow system–such as the influence of cold air on the glass facade.

To prevent cold-air downdrafts on the exhibition-hall glazing during extremely cold outdoor temperatures, special ventilation outlets for a tailored air-curtaining system were developed for the glass facade using warm air. They were functionally tested on location. The key aspect of the eight-meter high glass facade was always a fundamental consideration. Laboratory reports have been produced on the following themes:

- Study of the facade air-curtaining system
- Study of the shading curtain movement
- Assessment of facade temperatures and
  their effects on the formation of condensation
- Study of the interaction between the shading curtain and
  the conditioned air-curtaining

The documents recording the general overhaul present the working stages, diagrams, and measures, for instance recording the existing system, testing aspects including usability, re-acquisition, restoration, new acquisition, cost assessment, and also certification of the restoration and storage of the ventilation grilles until their eventual re-installation.

Using existing, preservation-listed components, a state-of-the-art air-curtaining system with conditioned-air inlets was developed and integrated into the existing architecture during the overhaul measures. Considerable improvements were achieved during the refurbishment measures using special, laboratory-tested air-flow elements. The enhanced system ensures acceptable air-conditioning for the single glazing during both summer and winter operations, thereby reducing the condensation to minimum.

2

3

2 Cooling cell in the laboratory, simulating outdoor temperatures acting on the exhibition-hall facade, 2018

3 The curtain was included in the simulation to test its influence when closed, 2018

IMPLEMENTATION | ENGINEERING

Andreas Schubert

Medium-voltage system

Power supply
for the entire Kulturforum

**Air-conditioning, lighting, elevators, and security systems–
no museum can operate without a reliable power supply. For decades,
there has been a high voltage station in the basement of the
Neue Nationalgalerie. Due to the refurbishment of the reinforced
concrete structure and the reorganization of its spatial uses,
it was essential to dismantle the technically outdated system.**

The medium voltage system of the Neue Nationalgalerie supplies not only the museum with power, but also the entire Kulturforum, including the Gemäldegalerie, the Kunstgewerbemuseum, the Kunstbibliothek, and the Staatsbibliothek zu Berlin (State Library) on Potsdamer Strasse (Fig. 1). To guarantee the power supply, two separate 10,000-volt lines are connected to the provider Stromnetz Berlin. Thus, in the case of a power failure, the second line can ensure the supply, which is why all building elements of the medium voltage system are doubled: including the supply cells, protective facilities for the input and output lines, transformers, and other system parts.

During the Neue Nationalgalerie's general overhaul, the energy supply had to be guaranteed both for the connected buildings and the building site. To that aim, a complete interim station was set up outside the building on the corner of Potsdamer Strasse and Reichpietschufer. For reasons of sustainability, it was equipped with many parts such as cells and transformers that could subsequently be reused in the refurbished museum building.

Installing the interim station

Setting up the interim station proved to be a challenge because its massive concrete parts weighed 44 tons. It also had to be equipped for fully functional operations immediately after installation, so a number of elements were fitted in advance. However, the sidewalk on Potsdamer Strasse had not been designed to support the enormous weight of the crane and the station, so the western lane of Potsdamer Strasse had to be closed to traffic. This was not a simple task, since it also required diverting public transport buses. The measure was carried out overnight from February 14 to 15, 2017, when a crane lifted the interim station onto the building site (Fig. 2).

The interim station was then fitted out, while a supply line from Stromnetz Berlin was diverted from the old medium voltage system to the interim station. Preparing the station for operations included the installation and testing of protective systems. In a next step, the power supply was patched to the Kulturforum and the State Library. To do so, one cable of each of double power supplies had to be disconnected and patched to the interim station. Both facilities had to be completely disconnected from the power supply for a short time, which demanded considerable advance coordination work to minimize disruptions to the operations of the supplied institutions. Furthermore, the timing of the repatching was critical, since during that period, only one cable supplied power to the Kulturforum and the State Library. A fault would have led to a total power failure.

Once that measure had been successfully implemented, the power supply could be provided from the interim station. The old medium voltage system in the Neue Nationalgalerie was decommissioned and the respective second power lines for the Kulturforum and the State Library were patched to the interim station. At the same time, the power supply for the building site was also connected to the interim station.

1

1 Original transformers in the medium voltage system of the Neue Nationalgalerie, before dismantling, 2016

Activating the new medium voltage system

In the spring of 2020, the general overhaul of the Neue Nationalgalerie had advanced sufficiently to prepare the spaces for the new medium voltage system. Following coordination with all the participants involved in repatching the power supply, part of the interim station was disconnected and transported to the Neue Nationalgalerie as the first part of the new medium voltage system. In May 2020, work to disconnect part of the interim station had been completed and elements of the interim station were re-installed in the museum's new medium voltage station. A second transformer was activated together with parts of the interim station. The disconnected outputs from the Kulturforum and State Library were then repatched to the museum's new medium voltage system. This was risky because no redundant power supply existed during the measure. However, everything went smoothly from the outset. At the same time, Stromnetz Berlin began preparatory work to provide power to the new medium voltage system, which also involved laying new input lines and testing the protection systems.

The interim station was disconnected in July 2020. Its final system parts were then integrated into the new station and activated. The empty station was finally transported away overnight from August 18 to 19, 2020. The new medium voltage station was commissioned in December 2020 (Fig. 3).

2 The interim station weighing 44 tons was lowered onto the building site by crane around midnight, 2017

3 The new medium voltage system after activation, again supplying the entire Kulturforum, 2021

Thomas Benk

Gray eminence

Suitability testing
for the granite

During the general overhaul, the facade of the Neue Nationalgalerie was treated as a monument of structural engineering. However, the refurbishment of the shell construction required all slabs to be removed. Before the slab's precise reinstallation, it was necessary to prove their structural stability and test their material properties.

The granite facade of the Neue Nationalgalerie is the second innovative natural stone facade planned by Ludwig Mies van der Rohe, the first being the mortared Travertine cladding of the Barcelona Pavilion in 1929. It is presumably one of the first back-ventilated, natural-stone curtain facades in Germany, which were produced before the introduction of applicable standards. [1] Thus it was debated whether to leave a limited area of the original facade untouched–for instance on the uninsulated exterior wall of the sculpture garden. However, this proved impossible to implement, due to extensive concrete refurbishment measures required on the shell construction.

The material used for the natural stone facade is known as Striegau granite (Fig. 1). The quarries are situated near Strzegom (German: Striegau) in Poland. The surface is coarsely ground and smoothly sawn into slabs with fair-faced surfaces that were treated using rotating steel plates and steel shot as abrasive materials. The slabs have a size of 119.4 × 64.4 × 3 centimeters, with 6-millimeter joints. Their holding and suspending anchors are made of stainless steel. Flat anchors, which are still standard today, were used as grouted anchors (Fig. 2). Only the web widths of 3 millimeters no longer conform to today's measurements, which are now generally 4 or 5 millimeters.

1 DIN 18515 "Cladding for external walls using natural stone, artificial stone and ceramic materials" dated July 1970, based on the 5th fully revised edition of the "Guidelines for moving and laying natural stone" developed by the German Natural Stone Association, June 1, 1964.

1 Striegau-granite natural stone facade, before refurbishment, 2016

2 Original flat mortared anchor, 2016

1

2

3

During the necessary refurbishment of the shell construction, all the facade slabs were dismantled (Fig. 3) and, following the shell's structural renewal–involving concrete refurbishment, sealing, and heat insulation–precisely replaced with the original 6-millimeter joint widths. From the perspective of the companies carrying out the task, the facade slabs are considered material provided on site. Thus, they not only needed structural-stability testing, but also confirmation of the reused slabs' required material properties with an appropriate performance declaration in accordance with the Construction Products Regulation (applicable since July 1, 2013).

In line with requirements defined by the standards for facade cladding made of natural stone, the Federal Office for Building and Regional Planning ordered eight material tests.[2] The test results were assessed with respect to reusing the facade slabs and summarized in a test report that acted as an expert statement confirming the material's suitability for use as back-ventilated facade slabs in accordance with DIN 18516 and DIN EN 1496. This provided proof that the original facade cladding could be reused after the refurbishment. The subsequent planning with respect to the load-bearing structure formed the underlying basis for legal approval of the craftsmanship tasks to implement the measures:

- *Measurement of the original anchor cross-sections* and the permissible joint widths of 6 millimeters in the specific context of thermal length changes and permissible installation temperatures (summer/winter)
- Coordination with an anchor manufacturer's application and production technique concerning the *custom production of anchors* in the original

3 Complete dismantling of the facade slabs on the northwest side, 2016

2 The relevant standards defining the required material properties can be found in Part II of the List of Technical Construction Regulations and in Building Rule List B, Part I of the Deutsches Institut für Bautechnik.
The following material tests were carried out on the natural stone:
• Determination of the linear expansion coefficient in accordance with DIN EN 14581
• Determination of the flexural strength in accordance with DIN EN 12372
• Determination of the rupture load at anchor pin in accordance with DIN 13364
• Petrographic testing in accordance with DIN EN 12407
• Determination of the raw density in accordance with DIN EN 1936
• Determination of the open porosity in accordance with DIN EN 1936
• Determination of the water absorption in accordance with DIN EN 13755
• Determination of frost resistance in accordance with DIN EN 12371

3 Proof of the properties of the cladding slabs in accordance with the requirements of EN 1469

dimensions with web widths of 3 millimeters

- *Assessment of the testing report by the MPA (Material Testing Authority)/ LGA (State Industrial Agency)* on the compressive strength, flexural strength, anchor-rupture load, and the expert statement on the suitability of the tested material[3] as back-ventilated facade cladding in accordance with DIN 18516 and DIN EN 1496
- Statement on the load-bearing structure with respect to testing reports concerning *the facade cladding's suitability in accordance with Construction Products Regulation*
- Coordination with the testing engineer regarding whether, in accordance with the official statement by the Deutsches Institut für Bautechnik–Part II of the List of Technical Building Regulations, *general construction-supervisory approval of the anchors is sufficient or whether approval of individual cases is required*
- Procuring *legal planning approval* for the reuse of the original facade cladding, the assembly of the facade with a joint width of 6 millimeters, which does not conform to DIN 18516, and the use of holding and suspension anchors as custom-made parts and reproductions of the original anchors
- Statement on the *suitability* and safety of the building's users with respect to the reused original facade cladding and on the structural stability of the facade in particular consideration of the current DIN 18516-3 and non-adherence to the construction-engineering recommendation provided by the German Natural Stone Association dated July 2012, which stipulated joints of 10 millimeters rather than the planned 6 millimeters
- Contributing to the *performance description* with respect to work on the natural stone material for the facade, e.g. formulating the admissible manufacturing and assembly tolerances for reinstalling the original facade cladding
- Spot-check *monitoring of implementation*

Although the original joint-widths do not conform to today's standards and guidelines, the appearance of the facade (joint pattern, joint widths) remained unchanged due to special monument-preservation considerations (Fig. 4). Preliminary measurements showed that using the original joint width of 6 millimeters and an anchor web-width of 3 millimeters provided sufficient gap sizes to cope with thermal length changes, as well as the low production tolerances. There was no indication of any constrictions or consequential anchor-pin ruptures. The anchors were therefore custom-produced as reproductions with the original dimensions and measurements, and used for the facade.

Due to the overall highly positive results of the material testing, reservations, limited liability or release from guarantee obligations could be avoided in coordination and mutual agreement with the implementing masonry company Gebauer with respect to the tendered performance. Thus, from the perspectives of construction and assembly, the way was clear for preservation-compatible refurbishment and re-assembling of the original natural stone facade.

4

4 Newly laid facade slabs with original and re-applied joint and anchorage widths, 2018

Michael Bauer

Natural stone facade

Restoring traces of time

The natural stone surfaces of the floor and wall cladding in the building, on the terrace, and on the building's base were exposed to very different influences–of natural or anthropogenic origin, significantly affecting the overall impression. One overriding aesthetic goal of the general overhaul was to restore much of the original appearance of the exterior facades, while also taking preservation of the historical context into account.

1 → Benk, "Granite suitability test", p. 236–240.

The restoration approach to refurbishing the natural stone facade involved reusing the original slabs wherever possible. To that aim, sample analysis and other tests were planned in advance, combined with parallel scientific studies.[1] Following the sampling, all specifications, assessments, and stipulations on the measures were made on the basis of preservation principles. Furthermore, depending on requirements, far-reaching decisions were made by a specific expert committee from among the relevant participants in different disciplines.

Status quo at the start of refurbishing measures

The back-ventilated granite-slab and ashlar curtain facades had been exposed to weathering influences for around 50 years (Fig. 1). Throughout that period, minor refurbishing measures had been carried out on a regular basis. However, some of them had actually damaged the building. Furthermore, the soiling ranged from biological growth to blackening, and also various coatings that had changed the appearance of the surfaces. Other damage included missing or broken slabs, cracks, penetration, flawed areas, breakage, and defect joints. The exact extent of the cracks and penetration on the slabs only became apparent after dismantling.

Restoration planning

The aim of the preservation-compatible handling of the ashlar stone in the exterior areas was to retain as much of the original material as possible, above all with respect to the facades. The slabs were re-applied taking underlying load-bearing considerations into account. However, broken facade slabs had to be replaced to ensure static safety. To achieve the preservation goals, a first step involved experiments on samples, sometimes in several stages. The sample areas were chosen in a way that covered, highlighted, or solved as many issues as possible. The sampling helped to transform preservation planning into realistic, feasible implementation. On the one hand, the aim of all sampling was to find a practicable method to treat the surfaces, while on the other, it helped define the intensity of implementation, for instance the extent of cleaning. Thus it was clear in advance how far the measures should reach and how the results would be defined. To ensure adherence to the prescribed parameters, it was necessary to carry out detailed implementation documentation and supervision.

Implemented sampling and tests for the refurbishing measures:
- Boring attempts on the original anchor pins
- Recreating the original surface
- Cleaning measures: wet cleaning, dry cleaning, and chemical cleaning
- Handling flawed areas
- New joints

The boring attempts on the severed anchor pins showed the extent to which the original mounting and boring could be reused. Flawed areas were only treated, preferably with mineral material, where water drainage was a factor or where it was necessary to recreate the original appearance, above all on the edges. The new joints were based on the original specifications, but could be technically improved by adapting them to today's standards. With respect to other themes, some of the implemented sampling measures and tests are described in detail below.

1 View from Sigismundstrasse before refurbishing, with clearly visible weathering on the facade slabs, 2016

Recreating the original surface

Over the years, several refurbishing and renovation measures, especially in the 1980s, involved replacing individual flawed slabs. These had gang-sawn, polished, acid-treated or flamed surfaces that differed considerably from the original slabs. Since the original coarse-grinding method is no longer used today, several masonry techniques were tested during sampling to create an alternative, yet similar surface (Fig. 2). The applied working methods included flaming and hammering in different stages, as well as brushing and combinations of the above methods.

Hammered surfaces came very close to the coarse character of the originally coarse-ground slabs and were therefore preferred. Wherever possible, the new slabs were to be produced in a larger format, hammered, and then cut to scale. If the older replaced slabs merely had a different surface, but were made of Striegau granite, the surface was adapted and subsequently treated. However, if the replaced natural stone was unsuitable, it was replaced completely.

Cleaning the surfaces

One of the main focuses of the facade restoration lay on cleaning the natural stone surfaces. Sampling was preceded by archive research, revealing that before the facade slabs were mounted in the 1960s, the steel shot had not been sufficiently removed from the surface of the stones. As a result, a number of slabs began to acquire a reddish stain soon afterwards. This unattractive change was tackled using drastic measures: All affected surfaces were sandblasted and some were also acid-treated. Furthermore, in a

1

measure with an indefinite time span, almost all wall surfaces of the natural stone facade were treated with a waterproofing agent.

A total of 69 cleaning samples were taken in advance for the general overhaul (Fig. 3). In a first step, a basic cleaning measure was implemented before dismantling, which achieved testable homogeneity. The slabs were only dismantled after examination of this cleaning step. At the same time, microscopic surface images were used to assess the damage to the outlines of the feldspars, to prevent excessive cleaning or damage during cleaning measures. Final and chemical cleaning (to remove rust stains) was carried out after the slabs had been remounted. The appearance was gently homogenized using the respective methods as required, while visually detrimental stains and coatings were removed. This non-invasive cleaning will also delay future dirt accumulation.

Adapting the concept while applying the measures

The cleaning process was applied both to surfaces with and without waterproofing, although not using the originally planned Joos method.[2] Instead, only dry-particle cleaning was used, since it is easier to handle and implement under the conditions on the building site. The results can be directly examined without having to wait for the surface to dry, also with respect to preserving the original material, and can therefore be improved or changed immediately. Adapting the concept in this way showed how essential it was to constantly re-examine the procedures determined during the planning stage–while always upholding the preservation guidelines on restoring the Neue Nationalgalerie.

2   The so-called "Joos method" is a particle-blasting technique with the simultaneous addition of water.

2   Samples of several mason's techniques to determine the treatment of new slabs and assimilate them to the original surface, 2014

3   Details of the laid sample surface to clean the facades, 2013

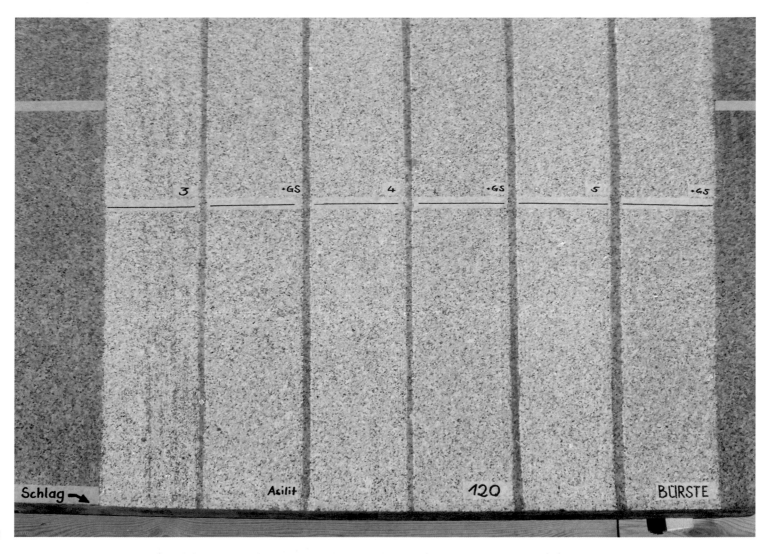

2

3

Rudolf Gebauer, Manuela Figaschewsky

Remounting

The granite returns

Following the concrete refurbishment, 14,000 natural stone elements had to be remounted. It was a great help that the process was supervised by an experienced craftsman who had already been involved in the work in the 1960s. In preparing for the reassembly measures, each individual slab had to be carefully checked, strengthened, and cleaned, as well as being tested for conformity to current technical standards, before being returned to its original location.

After the refurbishment of the building core and its extension, the Neue Nationalgalerie regained its familiar "protective" mantle including all ashlar slabs. Each element of natural stone was returned to its original position including its alignment at the time of construction. It was only necessary to replace the Striegau granite with new slabs in exceptional cases. The special aspect of the task was the fact that Rudolf Gebauer, Managing Director of Gebauer Steinmetzarbeiten GmbH, was able to supervise the task for a second time. In the 1960s, he had met the architect Ludwig Mies van der Rohe personally during work on the building site. In 1968, Gebauer himself produced catalogs of the implemented measures and order documents, supervised calculations for the right facade anchors produced by the company Lutz, and became acquainted with the new process of mounting a back-ventilated natural stone facade. He was able to contribute that experience when the slabs were repositioned following refurbishment.

1

1 → Benk, "Granite
suitability test",
p. 236–240.

Facades made of Striegau granite

One of the special challenges was to relay the original slabs made of Striegau granite in precisely the same positions after a period of 50 years. The demands for a back-ventilated facade in accordance with DIN 18516 have increased–owing to constant further developments in technical specifications, but also due to changing climate conditions. Before their reinstallation, the task involved standing up each of the over 2,500 natural stone slabs in the company workshop, checking them and preparing them for restoration to ensure they could be used without restrictions for the back-ventilated facade. During the planning process, strict regulations were defined for checking the slabs.[1] As a result, stainless steel tie bars were used to reinforce any small cracks on the rear side of the slabs before being remounted. The cracks were grouted with epoxy resin and flawed elements were sealed with a mineral artificial stone material. The flawed areas around the anchor-pin holes were repaired and new ones were created, or different anchor pins were applied if the originals were rejected. Wherever necessary, slabs were rotated for reuse, or rejected and replaced by new slabs if they did not fulfill requirements. Smaller slabs that needed replacing were cut out of larger slabs that could no longer be used entirely. All implemented measures were documented in the charting plans.

During the manufacturing company's checks, flexural strength tests were carried out on selected sample slabs in the company's own workshop or by TÜV Rheinland Würzburg.

1   Relaying the granite
slabs in the area of the
main stairs on Potsdamer
Strasse, 2020

2 → Figaschewsky, "Dismantling natural stone", p. 183–187.

Respecting the traces of time

Preservation measures for the natural stone in the outdoor areas had to address the many traces caused by weather, wear, and repairs over a period of 50 years. Since a renovation measure in the 1980s, the slabs in the terrace area had been embedded on coarse river gravel. The new type of bedding led to numerous ruptures, breakages, and cracks because it yielded under heavy loads and the slabs subsequently only rested on specific points of the gravel bed. For that reason, many slabs had already been replaced over time due to serious damage and the resulting risk to users. The facade surfaces were covered in blackened areas and all joints had sealant compounds containing toxic PCB.

The stone facade surface cleaning using a dry micro-blasting process produced a uniform surface appearance, but deliberately refrained from rejuvenating the overall impression or damaging the stone surface. The toxic PCB joint sealant was removed. In the interior, mortar joints for the floor slabs were carefully cut open using diamond hand-held grinders. The mortar joints of the wall cladding made of Tinos marble were opened using oscillating tools.

Remounting all natural stone elements

For a period of up to 4 years, around 14,000 natural stone elements, which had been professionally cataloged, packed, and stored, waited to be remounted.[2] They were then selected with their palettes according to the order of reinstallation and transported truck by truck to the building site. All the original facade lines and building axes were relaid on-site, slab by slab, section by section, in accordance with the original location. Differences dating back to the original condition were not corrected and allowed to remain. In this way, all participants were able to present the natural stone cladding with its original surface in the way that Mies had once planned.

Sophisticated small details, such as rear chamfered edges in the solid block steps, which reduce the intrusion of water into the horizontal joints to a minimum, and clearly structured joint divisions, as well as repeated axis dimensions, will continue to provide impressive evidence of the natural stone architecture in the future.

2 The expansion joint added in the 1980s was no longer necessary for relaying. Thus, new granite slabs were laid here. They were subsequently darkened to reduce their color contrast, 2020

3 Relaying of the granite slabs in the sculpture garden. The unconnected laying of the ground slabs was only carried out during work on the exterior grounds and planting, 2020

Alexander Rotsch

Light planning

Innovative renewal
of the existing systems

Light is a key factor for a museum, both in presenting the artworks and with respect to the architecture's effect. However, the current illumination concept for the Neue Nationalgalerie must provide even more: fulfilling the curatorial, preservational, energy-related, and heritage demands of a museum of the 21st century.

"The Museum of Twentieth Century Art [Neue Nationalgalerie] seems to us to be worth considerable effort, because it will attain great architectural renown and will relate well to our own strong activity in the museum lighting field,"[1] as Edison Price wrote in 1965 in a letter to a potential trading partner in Europe. The then President of Edison Price Lighting Inc., a lighting manufacturer founded in 1952, had already recognized that Ludwig Mies van der Rohe's Neue Nationalgalerie would become an outstanding piece of architecture—one that his company was keen to add to its list of references. 47 years later, the company Arup was contracted to refurbish the lighting of this architectural icon. Its task was to develop solutions that fulfilled the curatorial, preservational, functional, technical, and economic demands of a 21st-century museum, while also sensitively doing justice to the building's considerable heritage and architectural demands. Assessments from the many different professional disciplines, such as heritage preservation, art history, and engineering, had to be harmonized. Comprehensive research began on the original lighting plan.

1   Edison Price, letter to Walter Boissevain, Merchant Adventurers of London Limited, dated September 3, 1965.

2 Mies van der Rohe, cit. Franz Schulze, *Mies van der Rohe. A Critical Biography*, Chicago, London, 1985, p. 309.

3 Memorandum on the lighting samples, interlumen Lichtarchitektur GmbH by H. T. von Malotki, dated October 24, 1964.

4 Ibid.

5 Ibid.

Light as a part of Mies van der Rohe's architecture

The first design plans for the Neue Nationalgalerie, which Mies presented in 1963 together with the Senate Director of Urban Development Werner Düttmann, had already included a lighting concept. Until implementation planning, it was developed further into a lighting plan that was integrated into the architecture. Mies worked intensively on the interaction between light and space. Among others, the book *Architectural Lighting Graphics*, which was published in 1962 in New York by John Edward Flynn, presents museum illumination using wall floodlights known as wall washers. The principle served as a role model for the lighting system at the Neue Nationalgalerie. Mies was familiar with contemporary museum buildings in his chosen home of the USA. For instance, the Guggenheim Museum by Frank Lloyd Wright, which opened in New York in 1959, uses exactly the same wall-washer theme as the Neue Nationalgalerie. Furthermore, Mies had worked together with the most important lighting designer of the time, Richard Kelly, on the Seagram Building in New York, which had been completed in 1958. Kelly had held a lecture in 1952 entitled "Lighting as an Integral Part of Architecture," presenting his pioneering philosophy of a scenographic perspective, rather than merely a functional approach to the interaction between architecture and light. While planning the Neue Nationalgalerie in Berlin, Mies was supported by Hans Theo von Malotki from the Cologne-based company interlumen Lichtarchitektur GmbH.

Lighting for the exhibition hall

With its room-high, surrounding glass facade, the hall was conceived as an all-purpose space for art. Mies responded to the consequences of its use as a museum, also with respect to natural light, as follows: "It is such a huge hall that of course it means great difficulties for the exhibiting of art. I am fully aware of that. But it has such potential that I simply cannot take those difficulties into account."[2]

The arrangement of the downlights mounted in the ceiling follows the strict quadratic grid of the dark steel coffers. Four lights are integrated in each ceiling section for general lighting–making a total of 784 points of light. Mies found it extremely important that the lighting on the ceiling would be as inconspicuous as possible. Thus in 1967, while inspecting samples, it was determined that all lights should be produced with a matte black shading cone.[3] These so-called dark-cone reflector lights were designed for 150 or 200-Watt all-purpose light bulbs. Plans initially envisaged suspending dark-cone spots from the ceiling grid as required to provide flexible accentuating light.[4] When inspected by Dirk Lohan from the office of Mies van der Rohe, the rotatable and swiveling lights were equipped and assessed with a narrow-beam 300-Watt PAR 56 bulb.[5] However, this flexible, highlighting concept failed to impress and was not subsequently implemented.

1

Lighting for the collection rooms

The introverted spaces on the basement level focus exclusively on the presented art-works. Further reference to the outside world is only provided by the sculpture garden after having walked all the way through the spatial sequence–although the retaining walls clad in light-gray Striegau granite are room-high, thereby reflecting and diffusing the natural light.

The arrangement of the lighting inside relates to the grid of the omnipresent modular ceiling, whereby the individual 60 × 60 centimeter ceiling panels had originally been planned as replaceable timber elements (Fig. 1). This concept would have allowed the lighting arrangement to adapt flexibly to the relevant exhibition and changes to the exhibit walls. As part of a modular ceiling design, all lights in the basement therefore had the same diameter and a matte black shading cone. Even the original loudspeakers were designed in a way to allow them to be integrated into the uniform appearance.

A further grid of dark-cone downlights at the center of the space provided basic light. Tight rows of a total of 1,300 dark-cone wall washers along the picture walls ensured the homogeneous illumination of the artworks, true to the American principle. Mies highly valued even illumination for the basement walls. In 1996, the lighting planners from inter-lumen proposed a wall washer with a glass diffusion lens and a shovel reflector to flood-light the walls in the basement. The light was designed to be equipped with 300-Watt soft-glass bulbs or 150-Watt pressed-glass bulbs as floods.[6]

6 Letter from Licht-architektur GmbH by H. T. von Malotki, dated February 25, 1966, p. 2–3.

1 Original ceiling with downlights and wall wash-ers without additional fittings in the basement, 1972

2 Technical diagram of a
dark-cone reflector light

1 Ceiling grid system
(original)

2 Black shielding cone
(original)

3 Reflector (original)

4 Luminaire housing
(original)

5 Mounting brackets
(original)

6 Custom-made reflector

7 LED module

8 Heat sink

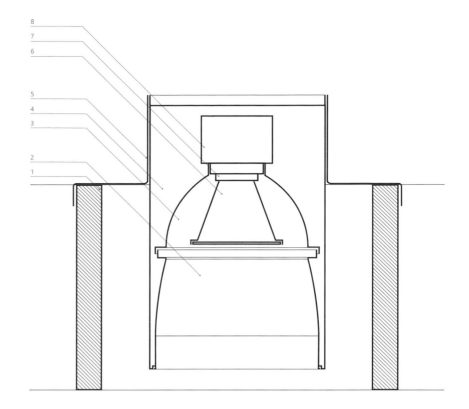

3 Technical diagram of a
multigroove wall washer

1 Modular ceiling system
(original)

2 Black shielding cone
(original)

3 Structured glass lens
(original)

4 Reflector (original)

5 Luminaire housing
(original)

6 Custom-made reflector

7 Custom-made
optical diffuser

8 LED module

9 Heat sink

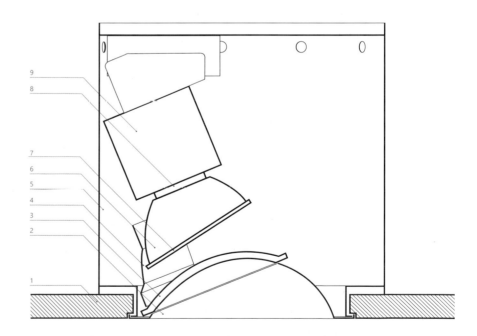

On July 25 and October 5–6, 1966, during light testing using a 1:1 model structure, Mies criticized the irregular light development on a vertical test section. To be able to project the light onto the wall as closely to the transition from the wall to the ceiling as possible, and allow it to diffuse there softly, it was decided during tests that "pressed-glass bulbs should have matte etching on the lower side of the lens."[7] In late October 1966, the lighting planners had finally found a satisfactory solution by changing the position of the reflector and partially sand-blasting the lens. The Berlin company Semperlux Lichttechnisches Werk GmbH, today's Selux AG, was awarded the contract for virtually all the lights.

7 Note, VI F 31 SP/4923 by Spange, SenBauWohn, dated October 27, 1966, p. 3, par. 2.

8 → Lipka, "Lighting-manufacturer selection process", p. 256–259.

Invisible innovation

The general overhaul of the lighting at the Neue Nationalgalerie was not least a challenge because it had to remain as invisible as possible. The approximately 2,400 existing lights had to be carefully restored, while retaining their position on the ceiling grid. The lighting scheme of the original illumination in the space and on the walls was just as worthy of preservation as the lamps themselves. The main task was to retrofit the 1960s light sockets, which had originally been designed for various bulb types, as well as optical components using state-of-the-art lighting technology that was compatible with museum use, in a way that preserved the original distribution of light (Figs. 2, 3). As was the case when the building was first constructed, numerous samples and a number of laboratory tests were required for the task.

Following initial samples to determine the basic planning for the Neue Nationalgalerie in 2013 and 2015, one of the most important practical tests was carried out in 2018 in the special exhibition rooms of the Kulturforum, after the laboratory measurement of selected lighting prototypes by various manufacturers.[8] Three wall washers and one dark-cone downlight by each manufacturer were assessed on an extensive testing structure (Fig. 4). A delegation consisting of representatives of the user, client, architect, heritage authority, expert planners, specialists, and Mies experts assessed the lights, both on the basis of the objective measurement values and with respect to subjective perception. Dirk Lohan, the consultant and grandson of Mies van der Rohe, was also able to gain an impression of the expected lighting quality of the retrofitted original lights.

Ultimately, the theme of the light's tone revealed the field of tension between preservation goals and curatorial demands. In accordance with the continuation of the original lighting design, a lighting tone was discussed in detail, and also sampled, that was similar to the original bulbs for the entire interior area. The original bulbs had a warmer tone, while the user's representatives called for light that appeared fresher and more contemporary, with a color temperature of 3,000 Kelvin, instead of the original 2,700 Kelvin. Despite the high illumination level, the new lighting technology achieves a drastic

4

reduction in energy consumption compared to the existing lighting system. This aspect is combined with the flexible, individual adjustment of every light using the new lighting control system. Fixed lighting scenarios, such as guard lighting, can also be set. Selected, retrofitted lights additionally assume the function of security lighting. Accentuated lighting using conductor rails and floods in a uniform design should be regarded as an additional element to the lighting concept by Mies and therefore only appear in relation to the respective exhibition.

4 Examining the illumination produced by various sample lights during the procurement process, 2018

Andrea Lipka

"The boy has mumps"

Choosing the right light
for works of art

Red cheeks or a pale complexion? The way a painting's color is perceived essentially depends on the lighting. Thus, the color reproduction of lights for the Neue Nationalgalerie was one of the most important aspects in procurement decisions to convert the lighting to LED technology.

As the classic "light bulb" has slowly disappeared from stores, the question of appropriate lighting technology has become a household quandary. Today's range on offer mainly includes LED lights, which save energy, but produce light that is a far cry from the homely, immediately available radiance of yesteryear. Roughly speaking, the task to retrofit the lights during the general overhaul of the Neue Nationalgalerie involved the same challenge: replacing the old "light bulbs" with new LED models. At the same time, contemporary museum lighting must fulfill curatorial, technical, and preservational demands–not to mention addressing the fear of presenting exhibits in a "poor" light.

Developing a procurement process

During the general overhaul, the user not only demanded contemporary museum lighting, but also defined specifications on color reproduction, the light color, and its potential to damage the artworks. At the same time, the lamps had to be low-maintenance and energy-efficient. For preservation reasons, following the principle of "As much Mies as

1 → Rotsch, "Light planning", p. 250–255.

2 784 downlights in the exhibition hall, 1,416 wall washers and 211 downlights in the basement. In a further project, almost 450 additional lights in public and non-public areas were retrofitted, albeit using a less extensive procurement process.

3 Special thanks to Ingbert Zimmermann (†) from the TU Lighting Laboratory for his outstanding commitment to this task.

possible," the outward appearance of the lights could not be changed and the light incidence on the wall had to remain identical to the original system.[1]

The contractual volume of the new lighting concept comprised a total of over 2,400 lights in three different lighting types for the public area of the museum. [2] Normally, public contracts of this size are awarded to the most economic offer. However, the Neue Nationalgalerie had to achieve the best possible quality according to user requirements. Thus, within the means of the procuring EU-wide contracts from public clients, a suitable procurement process was sought to decide the competition that was not simply based on the offered price. A two-stage procurement process was implemented that contributed development work in an iterative method. The development procedure was supervised and steered during each project stage of the procurement process. This enabled the greatest possible control over the necessary steps to transform the "old" lighting into a "new" system.

During the first process stage, the appropriate companies were selected on the basis of defined criteria regarding technical and economic performance. A second step focused on quality-tests in the form of curatorial sampling and technical light measurements on the lamps. Each of the selected tenderers received procurement documents and five existing lights in three different types (three wall washers for the basement, one downlight for the basement and one downlight for the hall) as samples for the technical retrofitting measures.

Minimum standards and evaluation criteria were defined for both curatorial and technical tests. The content of the minimum standards had to be fulfilled, otherwise the tenderer was rejected. The evaluation criteria awarded marks to the lights according to their results. The sample lights submitted by the tenderers underwent technical measurements at the lighting laboratory of the Technische Universität Berlin, an independent lighting laboratory.[3] The assessed parameters included color reproduction, color consistency, light color, damage potential, and lighting-system efficiency.

The curatorial assessment involved the visual inspection of the craftsmanship and structural quality of the retrofitted lights, as well as an evaluation of the illumination of artworks after the light had been installed. A special model structure was constructed in the special exhibition rooms of the Kulturforum, representing a 1:1 copy of an exhibition wall in the Neue Nationalgalerie, where the four invited companies each presented three wall washers in alignment. This produced coherent incident light by each manufacturer. The existing light from the 1968 system served as a reference. The lighting concept from the 1960s had also been assessed using such a model structure.

1

2

1 Examining the illumi-
nation and especially the
color properties of the
new lights in real condi-
tions with paintings from
the Nationalgalerie, 2018

2 Retrofitted lighting
using a wall washer, 2018

4 HP Zimmer, "Traum" ("Dream"), 1963, oil on canvas, 170 × 130 cm, Berlin, Staatliche Museen zu Berlin, Nationalgalerie.

5 Georg Schrimpf, "Selbstbildnis mit Sohn" ("Self-portrait with son"), 1932, oil on canvas, 56 × 50.5 cm, Berlin, Staatliche Museen zu Berlin, Nationalgalerie.

Assessment using artworks

A committee of representatives from the Federal Office for Building and Regional Planning, the museum, the preservation authority, and the fields of engineering (W33 mbH) and planning (Arup, DCA), together with the Mies-expert Fritz Neumeyer and, in a second round, Dirk Lohan, who represented the joint heirs, inspected and graded the installed sample lights in two stages. First, the light was assessed on a white wall. Aspects such as the light evenness and light incidence at the transition to the ceiling areas were considered, along with the perceptibility of color blots, color differences, and flickering. Secondly, the subjective color qualities of the LED modules were compared using two paintings from the Neue Nationalgalerie's collection (Fig. 1).

The red tones, which were critical to the inspection, were assessed using the painting "Traum" by HP Zimmer.[4] A comparison of the nuances of light tones was carried out with the painting "Selbstbildnis mit Sohn" by Georg Schrimpf.[5] During the inspection, a committee member examining the light produced by one tenderer–not the eventual winner–exclaimed: "The boy has mumps." The statement succinctly pointed out how significantly light can affect the colors of a painting. When inspecting the illumination provided by one light, the boy in "Selbstbildnis mit Sohn" appeared red, almost feverish, as if he had contracted mumps. By contrast, the boy looked almost pale when illuminated by the other lights.

Due to preservation concerns, the lights on the ceiling were also considered: The original light bulbs have a larger volume than today's LEDs. Once installed, the new lamps had to have the same appearance as the originals (Fig. 2).

A combination of price and grade from both curatorial and technical perspectives led to the result. In the end, the tender with lights that fulfilled all requirements was selected: Selux AG produced the highest quality. Interestingly, Semperlux (the company's predecessor) had been the original lighting supplier to the Neue Nationalgalerie at the time of its construction. Thus, artworks at the Neue Nationalgalerie will be exhibited using contemporary lighting technology–while nevertheless fulfilling Mies's original intentions.

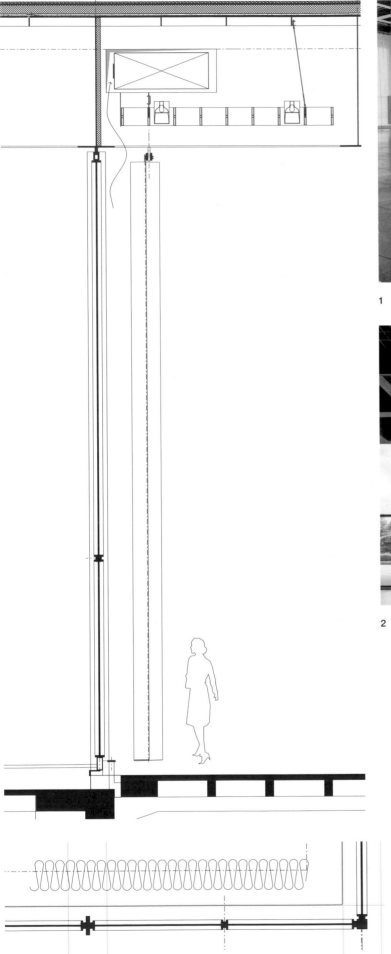

1 Original curtain in the exhibition hall, Wilhelm Lehmbruck exhibition, 1973

2 Inspecting samples to reconstruct the curtain during planning, 2013

3 Sectional detail, facade with curtain, M 1:50

Michael Freytag, Martina Betzold

Interior finishing

Between reproduction
and preservation

At the start of refurbishing work, elements of the original interior fittings were either missing, contaminated with toxic substances, or no longer usable for technical reasons. The challenge lay in searching for points of reference with respect to no longer existent objects in order to reproduce them, or to preserve their original appearance for reconstructions.

Curtain

1 Letter from Ludwig Mies van der Rohe to Dr. Stephan Waetzoldt, February 28, 1966, *Correspondence,* Folder 14-0017, The Mies van der Rohe Archive, Museum of Modern Art, New York.

The curtain in the hall was part of planning by Mies (Fig. 1). It was intended to "pleasantly enhance the architectural appearance of the great hall."[1] Together with the organic forms of the trees and the sculptures on the terrace, the curtain, which hung in a wavy form both in an open and a closed condition, provided a counterpoint to the geometry and clarity of the architecture. The curtain was transparent enough to experience the outdoor surroundings. A direct technical function regarding the light could not be proven. For preservation reasons, it was decided to install curtains again in the hall. A selection was made on the basis of samples inspired by the original curtain, although it no longer exists (Fig. 2). Thus, attempts to resemble the original were based on the details on the extant invoice, photos, and witness statements (Fig. 3). Fortunately, the motors and cord rails had survived and could be repaired by the company that had installed them in 1968. Unlike in the hall, the curtain and blinds in the garden room in the basement were selected with technical lighting conditions and curatorial requirements in mind. However, it was decided that at least the curtain should allow a visual relationship to the sculpture garden.

Carpet

During the original period of construction, a carpet was laid in the exhibition space in the basement, yet this is unusual for the standards of interior fittings in museums today. The material was a Bouclé carpet made of pure new wool. The color was described as "pepper and salt," making it very similar to the granite in the foyer, cabinet, and sculpture garden (Fig. 4). To maintain a uniform appearance from the garden, a carpet was also laid in the two Director's offices. The originally fitted carpet was replaced several times over the years. No pieces of the original material exist in the building or the producer's factory. Thus, it was necessary to rely on photos and witness reports for a reproduction. Already during design planning, we commissioned the company that had manufactured the original fabric in 1968 to produce a number of samples and decided in favor of a carpet made of a mixture of wool and polyester.

Floor-flex tiles

In the staff rooms, the entrance gate, the halls, the storage areas, and the technical rooms of the non-public part of the building, an affordable flooring material was mainly used that was typical of the period: so-called floor-flex tiles, which were one of the many newly emerging artificial surface materials at the time and consisted of a mixture of vinyl and asbestos.

The floor-flex tiles, which were black with a white marble effect and were produced in a 25 × 25 centimeter format, had a regular pattern and were laid in alternating alignment to that design, accentuating the individual panels (Fig. 5). They still existed in some rooms, but had to be painstakingly lifted during measures to remove toxic substances. It was even impossible to retain one storage surface in situ due to asbestos contamination.

It proved difficult to replace these tiles. The original format and the regular marble pattern could not be found on the market. Only one product from the USA largely conformed with the envisaged design, but, following tests on the material, did not fulfill German standards with respect to the substances it contained and their emissions, and was therefore not approved on the German market. Instead, bands of a linoleum product with a slightly regular structure were cut into flooring tiles.

4 Carpet reproduced according to the original while being laid in the exhibition areas of the basement, 2021

5 Reproduced floor-flex tiles in the communal areas of the basement, 2021

4

5

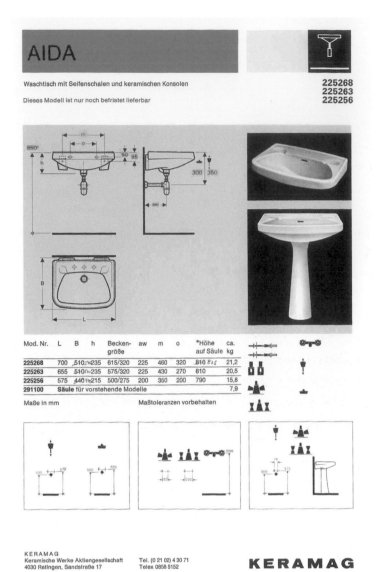

6 Original AIDA catalog by Keramag, 1960s

7 Reconstructed wash basin, 2021

8 Samples of the flat switch program, 2017

2 "Flat surface switch" range by the manufacturer GIRA Elektrotechnische Industrie Gustav Giersiepen KG, source: catalog "Schalter- und Schukomaterial", 1967.

Sanitary ceramics

The original fittings for the public and employee toilets used sanitary parts that were standard on the market at the time. Over the years, the original standing WCs were replaced by wall-mounted units and the urinals were exchanged. The new installations in front of the walls reduced the size of the toilet areas. Although it was possible to determine the precise original products in documents from the time, they were no longer manufactured and the original producer had no more available in stock, nor do plaster casts of the models exist. Major retailers with considerable warehouse stock were contacted, but to no avail.

In the Director's offices, two original washbasins (product: AIDA, washbasin with soap receptacles) were identified as the ceramics used for the entire building (Fig. 6). Molds were made of these original washbasins, to produce new plaster casts in order to reproduce the basins (Fig. 7). The products for the WCs and urinals were selected according to today's hygiene standards. The sanitary areas have regained their original proportions after the installation in front of the walls was dismantled, thereby recreating the original spatial impression.

Switch range

The original fittings used a range of flat surface switches that had just appeared on the market in the 1960s, which involved mounting them beneath the plaster. Most parts of the original flat surface switch range still existed in situ. However, tests on the original switches [2] by the manufacturer showed that the sockets and the light switches could not be reused for safety reasons. From a preservation perspective, only technically modified reconstructions and additions using special elements were feasible. To integrate data sockets, room temperature regulators, emergency alarms for the disabled, key switches, and other special elements, the series was supplemented with a rack frame. A large number of low-voltage and computer sockets added over time had led to a disorganized accumulation of the existing fittings, so one of the aims of the general overhaul was to restore their orderly appearance. The sockets and switches will be replaced. Additions are ordered in a vertical line beside the doors, beneath the original fitting locations.

In the 1960s, switches were produced using a Duroplast compression process that is no longer used today. The method makes the surfaces slightly shiny and gives them a somewhat irregular color development. To make the surface of the reconstructed range of switches resemble the original surfaces, a Thermoplast injection process was used, followed by subsequent surface varnishing (Fig. 8).

Michael Freytag, Gunter Schwarzbach

Modular Ceiling

Improved for
exhibition operations

The idea of the original modular ceiling in the basement was to install as flexible a ceiling system as possible. A new construction and materiality have improved such flexible use and its maintenance. At the same time, the aesthetic impression remained unchanged.

1 → Dechant, Trembowski, "Concrete refurbishing", p. 196–199.

In the basement of the Neue Nationalgalerie, a glance at the ceiling reveals two systems from the time of the building's construction: All publicly accessible areas–exhibition spaces, the staircase hall, and the café–use a modular ceiling system, while almost all non-public spaces and the user toilets have a Rabitz-wire ceiling. There is also a third ceiling type: The former depots, which were converted into a cloakroom and museum shop during the general overhaul, still use the reinforced-concrete coffered ceiling as an aesthetic indication of the new planning from the perspective of the shell construction.[1] The modular roof system serves as cladding for the technical infrastructure (supply air, exhaust air, lighting, and security systems) that is concentrated in the ceiling areas and needs to provide a high degree of flexibility in fulfilling the demands of exhibition operations. At the same time, it highlights a fluent space through a uniform, geometrically clear ceiling structure. Due to its technical and aesthetic function, the modular ceiling was the subject of special attention during the general overhaul.

The original modular ceiling consisted of a simple grid made of timber beams–all on one level (Fig. 1). The ceiling panels made of a composite wooden material were placed upon the beams in a grid of 60 × 60 centimeters and fixed to each of the four corners with countersunk screws. The screws were plastered over and the ceiling was evenly coated

1 Original wooden substructure of the modular ceiling during dismantling, 2017

2 Reconstructed modular ceiling with retrofitted lights, loudspeakers, and restored ventilation grilles, 2021

in white. The surrounding walls were made of a joint-free frieze. The general and exhibition lighting was permanently installed flush with the modular ceiling panels, together with the loudspeakers and ventilation grilles (Fig. 1, p. 252).

However, the ceiling did not fulfill the demands of flexible use and maintenance. The panels' fixed, screwed installation onto the underlying structure made changes cumbersome. Furthermore, the wooden structure represented a considerable fire load. Conductor rails retrofitted to the ceiling supplemented the original, fixed, integrated lighting, thereby disturbing the calm, clear ceiling appearance.

The aim of the general overhaul was to improve the structure with respect to fire protection and usability, while also preserving the original appearance of the ceiling.

Planning and installing the modular roof

Following initial planning discussions, a 1:1 model ceiling was erected in the special exhibition rooms of the Kulturforum (Fig. 3). It was used to test the appearance, usability, and technical feasibility, as well as to improve the construction. This was followed by CAD presentation and animation to support the construction of a special system of suspension profiles covering a distance of 7,000 linear meters.

A flexible ceiling system made of metal grids has now replaced the original wooden construction. The installed ceiling system consists of a metal ceiling panel [2] and vermiculite panels attached to its underside using adhesive and screwed connections (Fig. 4). The metal cassettes with wooden panels can be dismantled and exchanged, ensuring simple maintenance of the technical components behind the suspended ceiling and enabling flexible lighting. The panels contain numerous apertures to integrate technical components. To limit the number of conductor rails, they were fitted flush with the ceiling parallel to the exhibition walls, allowing lights to be used flexibly without significantly undermining the appearance of the ceiling.

2 Lindner ceiling system LMD-E 200 Type 2 (suspensions, bearing).

3

4

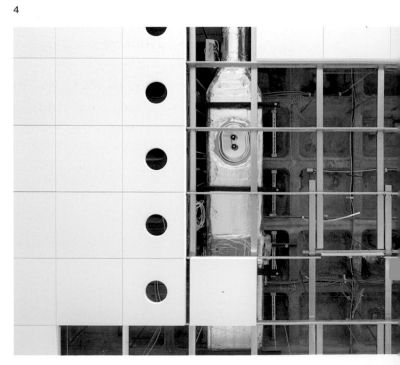

5

Due to the great installation density in the hollow spaces behind the suspended ceilings and the limited means of attachment to the coffered reinforced concrete ceiling, the ceiling structure had to be optimized using additional wide-span profiles. A variety of steel tubes with square hollow sections of 50 × 50, rectangular hollow sections of 70 × 40, and square hollow sections of 90 × 90, with spans of up to 4.80 meters, were installed for this purpose. The assembly team discussed appropriate special solutions with the project management for additional suspension points and installed them on site.

Another challenge was adherence to the regular joint pattern over a length of up to 100 meters and the width of 75 meters, while taking into account the even connectors of the ceiling panels to the regularly recurring existing supports (Fig. 5). Furthermore, the desired axis geometry of the ceilings and joints had to be implemented simultaneously through four rooms.

3 Installation of the sample ceiling in the special exhibition rooms of the Kulturforum

4 New ceiling system during the assembly process, 2020

5 The assembly sequence of ceiling slabs used reference axes through the entire building to ensure adherence to the joints and axial geometry, 2020

The logistical task consisted of coordinating the tight schedule to implement the building technology systems with the delivery of the approximately 11,200 ceiling panels and the 11,100 vermiculite panels. The technical components also had to be installed in the ceiling panels within a short time following delivery.

The new suspended ceiling is able to accommodate the required technical improvements and innovation, while also restoring the intended spatially formative impression of the ceiling (Fig. 2).

IMPLEMENTATION | INTERIOR FINISHING

Wolfgang Dambacher

Brown oak surface

Restoration preparations

Whether on partitions, cloakroom counters, or doors: Sooner or later, the traces of intensive use during museum operations could no longer be overlooked. After almost five decades, the brown-oak veneer on furniture and fittings needed thorough restoration.

Restoration work on the brown oak surfaces posed the question: What should be the aim of such measures? To remove the traces of use, to replace or repair damaged parts, or to preserve the existing patina and accept the material's aging appearance. Before the decision was made, Dirk Meier and I were contracted to carry out extensive preliminary examinations for the subsequent carpentry work, due to our many years' experience in the field.

Dismantling the wooden fittings

We first assessed whether the partition units could be dismantled without damaging them or would have to be restored in situ. We received copies of the original architectural drawings for the elements, which indicated that the substructures had been screwed in and the panels suspended. At least that was the theory. But nobody really knew whether glue, nails or screws had been used nevertheless in attaching the panels. So we followed the motto *facit indicium captiosus*, evidence leads to intelligence. We met the building management on site and attempted to dismantle one panel in the exhibition hall behind the cloakroom with our bare hands. Nothing moved. The gentle use of crowbars was equally ineffective. So we investigated whether panels could be lifted elsewhere and made a discovery in the basement, where some panels were easy to remove and others required a crowbar. As stipulated in the architectural drawings, the revealed substructure had indeed been screwed down, allowing the complete, damage-free dismantling of the wooden parts (Fig. 1).

Preliminary investigation of the brown oak's color qualities

In early 2015, I was commissioned to examine the color qualities of the partitions' faded brown oak surfaces in the hall. It was possible to derive the original appearance of the cloakroom surfaces from the original documents, which were instructions for work on the surfaces. Since the brown oak was mainly used in the English speaking world at the time, the wood for the Neue Nationalgalerie had been imported. In England, this special brown surface color is achieved by infecting oak trunks with a specific fungus. The wood is then cut into veneer. As far as we know, this method has never been applied in Central Europe.

As a reference, I prepared sample pieces of brown-oak veneer and treated them with linseed oil in accordance with the documents. This created a rich brown tone, similar to the one preserved in parts of the cloakroom interior that had been shielded from direct sunlight. The color, a warm brown, contrasts with the cool black of the steel structure and the gray of the natural stone floor, which had undoubtedly been intended. However, by the time of the refurbishment, the visual effect had ceased to exist. In addition to damage

1

1 Condition after complete dismantling of the attached panels, 2016

through imperfections and replaced veneer sections, the original color of the brown oak had disappeared in many areas. Wherever direct sunlight shone onto the surfaces of the partitions–and due to the surrounding glazing, this was almost everywhere–the surfaces had faded significantly (Fig. 2).

It was my task to show how and with which processes the original color of the faded surfaces could be restored. We began on sample panels with the original color in the interior sections of the cloakrooms. We were unable to experiment on the original pieces, due to the risk of damaging them irreparably. Thus we worked on oak-veneer sample panels using European wood.

A range of solvent and chemical staining substances can be used to change the color of wooden surfaces. Solvent staining is a good way of restoring the original color. However, it is hardly light-fast and was therefore unsuitable. By contrast, chemical staining using ammonia or potassium permanganate is described in the literature as remaining light-fast in the long term. So we stained the sample panels by applying different concentrations of chemical staining agents (Fig. 3). It became apparent that no warm brown tone can be created using ammonia, but potassium permanganate worked very well.

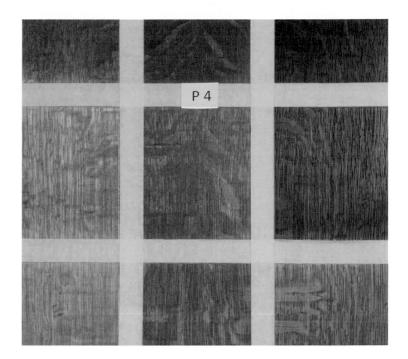

3

2 Heavily bleached
veneer of the brown-oak
cloakroom, 2016

3 Sample panel P4,
applying potassium
permanganate in varying
concentrations, 2015

4 Wolfgang Dambacher
and an employee treating
sample sections, 2016

4

IMPLEMENTATION | INTERIOR FINISHING

Inspection of the preliminary results

The samples were inspected on site in the presence of representatives from the Federal Office for Building and Regional Planning, the Neue Nationalgalerie, David Chipperfield Architects, and the Berlin Monument Authority, as well as the consultants Dirk Lohan and Fritz Neumeyer. Very quickly, it became apparent that there were strongly differing opinions on the restoration measures. Since the faded brown oak panels had not been the intention of Ludwig Mies van der Rohe, the question arose: To what lengths should restoration measures go to reproduce the aesthetic demands of the original builder with respect to recreating colors and their gloss? Are changes to the surface a form of patina that deserves preservation, or do they represent damage? To what extent should damage be repaired? Should one restore the original condition? The opinions of those present ranged from a conviction that today's patina should be preserved as a document of the times, to the opinion that the original condition should be restored as authentically as possible. At the end of the discussion, two decisions were made:

1.) The slightly faded tone on the inner sides of the cloakrooms should serve as a reference for the color of the faded partition surfaces.

2.) The desired color can be achieved through staining with potassium permanganate, but should not be applied because the process is irreversible.

Instead, I proposed an alternative method of adapting the color by applying pigmented shellac. Thus, oak-veneer sample panels were treated with differently pigmented shellac and presented on site. The color in various tones and the presentation of the measure's reversible quality convinced the project team. The method and scope of work was defined and documented in detail using a sample door. This process involved several project-team meetings in the carpentry workshop.

We applied selected tones to sample surfaces of the original front sides of the counters (Fig. 4). The surface was first washed with water and curd soap. Remnants of resinous varnish were removed using ethyl alcohol. We then smoothed the area with fine sandpaper and primed it with a linseed-oil varnish. In a final step, the pigmented shellac was applied in two color increments. This coloring fulfilled the stipulated requirements: reversibility, a controllable color tone for the differently faded surfaces, and a glazed coating that did not cover the structure of the wood.

Solution scenarios were discussed intensively and controversially, always with the aim of finding a compromise between heritage preservation and the museum's later intensive use—which was not always easy to achieve.

Dirk Meier, Martin Gaede

Restoration of the interior doors

Working report

The restoration of the interior doors involved not only treating the surfaces and repairing damage, but also and especially integrating technical components for fire-safety and burglary protection, without undermining the appearance or causing a relevant loss of original material.

A number of preparatory measures were necessary before beginning work on restoring the interior doors. Like all other technical parts, the interior doors of the Neue Nationalgalerie were dismounted before building measures began and placed in well-protected storage. Documentation of the dismantling measures, including appropriate coding and descriptions of the implemented dismounting work, made it easy for us to find the objects we needed to work on. In one complex measure, the doors and accessories were transported to our workshop and stored there in a specially prepared hall. We arranged the doors in a way that guaranteed access to any of them at all times.

The actual practical work was preceded by intensive planning based on measurements at the location–in so far as door apertures existed–and the examination of the respective door itself, since planning had to include all the actual properties of the frame and the door leaf. This procedure required multiple access to every single building part.

Intensive discussions and the search for solutions

1 → Dambacher, "Brown oak surface", p. 270–274.

Initially however, we worked on only one sample door to demonstrate all the restoration and technical problems, as well as their solutions. The approach allowed us to determine and document the scope of the work. There were several meetings at the workshops for this purpose, in the presence of representatives of the Federal Office for Building and Regional Planning, the Neue Nationalgalerie, David Chipperfield Architects, the building management, and the preservation authority. We controversially discussed the various solution possibilities in detail, weighing up heritage preservation and future utilization. At times the task was like an attempt to square the circle. There were struggles concerning the approach to every deficient or damaged area. What undermines the appearance and which traces of use should be allowed to remain (Figs. 1, 2)?

One aspect that was important to us was the work by Wolfgang Dambacher.[1] His insight and solutions prior to the restoration work allowed us to implement tasks on the surfaces relatively quickly and efficiently. All findings and specifications were recorded in an extensive report, were jointly authorized, and served as a guideline for action concerning the restoration work on the doors.

Fire-safety and burglary protection

One focus of our work was to integrate technical components for fire-safety and burglary protection without undermining the appearance of the building or cause any relevant loss of original material. These systems ensure that the original elements conform to contemporary legal requirements (Fig. 3). For instance a connection to the central fire alarm system and a smoke extraction system had to be prepared. It was important that the technical components, such as floor springs, were included in the approval documentation of the smoke extraction system and that their proper interaction had been approved. Before transportation back to the building site, the restored doors were mounted on a specially developed testing stand to assess their functions and the smooth interaction between all installed components (Fig. 4).

1 Original glass rails of the wooden and glass elements with asymmetrical, original fixing holes, before treatment, 2019

2 Producing fitting pieces to repair missing or damaged areas, 2019

3 Damage repair and integration of security systems in a wooden and glass element, 2019

4

5

4 Interior test stand for transporting and assembling the doors to the building site, 2019

5 After being assembled, the door frames were protected on the building site, 2020

On-site assembly

The on-site assembly work was a technical challenge. All dismounted parts of the door environment had to be meticulously measured and reassembled according to those measurements. "Our" doors then had to be mounted, at times in newly constructed masonry. In doing so, we had to avoid non-measurable warpage, especially in the case of the existing multi-winged elements. In the end, the frame and the door leaves had to form a vertical plane to allow the relaid hard flooring to meet at the same place beneath the door leaves, while ensuring that the sides and the ceilings were also congruous. The reinstalled original skirting boards also had to fit precisely again. At this point, the precision and quality of our preparatory work and our own documentation of the existing elements proved invaluable, since there was never the option of adapting the original material to the conditions. Once the door elements were fully mounted, the door leaves were dismounted again, returned to the workshop, and safely stored. The frames stayed on location, naturally well protected from the building site (Fig. 5).

Roland Sommer, Andreas Oberhofer

Furniture restoration

Museum objects
for daily use

The use of high-quality furniture over a period of decades at the Neue Nationalgalerie has left significant traces. However, exchanging the furniture with new models was not an option. Planning and implementation of the furniture's restoration therefore operated in the field of tension between preserving the original fabric and the furniture's continued long-term use in the museum.

The Neue Nationalgalerie is a universal work consisting of a building and its fittings, which were coordinated in detail to achieve an overall harmony. Individual furniture pieces are even regarded as unique objects, especially the tables produced according to plans by the office of Ludwig Mies van der Rohe. The majority of the furniture formed part of the building's original fittings and had to remain part of the new furniture stock. This presented a special challenge to the process of planning and implementing the furniture's restoration. The aim was to ensure its preventive conservation, enhancement, and prescribed maintenance and care, as well as the long-term preservation of the furniture, while also ensuring its lasting, continued use in the museum. The guiding principle was always to preserve as much of the original material as possible, while also accepting patina and traces of use.

Furniture with brown-oak veneer

Around 1968, the office of Mies van der Rohe produced detailed plans for furniture in brown-oak veneer, which included artificial leather surfaces and metal elements. The reduced, functional design highlights its timeless, modern expression. The surviving furniture comprised six reading and three reception tables, two so-called Director's and two conference tables (Fig. 1), a large table for layouts, seven file trolleys, a shelf, and two wall consoles. After almost 50 years, the furniture had according traces of use. In addition to sagging, some adhesive joints had come apart, leading to unstable table structures and necessary repairs. Numerous deficiencies developed on the veneer, ranging from the smallest blemishes to lengthy broken-off edges. Some of the earlier restoration work had used the wrong type of wood. The wooden surfaces also had typical traces of intensive use: soiling, worn surfaces, and gaps in the protective linseed oil coatings. The artificial leather also had damage including holes, cuts, scuffs, and burns.

The following restoration measures were necessary:
- Furniture cleaning
- Strengthening, veneer repair, cementing, retouching
- Structural enhancements
- Surface treatment
- Restoration of the artificial leather and metal surfaces

Slight traces of use that were not unsightly were left unchanged. Larger deficiencies and traces of use were improved or retouched professionally to resemble the existing objects. The retouching measures' tonality and level of shine had to conform to the nearby existing structures. The aim was to integrate the additions as well as possible into the existing surroundings. Above all, the methodical approach to additions to the brown-oak veneer required considerable prior testing. First, various versions of the additions were defined depending on the form and size of the deficiencies. The fitting pieces made of brown oak for insertion were adapted to suit the grain structure of the surrounding veneer. A brown-oak veneer was selected that had been artificially aged using citric acid. Very small deficient areas could be slightly interleaved along the damaged structure. The process of repairing small to medium-sized damaged areas proved to be more work-intensive. Assessment and sampling by all the involved expert representatives, including the preservation authority, showed that best results were achieved by comb-like interlocking for the veneer–thereby leaving the least conspicuous impression while taking the lost existing veneer into account. The exposed, deficient veneer areas were cut into a pointed form for this purpose, with the aim of removing as little of the original substance as possible. An exactly fitting counter-comb was incised into the subsequently inserted veneer piece. After its insertion and adhesion using animal glue, the additions were merged flush with the existing veneer. The broken-off edges were slightly straightened, before solid wood fitting elements were adhered to the edges and then leveled to ensure they were flush with the surface. Due to the furniture's high quality, it was decided that veneer additions made during improper repair work in the past, using the wrong type of wood, should be removed without damaging the existing objects and replaced to create a flat surface. Additions were treated with double watering measures and intermediate sanding, as well as single or double coats of a warm linseed-oil varnish. The original wooden surfaces were treated with a linseed siccative oil to strengthen them and enhance their saturation, before receiving two coats of primer with a matte shellac finish, as well as any required retouching of additions. Finally, two coats of hard wax were applied.

The frames of the reading tables had previously received small supporting blocks that were visible from the outside. However, the blocks undermined the purist appearance of the structures. As an alternative, more recent planning tested supporting joints as implants on the specially reconstructed table structure. However, the plan was rejected due to the significant interference with the original material this method would involve. Ultimately, reversible metal frames were chosen to strengthen the unstable tables. They cannot be seen from the outside and are screwed to the frames on their inner sides. These metal frames also help to straighten the sometimes sagging longitudinal frames of the tables. The existing artificial leather was restored in its current, spanned condition. The restoration of the file trolleys involved the maintenance or exchange of the trolley rollers, as well as producing replicas of the missing lateral bars and metal folder supports.

1

2

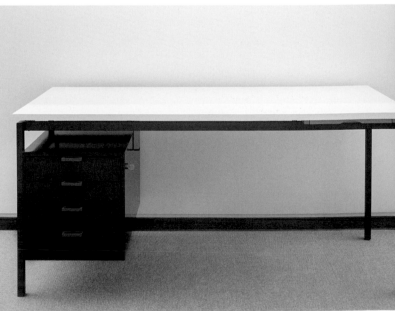

Furniture by the company Holzäpfel and other equipment

The furniture series purchased for the Neue Nationalgalerie was also restored as part of the overall work. This group of objects includes 9 desks by the company Holzäpfel (Fig. 2), 3 filing and 3 hanging-file cabinets, two photo cupboards, and 20 Thonet chairs. Instead of brown oak, this group of objects was characterized by laminated surfaces and metal frames. The pieces include wooden materials such as HPL or décor chipboard, metal elements such as frames, locking mechanisms and drawers, plastic elements such as handles and pen trays, as well as rattan materials for seating.

The following restoration measures were necessary:
- Furniture cleaning
- Structural enhancements
- Reproductions of laminated edges, cementing, and retouching on the laminated surfaces and lacquered metal
- Addition of missing elements and surface coatings
- Mobility maintenance for opening and closing mechanisms

The restoration measures focused on the Holzäpfel desks. The tables had a dark-gray lacquered substructure made of rectangular tubular steel. The composite wood tabletop with a white HPL coating is attached to this frame, separated by plastic spacers. On the left hand side, another dark-gray lacquered volume with four drawers is attached. On the right side, directly beneath the tabletop, there is a plastic drawer for writing utensils. Despite the damage to the HPL coating, the lacquered parts, and the hard plastic of the drawer, the restoration work was carried out while tolerating a certain amount of aging traces. Only heavily damaged melamine resin edges were renewed.

A maintenance and care concept is essential to ensure that the restored furniture remains preserved in the long term despite its continuing use in the museum. Ideally, the enhanced appearance of the restored furniture inspires a certain sense of reverence that encourages its sensitive handling and long-term preservation.

1   Reading desk with brown-oak veneer, specially designed by Ludwig Mies van der Rohe for the Neue Nationalgalerie, after restoration, 2021

2   Desk by the company Holzäpfel, part of the original furnishing, designed by Herbert Hirche, after restoration, 2021

Roland Sommer, Franziska Schlicht

Barcelona chairs

Restoring design classics

The furniture designed by Ludwig Mies van der Rohe and produced by the company Knoll International is a key element of the original fittings for the Berlin museum. The aim of the restoration was to preserve as much as possible, while also ensuring the continued use of the design classics at the Neue Nationalgalerie.

In addition to the famous Barcelona chairs, the furniture at the Neue Nationalgalerie included matching stools, tables, benches, and Tugendhat chairs. Ludwig Mies van der Rohe also developed a special bench with a hallmark structure–like the 1929 Barcelona chair–of crossed, chromium-plated steel profiles and upholstery divided into squares. While a total of 94 frames of seating furniture and glass tables had survived in relatively good condition, the upholstery from the 1960s had been more heavily worn by intensive museum use. It consists of black cowhide leather with leather-covered upholstery buttons. At the start of restoration measures, most of the rectangular leather segments were significantly worn and also torn (Fig. 1), while the flax welting had largely been destroyed. The original filling consisted of a polyurethane foam that had hardened over the years and disintegrated into powder (Fig. 2). Some of the tensioning belts that act as cushion supports sagged considerably, were torn, or no longer existed (Fig. 3). Thus many of the original upholstery and some unstable frames had been placed in storage for many years. The frames that continued to be used in the exhibition area had been retrofitted with upholstery of varying quality from different manufacturers.

After recording the furniture's current condition, the subsequent use of the historical furniture elements was coordinated on the basis of sample restoration work. The declared aim was not to buy any additional frames. By contrast, the heavily worn upholstery could not be reused in the long term in view of the preservation responsibility. A compromise between preservation, restoration, and reconstruction formed the basis of further plans.

Work on the frames

The frames for the seating furniture and tables consist of welded, screwed steel strips in several layers. They were copper-plated, nickel-plated, and finally given a glossy chromium-plated finish. The leg elements and lateral supports of all seating furniture frames are joined using dovetails and Allen screws. Frames were restored for 37 stools, 25 Barcelona chairs, 19 benches, 4 Tugendhat chairs, and 9 tables. After dismantling all straps and breaking down the frames into their individual parts, various methods of cleaning were applied, depending on the type of soiling. The metal restorer mixed tailored polishing materials to prevent abrasion to the chromium finish. This gave the surfaces a refined appearance, without removing all damage such as small scratches or individual deficiencies. Only clearly unsightly damage was retouched. After reassembly, concluding restoration measures included surface finishing, preparation of the furniture's location to prevent further wear, and ultimately the remounting of the leather strapping. Restored straps are used in the Director's offices, while specially reconstructed new strapping is used for the public areas.

Restoring the original upholstery

Some of the original upholstery and strapping was cleaned and packed for permanent storage in the depot of the Neue Nationalgalerie. 19 pieces of upholstery were so well preserved that they could be restored for the seating furniture in the Director's offices. The aim was to produce upholstery that was suitable for daily use, albeit for limited loads, without removing all traces of aging. An intensive sampling process was carried out in advance on the themes of exchanging segments, additional materials, and leather care. Considerable measures were necessary since the furniture's initial condition contrasted so greatly with user requirements. Many seams and button attachments had to be opened and detached in order to remove the filling material (Fig. 4). The covers were cleaned on all sides using a variety of methods. Individual, heavily damaged central and peripheral welting, as well as leather segments, were exchanged, while small deficiencies and cracks were retained. The upholstery was resewn, lateral seams were strengthened, new filling material was inserted, and buttons were reattached. Finally, a

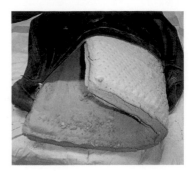

1 Original, heavily worn leather upholstery before restoration

2 Original filling made of polyurethane foam

3 Original torn straps before restoration and repair

4 Detached seam to remove the filling

5 Restored Barcelona armchair during an inspection, 2016

transparent care product was applied. During the restoration work, small attachment straps with clasps and the original frame straps were also refurbished (Fig. 5). The set was completed by reconstructing the seating upholstery for a Tugendhat chair.

Reconstruction of the upholstery, straps, and glass plates

The company Knoll International, who had originally produced the furniture, reproduced 91 pieces of leather upholstery for the museum's public areas. However, the measurements of the historical upholstery do not conform with the modern serial products–including the bench model, which was a small series produced for the Neue Nationalgalerie. Thus, all upholstery had to be remeasured and individually tailored by hand. Knoll International transported historical samples of upholstery and frames from the Neue Nationalgalerie to its factory in Italy in order to enable the upholstery's detailed reproduction. The frame straps are also specially tailored items. In accordance with the original straps, these remain black on three sides and natural-colored on the underside. Further reproductions were required for the tables, since the original glass tabletops had not survived. The existing 15 millimeter thick glass plates were replaced by 9 plates in the original thickness of 20 millimeters.

All these measures combined to ensure that the international design classics achieve an authentic expression of the original fittings, consisting of frames, upholstery, clasps, straps, and glass plates.

1

2

Bettina Bergande, Angela Kauls

Sculpture garden and landscape

Recreating
the preservation-listed exterior grounds

The Mies design comprises the entire exterior grounds of the Neue Nationalgalerie up to the adjoining streets, including the famous sculpture garden. The character of these facilities, especially the sculpture garden, had changed for the worse over the decades. All of these areas have now been restored according to preservation guidelines.

1 Plan of the Neue Nationalgalerie in the presentation portfolio of Ludwig Mies van der Rohe, 1963

2 The sculpture garden shortly after the Neue Nationalgalerie's opening, 1968

Since 1995, the Neue Nationalgalerie and its sculpture garden have enjoyed protection as a listed monument. However, Ludwig Mies van der Rohe's concept for the relationship between the architecture and nature was far more comprehensive. The starting point for the restoration planning with respect to the exterior grounds was therefore an interpretation of the site plan by Mies from his 1963 presentation portfolio (Fig. 1). In it, Mies aligned the building ground-plan towards the reconstructed Matthäuskirche, while the building geometry was oriented towards the orthogonal urban plan of the former Tiergarten district. At the same time, he presented a fabric of tree plantations, starting at the large terrace and the sculpture garden, the landscape-reference to the Grosser Tiergarten park to the north, and the Landwehrkanal by the urban planner and garden architect Peter Joseph Lenné to the south.

During the 1960s, the building site for the Neue Nationalgalerie in Berlin was a cleared area that had previously been destroyed by war. However, historical photos bear witness to a preserved landscape environment: as the Grosser Tiergarten was already regrowing in the north, and with the old tree population in the south, supplemented by newly planted vegetation along the bank of the Landwehrkanal.

At the heart of the garden grounds around the building to the east, south, and west, the sculpture garden is only separated from the collection rooms in the basement by glazing over the entire width of the building. Mies had already indicated in his collage sketches that the future sculpture garden would be a garden space that outwardly extended the museum areas. Despite the introverted character with its oversized surrounding walls, it appears connected to its environment due to the forest-like scenery. The attraction of a contemplative encounter with art is above all expressed in the sculpture garden of the Neue Nationalgalerie through the interaction between water, light, and vegetation (Fig. 2). Mies's design principles in integrating the landscape and garden are also clear in the case of the Neue Nationalgalerie: firstly in the close connection between interior and exterior spaces, as expressed through the sculpture garden in the basement, and secondly due to the framed view through the large glass windows of the exhibition hall into the surrounding natural and urban landscape.

Powerful roots

Mies collaborated with a landscape architect on most of his projects. This reflects the great importance he placed on gardens and the landscape environment with respect to his buildings. Eberhard Fink, a garden architect and Head of the Garden Authority of the District of Tiergarten, supported the office of Mies when implementing the planning measures for the exterior grounds of the Neue Nationalgalerie. In the nearby Tiergarten, the two of them sought tree varieties that were suitable for Mies's ideas. The trees were to have fine structures and feathery leaves, with large, irregular, and slightly translucent crowns, in order to envelope the geometrically designed architecture with a vegetable, organic element. In the majority of cases, honey locust and silver maple trees were chosen.

At the start of restoration planning, considerable parts of the exterior grounds no longer conformed to the original plan as implemented in 1967/68 and also revealed severe security flaws. Over the years, the fact that honey locust and silver maple trees have fibrous root systems proved problematic (Fig. 3). In terms of their appearance, the trees fulfilled Mies's concept. However, when they were planted, the aggressive and freely encroaching root growth had not been taken into account. Slabs were lifted off the ground and the surface of the floor buckled (Fig. 4). Combined with air-conditioning complications, this unhindered root growth made it impossible to provide access to the sculpture garden for many years. The type of garden care had also decisively changed the character of the facility: While the pyracantha plants in the sculpture garden and on the terrace were originally conceived as a loose undergrowth beneath the trees, with shrubs and grasses, pruning had in the meantime transformed them into compact, geometric forms, which obstructed important visual perspectives (Fig. 5).

3

4

3 Upright roots lying directly beneath the removed natural stone slabs, 2016

4 Lifted, broken, tilting slabs and a warped ground surface due to tree roots, 2016

5 Improperly pruned pyracantha in unwanted geometric forms create dense shrubbery in the sculpture garden, 2015

5

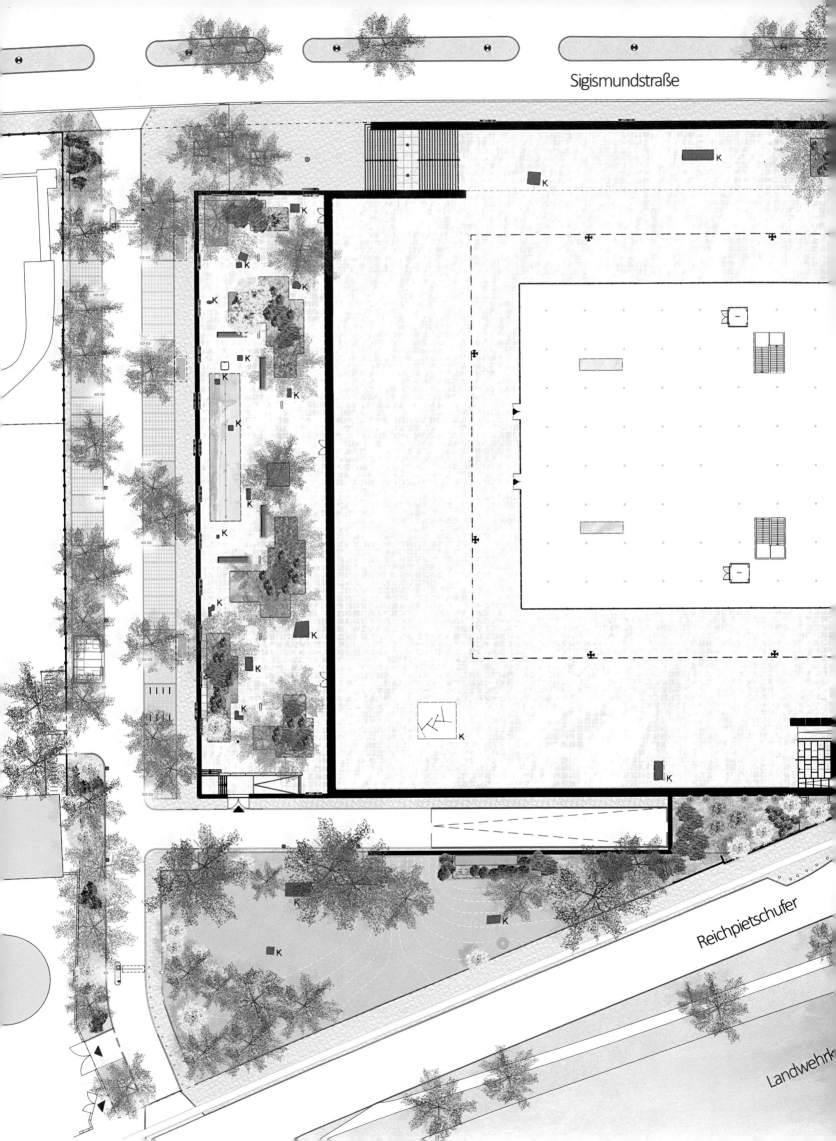

Sigismundstraße

Reichpietschufer

Landwehrk

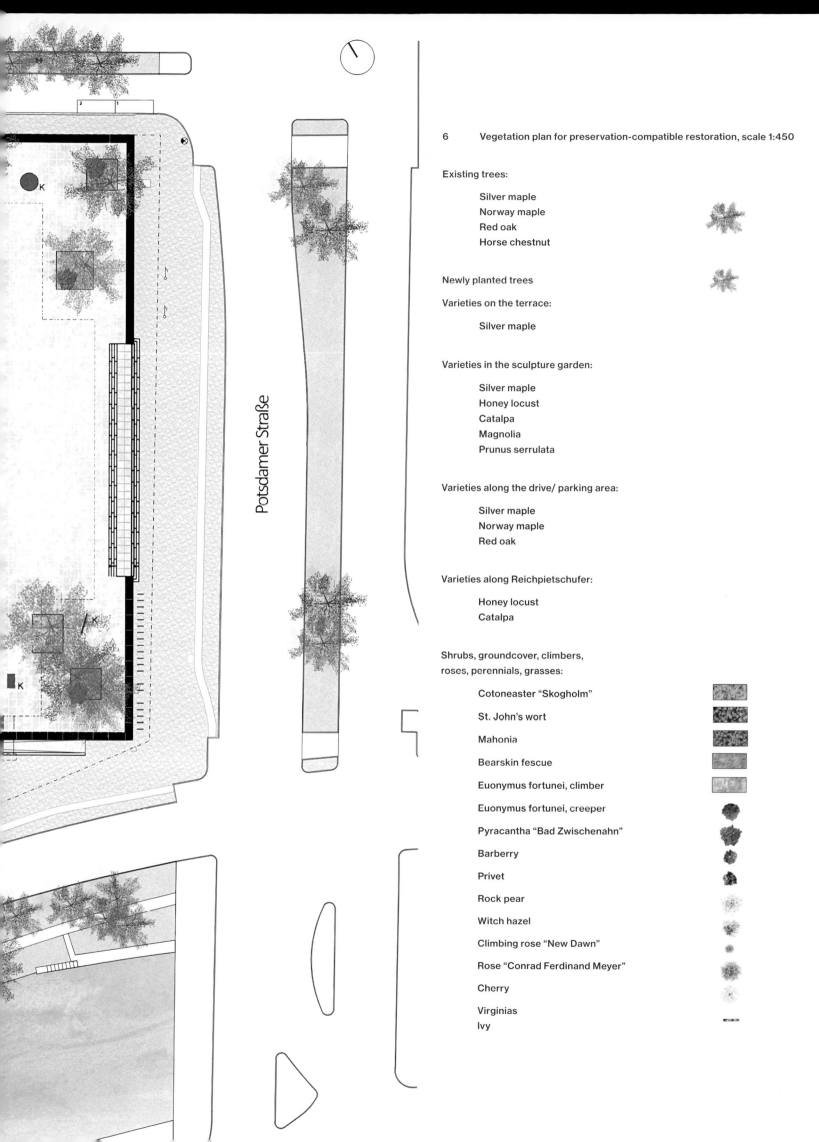

Potsdamer Straße

6   Vegetation plan for preservation-compatible restoration, scale 1:450

Existing trees:

    Silver maple
    Norway maple
    Red oak
    Horse chestnut

Newly planted trees

Varieties on the terrace:

    Silver maple

Varieties in the sculpture garden:

    Silver maple
    Honey locust
    Catalpa
    Magnolia
    Prunus serrulata

Varieties along the drive/ parking area:

    Silver maple
    Norway maple
    Red oak

Varieties along Reichpietschufer:

    Honey locust
    Catalpa

Shrubs, groundcover, climbers,
roses, perennials, grasses:

    Cotoneaster "Skogholm"

    St. John's wort

    Mahonia

    Bearskin fescue

    Euonymus fortunei, climber

    Euonymus fortunei, creeper

    Pyracantha "Bad Zwischenahn"

    Barberry

    Privet

    Rock pear

    Witch hazel

    Climbing rose "New Dawn"

    Rose "Conrad Ferdinand Meyer"

    Cherry

    Virginias
    Ivy

Status-quo analysis, assessment, and conception of preservation goals

In 2013, preliminary planning involved a comparison of the existing situation with the plan for the exterior grounds approved by Mies in 1967, as well as the 1968 implementation plan. The analyses of the existing garden and its losses led to a preservation assessment and the definition of the preservation goals. This formed the basis for the recommended tree-felling and clearance measures, always under the premise of retaining as much of the building fabric as possible while carrying out its essential general overhaul. Based on coordinated urban-planning and preservation guidelines, the sculpture garden was restored with wall climbers and plantation on staggered heights in modeled beds, in accordance with the original combinations of plant varieties, including measures to repair the water basin and all granite floor slabs, and restore the framing planted vegetation with deciduous trees along the private road outside the wall (Fig. 6). Finally, the plants in the beds on the terrace had to be replaced. The measures also enabled improvements to the planting locations–allowing larger root-growth areas, suitable substrate, an irrigation system, and edging for the beds using steel bands, which prevented roots from raising the slabs on the ground. The selected plants such as silver maple, accompanied by amelanchier, a variety of pyracantha known as "Bad Zwischenahn," and cotoneaster dammeri "Skogholm," conform with the original mixture of varieties and are typical for the greenery of post-war Modernity. In the sculpture garden, silver maple and honey locust are accompanied by ornamental cherry, catalpa, pyracantha, and groundcover such as bearskin grass and St. John's wort, while the inner and outer sides of the walls are covered in ivy and Virginia creeper. On the south side of the building, hedge and climbing rose varieties are being planted. The art historian Christiane Kruse commented on their use by stating that Mies "always favored rose gardens [...]. Beds with [...] roses, the quintessential noble plant variety, suited the aesthetic perception of Mies van der Rohe, who always chose refined materials for his buildings [...] and deliberately placed them as an accentuating detail."

Sustainably planned exterior grounds

Together with the demands of heritage preservation, plans for the exterior grounds also had to fulfill the Federal Government's sustainability standards as far as possible. These are formulated in the brochure "Sustainably Planned Exterior Grounds" and the "Assessment System for Sustainable Building, Exterior Grounds" ("BNB_AA"). One key aspect is to preserve as many trees as possible in the long term. In parallel with the preservation analysis and an assessment of the existing situation, early planning involved a tree expert to evaluate the existing trees and study them in detail if necessary, as well as examining critical locations through extensive root exposure, and providing the building project with expert advice. Based on this survey, the vitality and condition of each individual tree could be assessed in depth. The quality of the locations was also examined, some of which was very poor, especially with respect to the growth of the indicator species and the damage this entailed, as well as the forthcoming building measures. The aim was to create a stable growth of trees and shrubs for the next 50 years. In close collaboration with the Berlin Monument Authority, 13 of the 40 originally planted trees could be preserved. A total of 51 trees were additionally planted, thereby almost achieving the original number of 69 trees, some of which had multiple trunks. The safety and convenience of pedestrians and cyclists on the green connection between the Kulturforum and Landwehrkanal via the adjacent private road was improved, since the installation of barriers now prevents through-traffic. The green areas on the private road are significantly larger because only a third of the car parking spaces still exist. This also improves the quality of the location with respect to increased number of planted trees, in accordance with the original plans. Furthermore, the Neue Nationalgalerie's exterior grounds have been enhanced with cycle stands and wheelchair-friendly access to the building, since the ramp on the southeastern side of the terrace has been modified. The reuse of the original floor slabs and wall cladding in accordance with preservation principles represents a further contribution to sustainability.

To fulfill preconditions for the meaningful, efficient use of the exterior grounds and to prevent the above-described detrimental consequences of the past, a three-year development program was produced including documentation and a care and development concept. It formulates in detail the care measures for trees and green areas, as well as maintenance, cleaning, and repair guidelines for paths, installations, and technical facilities. The concept also clearly describes the specific fields of tasks and working procedures of those responsible for caring for the grounds in future. These measures fulfill the key requirements for a sustainable and preservation-compatible development of the exterior grounds at the Neue Nationalgalerie.

1

Thomas Lucker

Restoration of Calder's sculpture "Têtes et Queue"

Taking artistic intention into account

While planning the Neue Nationalgalerie, Ludwig Mies van der Rohe always took the installation of outdoor sculptures into account. However, like the building itself, around 50 years of environmental influences have severely damaged the artworks, which had not been apparent before the general overhaul. Special restoration measures were required for Alexander Calder's "Têtes et Queue."

1 → Neumeyer, p. 40–49.

The sculptures on the terrace of the Neue Nationalgalerie–for instance by Alexander Calder, Henry Moore, and George Rickey–continue to be visible from afar, characterizing the building's appearance in a speclal way. Their locations have remained unchanged since their installation in the late 1960s (Fig. 1).[1]

In principle, the restoration of artworks is the museum's responsibility and is therefore not part of the general overhaul implemented by the Federal Office for Building and Regional Planning. However, two exhibits on the terrace of the Neue Nationalgalerie are an exception in this respect: the kinetic object "Vier Vierecke im Geviert" (1969) by George Rickey and the steel sculpture "Têtes et Queue" (1965) by Alexander Calder. Before the area was completely cleared, both these multipart sculptures had to be professionally dismantled on the terrace and securely transported away (Fig. 2). Due to the age of the objects and their direct exposure to the weather over a period of many years, severe, previously undetected damage was discovered despite the great care with which they had been handled. The damage made it impossible to reinstall the sculptures without comprehensive technical restoration measures.

1 Installation of the sculpture "Têtes et Queue" (1965) by Alexander Calder for the museum's opening, 1968

Alexander Calder (1898–1976) is regarded as one of the most important Modern sculptors. He produced "Têtes et Queue" in 1965 as an abstract form consisting of six large, rib-reinforced steel plates, which are supplemented by a separate round plate positioned upon their highest point. The six roughly vertical plates are riveted with screws and welded together. The object was coated in matte black paint. Its dimensions are around 5 × 5 × 5 meters, with a plate thickness of 6 millimeters. The spatial effect of the sculpture is achieved through the form of the plates and their mutual arrangement. The sculpture's sweeping form strongly contrasts with the clear geometry of the museum building. The installation of "Têtes et Queue" on the terrace of the Neue Nationalgalerie was implemented in June 1968, in agreement with Ludwig Mies van der Rohe, for whom the connection between architecture and sculpture was especially important.

Significant damage

Since then, the sculpture had been directly exposed to the weather. An inspection after its dismantling in the autumn of 2015 revealed a rough surface and clear corrosion of the surfaces due to weather damage to the paint layers. Moisture had seeped into the metal joints, causing traces of pitting-corrosion and crevice corrosion (Fig. 3). Small-scale deformation of the steel sheets was also discovered (Fig. 4). The screws that served to connect the individual elements were also partially deformed, pitted, or affected by crevice corrosion and heel-and-toe wear (Fig. 5).

The aim was a restoration concept that did justice to the art-historical importance of the exhibit. It had to take both the ethical aspects of restoration and the aesthetic aspects of all measures into account, as well as ensuring the sculpture's structural stability. In view of the poor condition of the color scheme, a sustainable and durable paint had to be found that approached Calder's original artistic intention.

The Rathgen research laboratory was contracted to carry out scientific studies on the object's different paint layers, to underpin the professionalism of the measures. Furthermore, the restorer Anke Klusmeier was commissioned to carry out extensive research on "Têtes et Queue," providing valuable information on the production of the piece and its repair history. According to that research, the alkyd resin paint used for the artwork's first coat, which is known as "Philolaque Calder" and can still be delivered today, does not provide high levels of resistance to the influence of weathering and mechanical effects, thus requiring the sculpture to be repainted several times in the past using various paints. The same applies to other sculptures by Calder.

2

3

4

5

2 Professional removal of the sculpture, 2015

3 Traces of pitting corrosion and crevice corrosion at the sheet-metal connectors, 2015

4 Loss of color, surface corrosion and local deformation, 2015

5 Corroded and deformed original screw, 2015

Collaboration with the Calder Foundation

In recent years, the Calder Foundation, based in New York, has researched color value and matte paint levels that largely conform to the paint used by Alexander Calder and which is nevertheless resistant to damaging airborne substances and mechanical influences. The Calder Foundation was contacted to discuss the use of this paint, leading to a lively exchange, above all with respect to the required new version of "Têtes et Queue". The discourse was initially held via email and telephone, but in the autumn of 2019, the parties met personally in New York. The Calder Foundation recommended involving the New York conservator Abigail Mack, who had participated in the research and development of the paint and had already repainted a number of Calder sculptures using the system. Following an initial meeting in New York, she became a consulting member of the Berlin planning team, consisting of Thomas Lucker, Stefanie Dannenfeldt, and Alberto Gil Ricart.

The definition of a new color scheme represents the centerpiece of restoration planning for "Têtes et Queue". The paint is quasi the skin of the sculpture. To Calder, it was almost as important for the work's intended impact as its form. Thus the preservative treatment of the existing coat of paint was not an option, since additions and retouching would never have been able to ensure a lasting, homogeneous, and satisfactory appearance. This aspect was all the more relevant since the last visible coat of paint had been applied almost twenty years after the work had been produced and in no way corresponded to the original matte black paint.

The restoration strategy was discussed in themed workshops. In addition to questions concerning the color scheme, the approach to the damaged bolts and corrosion also had to be assessed. As a result, it was determined that, in the interests of long-term structural stability, the existing bolts should all be replaced by new bolts that are identical to the originals, drawing from the resources of the Calder Foundation. Finally, the participants agreed that the sculpture should be reassembled without the flat base that had been used for several decades, thereby restoring the original appearance of "Têtes et Queue" on the terrace.

The restoration concept fulfills the demands of the Staatliche Museen zu Berlin concerning the appropriate refurbishment of this important artwork, while also taking into account the stipulations of the Calder Foundation, which represents the rights to the artwork. Furthermore, the measures ensure that the sculpture can be installed safely on the publicly accessible terrace of the Neue Nationalgalerie for the long-term future.

6   Dismantling the sclupture "Têtes et Queue", 2015

Joachim Jäger

Reopening program

The Neue Nationalgalerie building and its history stand for US-American Modernity. The open hall, to a certain extent the legacy of Ludwig Mies van der Rohe, is an ideal place to present a contemporary of the architect at the museum's reopening: Alexander Calder. Many aspects connect Mies and Calder. The biographies and works of both men are prime examples of the western avant-garde and of an artistic blossoming in the 20th century. Both were committed to open concepts in their work, which in the case of Calder's art went as far as participation. Both spent their lives researching spaces and spatial experiences. In many ways, Alexander Calder therefore appears to represent an ideal artistic position with which to re-inaugurate the Neue Nationalgalerie following its preservation-compatible refurbishment. For decades, Calder has been closely associated with the Neue Nationalgalerie due to his key work "Têtes et Queue" (1965). Other than that, the sculptor's work has not been presented in an exhibition in Berlin for over 50 years.

The opening presentation will be entitled "Minimal. Maximal," since the three-dimensional and often movable objects by Calder range from tiny miniatures to monumental sculptures, including stabiles and mobiles. The exhibition investigates the special relationship between size, scale, and spatiality, using the confrontation between the organic forms in Calder's art and the stringent geometry of Mies van der Rohe's building to initiate a special dialogue. The exhibition, which was specially designed for the glass hall of the Neue Nationalgalerie, takes an open and experimental stance involving the principles of participation, allowing the general public to experience some of Calder's works in action. After six years, the art collection is finally returning to its designated floor, presenting major works of classic Modernity from the collection of the Nationalgalerie. Entitled "Die Kunst der Gesellschaft" ("The Art of Society"), around 250 paintings and sculptures from the period between 1900 and 1945 are presented, including pieces by Otto Dix, Hannah

Höch, Ernst Ludwig Kirchner, Lotte Laserstein, and Renée Sintenis. The artworks' collection in the exhibition reflects the social processes of a turbulent time: reform movements during the imperial period, World War I, the "golden Twenties" of the Weimar Republic, the persecution of the avant-garde during National Socialist rule, World War II, and the Holocaust are all present in the works. Going beyond a pure aesthetic history, the collection also impressively demonstrates the connection between art and social history. The open floor-plan of the iconic architecture by Mies van der Rohe offers diverse perspectives on the different branches of the avant-garde. Special "changes of perspective" establish connections to current discourse in today's society, while, for the first time, a separate temporary educational space within the exhibition route supplements the retrospective on the early 20th-century art.

Furthermore, the Berlin-based artist Rosa Barba presents a highly architecturally related exhibition in the "Graphics Cabinet" entitled "In a Perpetual Now," which also enables multifaceted engagement with and reflection on "Modernity." In addition to key works in the overall oeuvre of Barba, a new film is also presented that was specially produced for the exhibition. The architectural structure of the three-dimensional steel construction refers to Mies van der Rohe's early project "Landhaus aus Backstein" ("Country house made of brick") and shows a total of 15 films and sculptural works. The spatial-architectural construction, which was specifically developed for the architecture of the Neue Nationalgalerie, follows the principle of cinematic montage, an aspect that plays a key role in works by the artist.

Events and numerous smaller programs will accompany the exhibitions. There will also be a separate series of events on architectural themes, as well as a special educational program for young people in Berlin. Furthermore, the "Jazz in the Garden" concert series will be revived in collaboration with several companies and sponsors.

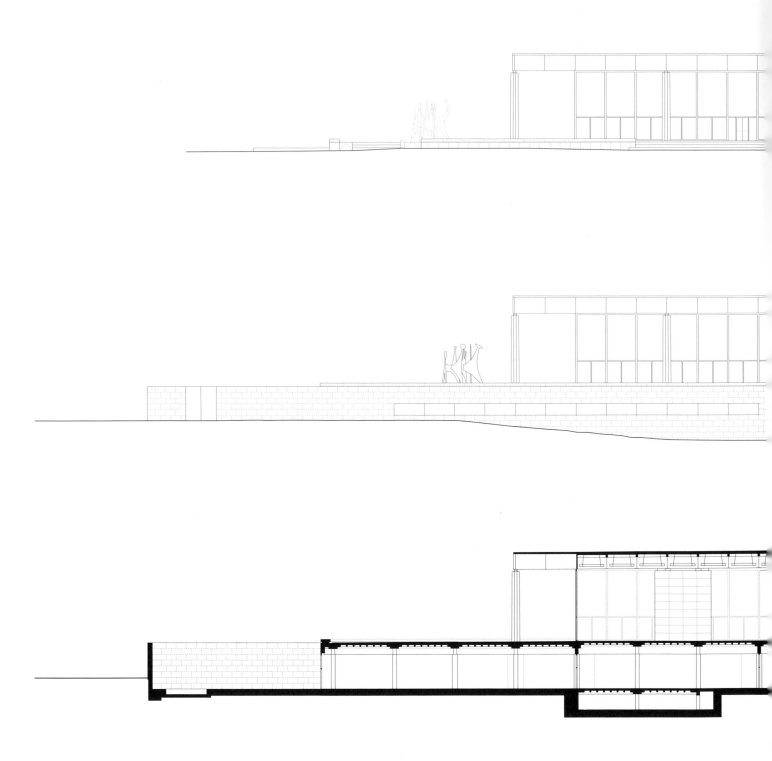

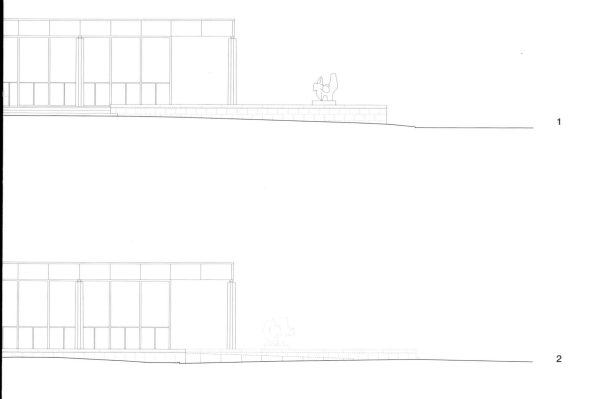

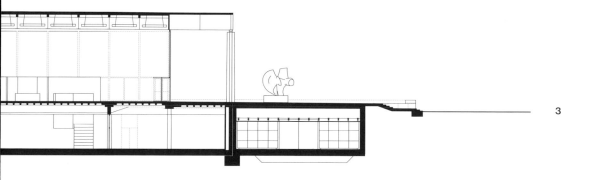

1 East view, scale 1:450

2 South view, scale 1:450

3 East-west sectional view, scale 1:450

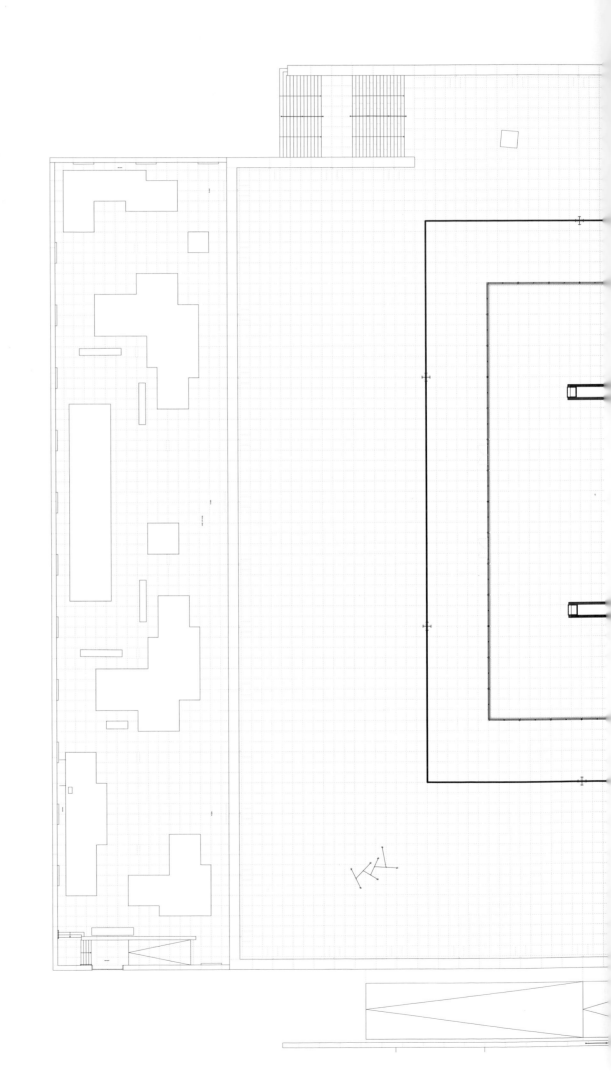

PLANS

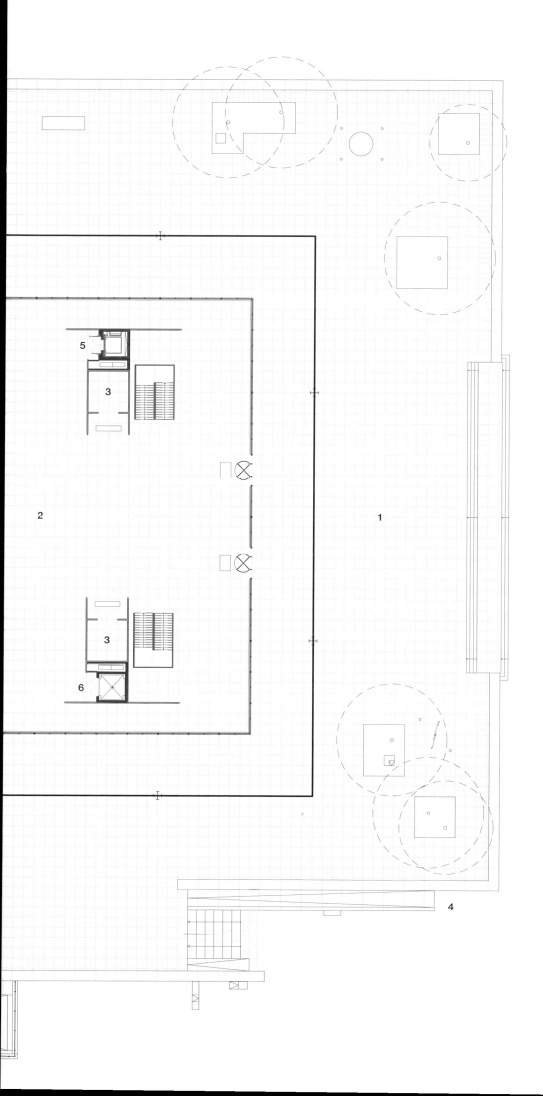

1   Ground floor plan,
    historical and new, scale 1:450

    1   Terrace

    2   Exhibition hall

    3   Cloakroom

    4   New barrier-free access

    5   New visitor elevator

    6   Freight elevator

PLANS

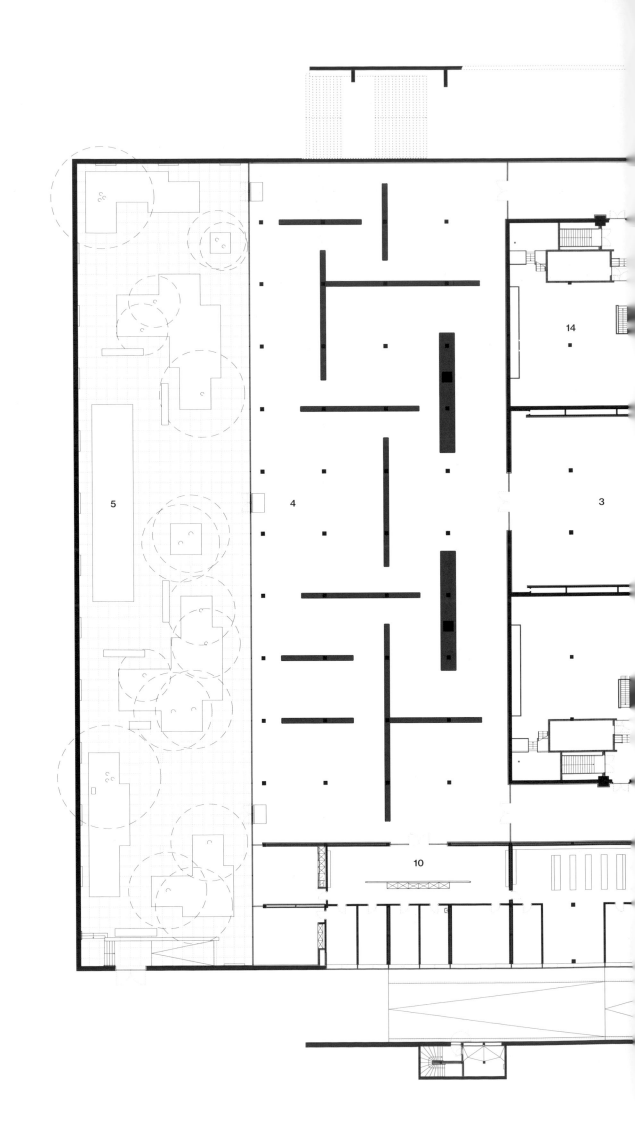

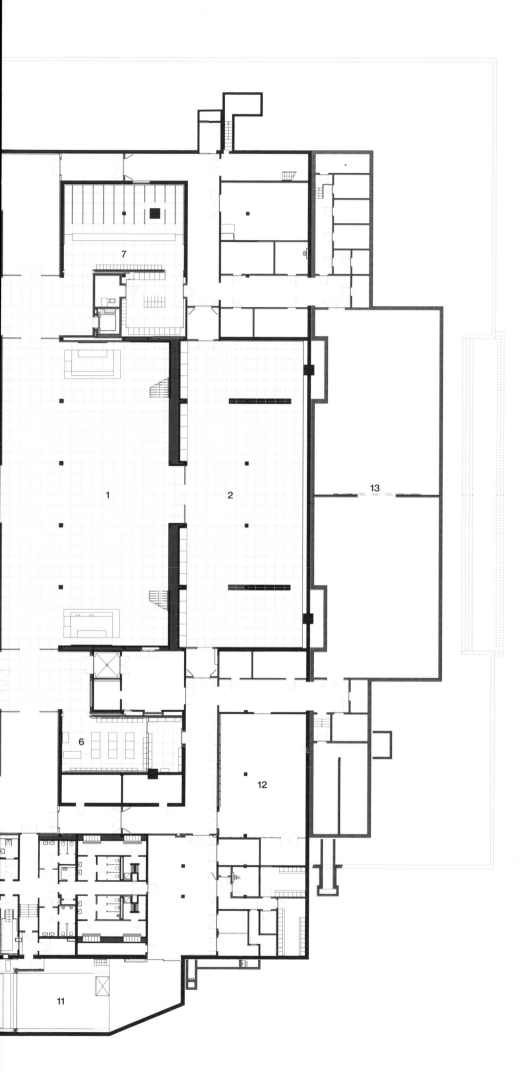

2　Lower ground floor plan,
　　historical and new, scale 1:450

　　1　Staircase hall

　　2　Graphics gallery

　　3　Smaller exhibition hall

　　4　Grand exhibition hall

　　5　Sculpture garden

　　6　Museum shop in the
　　　　former sculpture depot

　　7　Cloakroom in the
　　　　former painting depot

　　8　Visitor toilets

　　9　Café

　　10　Director's offices

　　11　Deliveries, service entrance

　　12　Exhibition preparation

　　13　New storage space

　　14　Central ventilation plant room

PLANS

Project participants

Owner, client
Stiftung Preußischer Kulturbesitz

Highest user authority
Federal Government Commissioner for Culture and the Media

Highest technical authority
Federal Ministry of the Interior, Building and Community

User representatives

Staatliche Museen zu Berlin
Building planning office
Dr. Ralf Nitschke, Daniel Naumann
Nationalgalerie
Udo Kittelmann (until 10/2020)
Neue Nationalgalerie
Dr. Joachim Jäger
Engineering Department
Uwe Heuer, Carsten Güth,
Hans-Jürgen Harras
Information and communication technology
Sabine Drexler
Department of Education, Communication, and Visitor Services
Heike Kropff

Monument preservation

State Monument Authority
Dr. Jörg Haspel (until 09/2018),
Dr. Christoph Rauhut
Norbert Heuler

Client representatives

Project management
Federal Office for Building and Regional Planning, Division IV 5
Annett Miethke, Head of Division

Arne Maibohm, Overall Project Manager
Susanne Manthey, project management, initial installations (from design planning onward) Katrin Bauer, Michaela Bauer, Arminius van Cleve, Jörg Fliegner, Tobias Heide, Angela Kauls, Norbert Klövekorn, Katja Kühn, Andrea Lipka, Gertrud Matthes, Mark Moammer, Alexander Niederhaus, Anke Offermann, Ulli Precht, Birgit Rössig, Andreas Schubert, Till Waninger
Procurement process
Marc Tenud, architect
Project steering
KVL Bauconsult GmbH
Sven Seehawer, project partner
Mathias Stieb, overall project management
Anja Pyka, initial installations management
Christian Flintrop, Bastian Geistler, Wajih Khalil, Sarah Lassika, Andreas Löbbecke, Mirko Moszynski, Frank Mütze, Jette Seifert, Thomas Weber, Gerrit Wegener, Teresa Wende
Representative of the joint heirs
Dirk Lohan
Monument preservation consulting
Prof. Dr. Fritz Neumeyer

Assessment of the existing monument

Preservation report
Büro adb, Michael Ewerien, Steffen Obermann GbR
Civil engineering report
Wetzel & von Seth
Fire-safety report
Halfkann+Kirchner
Report on toxic substances
KWS Geotechnik
Electrical engineering report
EGU Elektroingenieure
Heating, ventilation, and sanitary report
FWU Ingenieure

Planning and general overhaul

Building planning
David Chipperfield Architects Gesellschaft von Architekten GmbH (DCA)
David Chipperfield
Martin Reichert, Alexander Schwarz (Design Lead), Partner
Daniel Wendler, Michael Freytag, project management
Marianne Akay, Sebastian Barrett, Alexander Bellmann, Thomas Benk, Martina Betzold, Matthias Fiegl, Anke Fritzsch, Lukas Graf, Dirk Gschwind, Anne Hengst, Martijn Jaspers, Christopher Jonas, Franziska Michalsky, Maxi Reschke, Christian Vornholt, Lukas Wichmann; visualization: Dalia Liksaite, Simon Wiesmaier
Building supervision
DCA with BAL Bauplanungs- und Steuerungs GmbH
Kerstin Rohrbach, project management
Mona Azizi, Mario Barkewitz, Kira Bauer, Christian Böhme, Gunnar Brachmann, Babette Braun, Karlo Demrovski, Kilian Dörfler, Bea Forster, Ricky Götz, Dimitrios Katsamakas, Ulrike Küpper-Sommer, Matthias Pabst, Michael Schmitt, Ralph Seeling, Michael Slodowski, Wolfgang Streich, Ralf Thüre, Florian Völker, Joachim Würzburg
Load-bearing planning
GSE Ingenieurgesell. mbH, Saar, Enseleit und Partner
Dr. Jorg Enseleit, project management
Hans-Werner Boddenberg, Torsten Glitsch, Dr. Gabriele Henkens
Heating, sanitary, and electrical engineering planning
Ingenieurgesellschaft W33 mbH (heating and sanitary in partnership with Domann Ingenieure)

Afschin Tabassomi, project partner
Michael Moritz, overall project
management
Lukas Bernick, Michael Drung, Britta
Hartwich, Volker Koldewey, Björn Löbe,
Sabrina Matula, Parvis Mehrabiy-Pari,
Ulrike Niehaus, Alexander Reichhardt,
Torsten Ruthardt, Sven Schwiegelshohn,
Peter Seidler, Mostafa Takach,
Silvia Tarnow, Susanne Wagner,
Sabine Wasmann
Air-conditioning systems planning
Domann Beratende Ingenieure
(in partnership with W33 Ingenieure)
Stefan Domann, project management
Matthias Bahr, Tudor Ciortan, Maximilian
Domann, Rüdiger Holtz, Andreas Just,
Mieraf Mulugeta, Katharina Prost,
Regina Weiß
Fire-safety planning
HHP West, Beratende Ingenieure GmbH
Heiko Zies, project management
Hauke Fäseler
Landscape planning
TOPOS Stadtplanung, Landschaftspla-
nung, Stadtforschung
Stephan Buddatsch, project partner
Bettina Bergande, project management
Jürgen Liehr, Gerd Strütt
Lighting planning
Arup Deutschland GmbH
Alexander Rotsch, project management
Clearance planning–Preparatory work
Restaurierungsatelier Cornelia Rüth
Planning of inflow structure,
Landwehrkanal
Müller-Kalchreuth
Planungsgesellschaft mbH
Thermal structural physics
Müller BBM GmbH, Berlin branch
Building and spatial acoustics
Akustik – Ingenieurbüro Moll GmbH
Technical flow and thermal simulations
Arup Deutschland GmbH
Glass and facade consulting
DS-Plan Ingenieurgesellschaft für
ganzheitliche Bauberatung und
Generalfachplanung mbh

Transport planning
Hoffmann-Leichter
Ingenieurgesellschaft mbH
Surveying
Ingenieursozietät Zech/Ruth/Blasius
Testing expert, structural stability
Bernd von Seht, testing engineer
Testing expert, fire-safety
Sylvia Heilmann, testing engineer
Soil expert
GuD Geotechnik und
Dynamik Consult GmbH
Tree expert
Andreas Wüstenhagen
Toxin expert, health & safety coordinator
IUP Ingenieure GmbH
Testing expert, ventilation
Sachverständigenbüro
Dipl.-Ing. Johann Margulies
Testing expert, electrics
bap. Hans-Joachim Sylvester

Initial installations planning

Architect (until design planning and
overall artistic management)
David Chipperfield Architects Gesellschaft
von Architekten GmbH
Michael Freytag, project management
Yannic Calvez, Ute Zscharnt
Architect (from implementation planning)
buerozentral.architekten
Uli Lechtleitner, Michel Weber, project
management
Planning logistics, paintings, and interior
sculptures
Restaurierungsatelier Cornelia Rüth
Restoration management for furniture
metal, leather, and upholstery
ProDenkmal GmbH
Roland Sommer, project management
Andreas Oberhofer, Franziska Schlicht
Planning of storage and restoration of
outdoor sculptures and initial installation
Restaurierung am Oberbaum GmbH
Thomas Lucker, project management
Planning of IT systems
Berger Schallehn Ingenieure PartG mbB

Hanns-Werner Schallehn, project
management
Lighting planning, effects
Arup Deutschland GmbH
Alexander Rotsch, project management
Planning of guidance
and information system
fernkopie
Matthias Wittig, project management
Planning of screen design for media walls,
barrier-free guidance system
Polyform Planen und Gestalten Götzel-
mann Middel GbR
Dietmar Götzelmann, project management

Construction companies

Building-site preparation
Becker + Armbrust GmbH
Container facilities
B Plus L Infra Log GmbH
Container cleaning and winter services
RUWE GmbH
Central building waste disposal
Dare GmbH
Carpentry–Dismantling
Tischlerei Seeger GmbH
Metal construction work–Dismantling
F.R. Hauk Stahl-
und Leichtmetallbau GmbH
Demolition and dismantling work
REA GmbH
Excavation
Bietergemeinschaft PST Grundbau GmbH
and Stump Spezialtiefbau GmbH
Shell construction work
Dechant hoch- und ingenieurbau gmbh
Scaffolding
Döhne & Kreyß GmbH
Roof sealing work
AWD-Flachdach GmbH
Refurbishment of the steel and glass
facade, metal restoration work
FLZ Stahl- und Metallbau Lauterbach
GmbH
Metal building work–
New production of objects
Dörnhöfer Stahl-Metallbau GmbH & Co. KG

Restoration and refurbishment of
metal doors
ER+TE Stahl- und Metallbau GmbH
Metal building work–Production of
new steel doors
Jens Dunkel Bauelemente GmbH
Restoration and refurbishment of
wooden doors
Tischlerei Meier Betriebs-GmbH & Co. KG
Security systems
Weckbacher Sicherheitssysteme GmbH
Natural stone work–Interior and
exterior dismantling, outdoor laying
Gebauer Steinmetzarbeiten GmbH
Natural stone work–Interior laying
F.X. Rauch GmbH & Co. KG
Screed work
Freese Fußbodentechnik GmbH
Flooring work
IB Fußbodentechnik Berman GmbH
Tile work
Bauhütte 16 Ralf Beierle
Tile retro-flaming
GOLEM Kunst- und Baukeramik GmbH
Plaster work
Fuchs + Girke, Bau und Denkmalpflege
Dry construction work, special suspended
ceilings, hollow floors
Lindner AG
Carpentry work
RvH Restaurierung von
Holzobjekten GmbH
Carpentry, interior finish
Hofmann & Großmann GmbH
Paint work
Maltec Malerwerkstätten GmbH
Fitting-restoration on metal and wood
Sandstrahl Schuch GmbH
Sliding walls, depot
stabaArte GmbH

Water supply and drainage
Berliner Wasserbetriebe
Long-distance heating connection
Vattenfall Europe Wärme AG
Medium voltage power supply
Stromnetz Berlin GmbH Netzvertrieb
Netzanschluss

Construction electricity
Gewerbecentrum GCG GmbH
Sanitary systems, standpipes, heating,
and cooling technology
Apleona Wolfferts GmbH
Air-conditioning systems
Caverion Deutschland GmbH
Special air inlets
SLT Schanze Lufttechnik GmbH
Special air inlets for the exhibition space
in the basement
Georg Kiefer GmbH Luft und Klimatechnik
Medium voltage systems
Wahl Elektro Technik GmbH
Lightning conductors
Helmecke Blitzschutz- und
Erdungsanlagen
Active IT-system components
Computacenter AG & Co
Retrofitting of the existing lights,
exhibition areas
Selux AG
Retrofitting of the existing lights,
non-exhibition areas
Mawa Design Licht- und Wohnidee GmbH
High-voltage systems,
telecommunications, dismantling of
original technical equipment
Ritter Starkstromtechnik
Berlin GmbH & Co. KG
Elevator system–Personal elevators
Hans Lutz Maschinenfabrik
GmbH & Co. KG
Elevator system–Existing freight elevators
Tepper Aufzüge GmbH
Conveyor systems and lifting platform
Bühnentechnik Arnold GmbH
Building automation
Climtech GmbH
Insulation for technical systems
Huber + Jente Isolierungs GmbH

Inflow building
Bleck & Söhne, Hoch- und Tiefbau
Garden design and landscaping,
preparatory work
Rüdiger Brandenburg Garten-, Land-
schafts- und Sportplatzbau GmbH

Garden design and landscaping,
main services
Hartmann Ingenieure GmbH
Building-site surveillance
AWR Allwacht Rennwanz GmbH
Internal storage
Froesch GmbH
External storage
Bundeswehr Standortübungsplatz Storkow
Copying and reproduction services
Koebecke mediaprint c/o flying papers-
GmbH

Implementation, initial installation

Data cable laying
SSP Schwachstrom-Partner GmbH
Lighting rails
Leyendecker GmbH
Lighting
ERCO, Lichtblick Bühnentechnik GmbH,
Amptown System Company GmbH
Curtain
Pinder Veranstaltungstechnik
Newly procured upholstery
for Barcelona chairs
KNOLL International
Upholstery restoration
ArtDetox GmbH
Metal restoration,
volume lettering and signs
Stromlinie.eu
Showcase construction,
special steel-object tailoring
SEIWO Technik GmbH
Restauration, wooden furniture, laminate,
metal
Restaurierungswerkstätten Berlin GmbH
Office and special furniture
minimum einrichten gmbh
Sculpture restoration
Haber & Brandner GmbH
Workshop fittings, exhibition preparation,
and depot fittings
Scheidt GmbH & Co. KG, Regal Consult und
Handel GmbH, fintec – saugsysteme, BELO
Restaurierungsgeräte GmbH, Foto Meyer
GmbH, Leica Mikrosysteme Vertrieb GmbH

Library shelves
Körling Interiors GmbH & Co. KG
Direct labeling
Schilder Illig GmbH
Event technology
SIGMA & TBL
Kommunikationstechnik GmbH
Restoration and installation,
Calder sculpture
SICEM GmbH
Carpet
Tisca Object
IT workplace equipment
Human Art Computersysteme GmbH
Restoration and installation,
Rickey sculpture
Huiskens Kunstschlosserei GmbH
Outdoor sculpture transportation
Belaj Fine Art Service GmbH

Contemporary witnesses

Udo Beisert (Neue Nationalgalerie
Depot Manager)
Rudolf-Manfred Gebauer (Gebauer
Steinmetzarbeiten GmbH)
Lucius Griesebach (curator)
Andreas Grote (curator)
Klaus Israel (building management,
Senate Administration for Urban
Development and Housing, Berlin)
Dirk Lohan (project management,
Mies van der Rohe office)
Heinz Oeter (Krupp-Druckenmüller)
Paul Pätsch (Fliesen Pätsch)
Helmut Rogawsky (structural planning,
Dienst & Richter)
Angela Schneider (curator)

Photographers

Thomas Bruns
    studied Photography at the Folkwang
Universität der Künste, Essen, and at
the Hochschule für Grafik und Buchkunst,
Leipzig. His work focuses on interim
conditions of architecture, urban planning,
and urban brownfields. Many of his
works are produced together with exhibition projects and publications

Marcus Ebener
    studied Architecture at the Hochschule
für bildende Künste Hamburg. 2000 to
2011, worked as an architect for renowned
architectural offices in Berlin.
From 2010, part-time commissioned work
as a photographer. Since 2012,
full-time architectural photographer
focusing on cultural buildings

Ute Zscharnt
    Berlin-based designer and photographer
specializing in architecture and art.
Her works have been widely published and
exhibited

Authors

Marianne Akay

architect, employed at the office of Alvar Aalto, Helsinki, Finland, Project Manager of the Monument Preservation Department, Stiftung Preußische Schlösser und Gärten Berlin Brandenburg, Potsdam, employed at David Chipperfield Architects, Berlin

Michael Bauer

mason and restorer, ProDenkmal GmbH, 2011 to 2013 restored Magdeburg Cathedral, west section, expert building management, 2013 to 2015 restored the southeast pavilion/Orangery Palace, Potsdam, concept development, restoration planning, building management, 2013 to 2020 general overhaul of the Neue Nationalgalerie, underlying research, samples, and tests, expert building management

Thomas Benk

architect and Associate, David Chipperfield Architects, 2003 to 2008 reconstruction of the Neues Museum, Berlin, project management for existing shell construction, overall artistic direction, since 2013 Bötzow Brauerei, Berlin, monument preservation coordination, 2013/14 general overhaul of the Neue Nationalgalerie, underlying research, facade refurbishment

Bettina Bergande

graduate freelance landscape architect, studied Garden and Landscape Design (TH München-Weihenstephan) and Landscape Planning (TU Berlin), studied Sociology/Urban and Regional Planning (FU Berlin), since 1993 freelance landscape architect and freelance collaborator at TOPOS, Berlin, focusing on garden preservation, Project Manager, preserving and refurbishing the exterior grounds of the Neue Nationalgalerie

Martina Betzold

architect, David Chipperfield Architects, Literaturmuseum, Marbach, project management, overall artistic building management, interior refurbishment, Schiller-Nationalmuseum, Marbach, project management, overall artistic building management, 2015 to 2020 general overhaul of the Neue Nationalgalerie

David Chipperfield

architect, founder of David Chipperfield Architects in London, Berlin, Milan and Shanghai

Wolfgang Dambacher

carpentry tool maker and restorer, studied Physics and History of Art at the TU Berlin, lecturer at the Handwerkskammer Berlin, since 1979 owner and Managing Director of AMB Dambacher GmbH – Werkstatt für Möbelrestaurierung und Baudenkmalpflege, preparatory studies for the brown-oak surfaces at the Neue Nationalgalerie

Peter Dechant

civil engineer and specialist welding engineer, since 2000 Managing Director of dechant hoch- und ingenieurbau gmbh in Weismain. Shell construction work on the Neue Nationalgalerie

Stefan Domann

Managing Director, Domann Beratende Ingenieure GmbH, studied Engineering Management, and Supply and Energy Technology, TFH Berlin; projects: refurbishment of the Alte Nationalgalerie; new construction of the DHM temporary exhibition; Berlinische Galerie, air-conditioning planning; Neue Nationalgalerie, building automation

Manuela Figaschewsky

graduate civil engineer, studied at the TU Dresden, since 1990 specialist building management in natural stone restoration, including at the Staatsbibliothek Unter den Linden, Sophienkirche, Kaiserin-Friedrich-Haus, 2016 to 2021 specialist building management, dismantling and relaying the natural stone at the Neue Nationalgalerie as an employee of Gebauer Steinmetzarbeiten GmbH

Michael Freytag

architect and Associate, David Chipperfield Architects, 2000 to 2009 reconstruction of the Neues Museum, Berlin, subproject management, 2010 to 2012 Forum Museumsinsel, Berlin, project management, 2012 to 2021 general overhaul of the Neue Nationalgalerie, project management

Anke Fritzsch

civil engineer and Associate, David Chipperfield Architects, 2000 to 2009 reconstruction of the Neues Museum, Berlin, restoration planning, 2007 to 2017 Sanatorium Dr. Barner, Braunlage, restoration planning, 2013 to 2020 general overhaul of the Neue Nationalgalerie, restoration planning

Bernhard Furrer

Prof. Dr., architect, ETH Zurich, monument preservation officer of the City of Bern, Professor, Accademia di Architettura Mendrisio, monument preservation focusing on post-war architecture, Deputy Director, Berlin State Monument Authority

Martin Gaede

master carpenter, Tischlerei Meier since 2002, training as a journeyman carpenter, responsible for planning and building management for projects with high expert and organizational demands, project management for work by Tischlerei Meier on the Neue Nationalgalerie, restoration and strengthening of the interior doors

Rudolf Manfred Gebauer

master mason and stone engineer, publicly appointed and sworn-in expert for masonry and sculpture, 1965 to 1968 stone engineer for the construction of the Neue Nationalgalerie as an employee of Paul Becker Berlin, since 1981 Managing Director of the company Hans Meuser, since 1992 owner of the implementation company Gebauer Steinmetzarbeiten GmbH

Torsten Glitsch

civil engineer, TU Berlin, Research Assistant and doctorate at the Steel Construction Faculty of the TU Berlin in 2008, since 2005 civil engineer at GSE – Ingenieurgesellschaft mbH Saar, Enseleit und Partner, responsible for load-bearing calculation in steel, facade, and solid construction

Marc Gutermann

Prof. Dr. of Engineering, civil engineer, studied at the Universität Hannover, doctorate at the TU Dresden, since 2007, Professor and Head of the Institute for Experimental Statics, Hochschule Bremen, from 2008 Managing Partner of IGES mbH, Bremen; focus: analysis and experimental load-bearing safety assessment of buildings

T. Gunny Harboe

FAIA, Fellow US/ICOMOS, internationally recognized architect and teacher, over 30 years' experience in the conservation of the world's cultural heritage. His Chicago-based firm focuses on historical preservation and sustainable design, has worked on many iconic modern masterpieces including numerous works by Mies van der Rohe, Frank Lloyd Wright, and Louis Sullivan. Education: AB History, Brown Univ.; M.Sc.Hist.Pres. Columbia Univ.; M.Arch. M.I.T.; ICCROM, Arch. Conservation

Jörg Haspel

Prof. Dr., studied Architecture and Urban Planning, as well as History of Art and Empirical Cultural Science. From 1992 to 2018, State Preservation Officer in Berlin. President of the German National Committee of ICOMOS

Tobias Heide

graduate architect (FH), studied at the Technische Fachhochschule Berlin and the Universidade Federal do Rio de Janeiro, Brazil, employed at Sauerbruch Hutton Architekten Berlin and HAAS Architekten BDA Berlin, since 2014 project and operative consultant for the Neue Nationalgalerie at the Federal Office for Building and Regional Planning, Berlin

Uwe Heuer

Head of the Department of Engineering, Safety, and Internal Service, Staatliche Museen zu Berlin, graduate in Building Engineering, TU Berlin, user representative in all matters of technical building equipment and building operations

Martin Hurtienne

graduate mechanical engineer, studied at the Wilhelm-Pieck-Universität Rostock, 2002 qualified as a European specialist welding engineer (SFI), from 1990 employed at FLZ, since 2006 Managing Director of FLZ Stahl- und Metallbau Lauterbach GmbH, project management for restoring the steel and glass facade of the Neue Nationalgalerie

Joachim Jäger

art historian (PhD), studied in Tübingen, Munich, Philadelphia and Karlsruhe. Curator and Project Manager for numerous exhibitions. Since 2008, Head of the Neue Nationalgalerie. Since 2014 participant in plans for the new construction at the Kulturforum. Currently: Managing Director of the Nationalgalerie, Staatliche Museen zu Berlin

Angela L. Kauls

landscape architect, studied at the Technische Universität Berlin and Ball State University, USA, employed in several planning offices in the USA and Berlin, Research Associate at the TU Berlin, since 2004 Head of the Department of Landscape Architecture at the Federal Office for Building and Regional Planning, Berlin

Andrea Lipka

graduate architect, studied at the TU Berlin and the EPF Lausanne (CH), implementation planning for the Deutscher Dom Berlin in the office Pleuser Staab Architekten, construction supervision, new construction of the Akademie der Künste Berlin in the office BIG GmbH Berlin, since 2015 project consultant for the Neue Nationalgalerie at the Federal Office for Building and Regional Planning, Berlin

Dirk Lohan

FAIA, architect, studied at the Illinois Institute of Technology in Chicago, USA, and at the TU München. 1962 employed at the office of his grandfather Ludwig Mies van der Rohe and responsible for the construction of the Neue Nationalgalerie in Berlin. 1975 to 2019 Director of various architectural offices of his name. In recognition of many prize-winning buildings, became a Fellow of the American Institute of Architects AIA. Since 2020, founder and Chief Architect of the company Lohan Architecture LLC in Chicago

Thomas Lucker

sculptor and restorer, studied Fine Art at the Hochschule Hannover, Partner of RAO – Restaurierung am Oberbaum GmbH, expert planner for the restoration and re-installation of outdoor sculptures for the Neue Nationalgalerie

Arne Maibohm

architect, trained and worked as a carpenter, studied at the Bauhaus-Universität Weimar, employed at BAR Architects, San Francisco, USA, and Barkow Leibinger, Berlin, since 2009 project management for the Neue Nationalgalerie and Deputy Head of Department at the Federal Office for Building and Regional Planning, Berlin

Gertrud Matthes

graduate architect (Dipl.-Ing.), studied at the FH Oldenburg, project management for the Federal Office for Building and Regional Planning for the reconstruction of the Neues Museum in Berlin and for preparatory work on the Neue Nationalgalerie

Dirk Meier

owner and founder of Tischlerei Meier since 1990, certified craftsman (1994), certified restorer (1996), master carpenter (1990), since approx. 1993 increasingly focused on monument preservation, especially historically valuable buildings in Berlin, Brandenburg, Saxony-Anhalt, Saxony, and Mecklenburg-West Pomerania, restoration and strengthening of the interior doors of the Neue Nationalgalerie

Annett Miethke

graduate civil engineer, studied at the TU Dresden, Research Associate, Trainee at the Federal Building Authority, from 1992, expert on technical building equipment, including for the Foreign Office and the Deutsches Historisches Museum, since 2004 Head of Department, from 2006 responsible for building measures of the Stiftung Preußischer Kulturbesitz, including the Kulturforum

Mark Moammer

graduate engineer (FH), studied Building Technology at the TFH Berlin, Head of Department at the Federal Office for Building and Regional Planning, Berlin, since 2013 responsible for heating, air-conditioning, and sanitary engineering at the Neue Nationalgalerie

Michael Moritz

Authorized Officer and Partner of the engineering firm W33 mbH, graduate in Supply and Energy Engineering, TFH Berlin, projects: Kleistmuseum Frankfurt/Oder; Admiralspalast, Berlin; Augusteum, Lutherstadt Wittenberg; Museum für Naturkunde, Berlin; overall project management and planning, heating technology for the Neue Nationalgalerie

Konstanze von zur Mühlen

graduate restorer and heritage professional, studied at the FH Potsdam, postgraduate studies at UCL, London, project management in Angkor, Cambodia for WMF, New York, co-founder and Managing Director of Antony & von zur Mühlen GbR (AM-Restore), Berlin, since 2018 heritage-compatible restoration of the existing framework of the Neue Nationalgalerie

Fritz Neumeyer

Prof. Dr., architect, 1993 to 2012 Professor of Architectural Theory at the TU Berlin, author of "Mies van der Rohe. Das kunstlose Wort. Gedanken zur Baukunst", Berlin 1986 (Cambridge/London 1991; Madrid 1996; Paris 1996; Mailand 1996; Seoul 2009; Berlin 2016; Shanghai 2020)

Ralf Nitschke

art historian (PhD), studied at the Westfälische Wilhelms-Universität Münster. Professional positions include the Westfälisches Freilichtmuseum Detmold and Kleihues + Kleihues, since 2013 Head of the Building Planning Department at the Staatliche Museen zu Berlin

Andreas Oberhofer

specialist carpenter, Architecture BSc, Universität Innsbruck, Monument Preservation M.A., TU Berlin, project associate for the Neue Nationalgalerie, general overhaul and initial installations, ProDenkmal

Hermann Parzinger

Prof. Dr., archaeologist, from 2003 to 2008 President of the Deutsches Archäologisches Institut, since 2008 President of the Stiftung Preußischer Kulturbesitz

Martin Reichert

Architect and Partner, David Chipperfield Architects Berlin, focusing on cultural and heritage preservation projects. Together with Alexander Schwarz, responsible project Partner for the general overhaul of the Neue Nationalgalerie

Alexander Rotsch

graduate architect, studied at the Bauhaus-Universität Weimar and the École Nationale Supérieure d'Architecture Paris, employed at Kress & Adams Atelier für Lichtplanung, Cologne, project management at Licht Kunst Licht AG, Bonn, since 2012 Head of the Department of Natural and Artificial Light Planning Germany at Arup, Berlin, and project management for the Neue Nationalgalerie

Cornelia Rüth

graduate painting restorer, studied at the Hochschule für Bildende Künste Dresden, planning/building supervisor: relocation of the paintings, as well as interior and exterior sculptures, since late 2016, re-installation of paintings and interior sculptures at the Neue Nationalgalerie

Joachim Schanze

graduate engineer, studied at the FH Münster, Burgsteinfurt Department, Assistant to the Management and Head of Development for the field of air-conditioning at EMCO, Lingen, since 1984 entrepreneur and founder of SLT Schanze Lufttechnik GmbH & Co. KG, which was integrated into the SEGON Group, 2020

Jochen Schindel

1981 to 1996 worked as a glazier and window builder, publicly certified building engineer and master glazier, since 1997 facade consultancy expert at Drees & Sommer SE, expert planning and consultancy in the field of facades for the general overhaul of the Neue Nationalgalerie

Franziska Schlicht

restorer (M.A.), heritage preservation (M.A.), studied at the HTW Berlin and the TU Berlin, employed at the Leather Conservation Centre Northampton, GB, project associate for the Neue Nationalgalerie's initial installations, ProDenkmal

Andreas Schubert

graduate electrical engineer (FH), 20 years at the Tempelhof-Schöneberg district council as planner and building manager, as well as a representative of the client for various repairs, restorations, and new construction of kindergartens, schools, and official buildings, including Schöneberg Town Hall, since 2014 at the Federal Office for Building and Regional Planning, since 2016 its client representative in the field of specialist electrical engineering at the Neue Nationalgalerie

Alexander Schwarz

Architect and Partner, David Chipperfield Architects Berlin, Design Lead for the reconstruction of the Neues Museum, Berlin, the Literaturmuseum der Moderne, Marbach, and the James Simon Gallery, Berlin, among others. Together with Martin Reichert, responsible project Partner for the general overhaul of the Neue Nationalgalerie

Gunter Schwarzbach

FK Trockenbau (Handwerkskammer Dresden), Project Manager (IHK Niederbayern), modernization of Deutschlandradio FES 8, Berlin (studio fit-out), modernization of the Pergamon Museum, Berlin, (special lighting ceilings, under construction), new construction of the City Cube Berlin, Messegelände am Funkturm (textile facade and glass railings), Project Manager at the firm Lindner SE, Arnstorf, for the general overhaul of the Neue Nationalgalerie

Roland Sommer

PhD, graduate restorer (FH), M.A. in Preservation of European Cultural Heritage, studied at the HAWK Hildesheim and the Europa Universität Viadrina, project associate for the general overhaul Neue Nationalgalerie and project management for restoration planning of the Neue Nationalgalerie's initial installations, ProDenkmal

Mathias Stieb

civil engineer, freelance Project Manager and Lean Expert focusing on cooperative project processes, since 2013 Project Manager for the Neue Nationalgalerie at KVL Bauconsult GmbH

Marek Trembowski

civil engineer, studied at the Fachhochschule in Szczecin, Poland, building manager at dechant hoch- und ingenieurbau gmbh responsible for shell construction for the Neue Nationalgalerie

Till Waninger

graduate architect, building director, trained carpenter, studied at the TU Berlin, employed at Axel Schultes Architekten et al., project management for the Staatsbibliothek zu Berlin, Unter den Linden (1st building stage with the main reading room) for the Federal Office for Building and Regional Planning, Head of the Department of Planning and Building Regulations, project supervision for the Neue Nationalgalerie on public building regulations

Gerrit Wegener

graduate architect, M.A., project focuses: monument preservation and restoration work, since 2010 assessment of existing monuments (adb Ewerien und Obermann), subsequently on the project-steering side (KVL)

Ingo Weiss

1986 to 1988 draftsman's training, 1988 to 1993 studied Engineering (Universität Stuttgart), 1993 to 2001 structural planner at Werner Sobek Ingenieure, since 2001 facade and structural planner at Drees & Sommer SE, specialist planning and consulting in the field of facades and facade structures for the general overhaul of the Neue Nationalgalerie

Daniel Wendler

architect und Associate, David Chipperfield Architects, 2006 to 2007 Empire Riverside Hotel, Hamburg, spatially formative fit-out, interior planning, overall artistic management, project management, 2010 to 2012 conversion and renovation of the Kaisergalerie, Hamburg, 2012 to 2018 general overhaul of the Neue Nationalgalerie, since 2018 Elbtower, Hamburg

Petra Wesseler

studied Architecture and Urban Planning at the TU Braunschweig and the Universität Stuttgart. Following positions in London architectural offices, from 1993 project management and from 1995 Head of Division at today's Federal Office for Building and Regional Planning. Teaching position at the BTU Cottbus from 1994 to 1995. 2002 to 2015 Mayor and Head of the Urban Development Department of the City of Chemnitz, 2003 to 2013 member of the Scientific Advisory Board of the Stiftung Bauhaus Dessau. Since 2015, President of the Federal Office for Building and Regional Planning

Image credits

Photography

Dust jacket: photo: Ute Zscharnt for David Chipperfield Architects, **montage:** Studio Krimm; **cover:** BBR/Marcus Ebener; **p. 2–19:** BBR/Marcus Ebener; **p. 28:** BBR/ Thomas Bruns; **p. 31, 1:** © Marc J. Rochkind, 2016, CC-BY-SA-4.0; **p. 32, 2:** Constanze von Marlin; **p. 35, 3:** Ute Zscharnt for David Chipperfield Architects; **p. 36, 4:** David Chipperfield Architects; **p. 36, 5:** BBR/Thomas Bruns; **p. 36, 6:** Ute Zscharnt for David Chipperfield Architects; **p. 39, 7:** BBR/Thomas Bruns; **p. 40, 1:** Constanze von Marlin; **p. 40, 2:** BBR/ Thomas Bruns; **p. 43, 3:** Fritz Neumeyer; **p. 43, 4:** BBR/Thomas Bruns; **p. 43, 5:** Ute Zscharnt for David Chipperfield Architects; **p. 46, 6:** Ute Zscharnt for David Chipperfield Architects; **p. 49, 7:** BBR/Thomas Bruns; **p. 55, 1:** Frank Scherschel/The LIFE Picture Collection via Getty Images; **p. 57, 3:** HB-26347-Y, Chicago History Museum, Hedrich-Blessing Collection; **p. 58, 4:** bpk/ Staatliche Museen zu Berlin, Kunstbibliothek/Dietmar Katz; **p. 60/61, 5–8:** Bernhard Furrer; **p. 65, 9:** Staatliche Museen zu Berlin/Zentralarchiv/Reinhard Friedrich; **p. 67–73, 1–7:** T. Gunny Harboe; **p. 76, 1:** BBR/Thomas Bruns; **p. 79, 1:** Staatliche Museen zu Berlin/Zentralarchiv/Reinhard Friedrich; **p. 79, 2:** Großer Boss 1972 von Bernhard Luginbühl, Staatliche Museen zu Berlin/Neue Nationalgalerie/J. v. Waldhausen; **p. 79, 3:** Staatliche Museen zu Berlin/ Neue Nationalgalerie/Reinhard Friedrich; **p. 80, 4:** Staatliche Museen zu Berlin/ Zentralarchiv/Reinhard Friedrich; **p. 82:** BBR/Thomas Bruns; **p. 85, 1:** BBR/Büro adb, Michael Ewerien, Steffen Obermann GbR; **p. 86, 2:** Staatliche Museen zu Berlin/ Neue Nationalgalerie; **p. 88, 1:** Ute Zscharnt for David Chipperfield Architects; **p. 92, 2, 3:** BBR/Büro adb, Michael Ewerien, Steffen Obermann GbR; **p. 92, 4:** BBR/Thomas Bruns; **p. 95, 5, 6:** Ute Zscharnt for David Chipperfield Architects; **p. 95, 7:** BBR/Büro adb, Michael Ewerien, Steffen Obermann GbR; **p. 96, 1:** BBR/Thomas Bruns; **p. 103, 1:** David Chipperfield Architects; **p. 103, 2:** BBR/Büro adb, Michael Ewerien, Steffen Obermann GbR; **p. 103, 3:** Arne Maibohm; **p. 106, 4, 5:** Arne Maibohm; **p. 107, 6:** Sven Seehawer, KVL Bauconsult GmbH; **p. 108, 7:** David Zidlicky; **p. 112, 3:** Staatliche Museen zu Berlin/Zentralarchiv/Reinhard Friedrich; **p. 113, 4:** Staatliche Museen zu Berlin/Zentralarchiv/Reinhard Friedrich; **p. 113, 5, 6:** Heinz Oeter; **p. 114:** BBR/ Thomas Bruns; **p. 120, 1:** BBR/Thomas Bruns; **p. 125, 4:** BBR/Thomas Bruns; **p. 126, 1:** BBR/Thomas Bruns; **p. 128, 2:** Constanze von Marlin; **p. 129, 3:** Ute Zscharnt for David Chipperfield Architects; **p. 136, 6:** BBR/Thomas Bruns; **p. 139, 9:** BBR/Thomas Bruns; **p. 140, 1:** BBR/ Thomas Bruns; **p. 144, 3, 4:** BBR/Thomas Bruns; **p. 145, 6:** BBR/Thomas Bruns; **p. 147, 1:** BBR/Thomas Bruns; **p. 150–168:** BBR/Thomas Bruns; **p. 172, 1:** BBR/ Thomas Bruns; **p. 172, 2:** Ute Zscharnt for David Chipperfield Architects; **p. 172, 3:** BBR/Thomas Bruns; **p. 174, 4:** BBR/ Thomas Bruns; **p. 176, 1:** Mathias Stieb; **p. 179, 1:** Ute Zscharnt for David Chipperfield Architects; **p. 180, 2:** Cornelia Rüth; **p. 180, 3:** Ute Zscharnt for David Chipperfield Architects; **p. 182, 4:** Cornelia Rüth; **p. 184, 1, 2:** BBR/Thomas Bruns; **p. 185, 3:** BBR/Thomas Bruns; **p. 186, 4, 5:** BBR/ Thomas Bruns; **p. 188, 1:** BBR/Thomas Bruns; **p. 190, 2, 3:** BBR/Thomas Bruns; **p. 191, 4:** BBR/Thomas Bruns; **p. 191, 5:** Ute Zscharnt for David Chipperfield Architects; **p. 193, 1–3:** BBR/Thomas Bruns; **p. 195, 4, 5:** BBR/Thomas Bruns; **p. 197, 1:** BBR/ Thomas Bruns; **p. 198, 2:** BBR/Thomas Bruns; **p. 199, 3:** BBR/Thomas Bruns; **p. 200, 1:** BBR/Thomas Bruns; **p. 205, 1:** BBR/Thomas Bruns; **p. 205, 2, 3:** David Chipperfield Architects; **p. 211, 1–3:** BBR/ Thomas Bruns; **p. 214, 4, 5:** BBR/Thomas Bruns; **p. 217, 6, 7:** BBR/Thomas Bruns; **p. 218, 1:** BBR/Thomas Bruns; **p. 221, 2, 3:** Konstanze von zur Mühlen; **p. 221, 4:** BBR/ Thomas Bruns; **p. 222, 1:** BBR/Thomas Bruns; **p. 227, 3–5:** BBR/Thomas Bruns; **p. 228, 1:** Kiefer Klimatechnik GmbH; **p. 231, 2, 3:** Tobias Smolla/SLT Schanze Lufttechnik Lingen; **p. 233, 1:** BBR/Thomas Bruns; **p. 234, 2, 3:** BBR/Thomas Bruns; **p. 237, 1:** Ute Zscharnt for David Chipperfield Architects; **p. 237, 2:** BBR/Thomas Bruns; **p. 238, 3:** BBR/Thomas Bruns; **p. 240, 4:** BBR/Thomas Bruns; **p. 243, 1:** BBR/ Thomas Bruns; **p. 245, 2, 3:** Michael Bauer/ ProDenkmal GmbH; **p. 247, 1:** BBR/Thomas Bruns; **p. 248, 2, 3:** BBR/Thomas Bruns; **p. 252, 1:** Staatliche Museen zu Berlin/ Neue Nationalgalerie/Reinhard Friedrich; **p. 255, 4:** BBR/Thomas Bruns; **p. 258, 1, 2:** BBR/Thomas Bruns; **p. 260, 1:** Staatliche Museen zu Berlin/Neue Nationalgalerie/ Reinhard Friedrich; **p. 260, 2:** Ute Zscharnt for David Chipperfield Architects; **p. 263, 4, 5:** BBR/Thomas Bruns; **p. 264, 6:** Keramag; **p. 264, 7:** BBR/Thomas Bruns; **p. 264, 8:** David Chipperfield Architects; **p. 266, 1:** Ute Zscharnt for David Chipperfield Architects; **p. 266, 2:** BBR/Thomas Bruns; **p. 268, 3:** David Chipperfield Architects; **p. 268, 4:** BBR/Thomas Bruns; **p. 269, 5:** BBR/ Thomas Bruns; **p. 271, 1:** Ute Zscharnt for David Chipperfield Architects; **p. 272, 2:** BBR/Thomas Bruns; **p. 273, 3, 4:** BBR/ ProDenkmal GmbH; **p. 277, 1–3:** Dirk Meier/ Tischlerei Meier; **p. 278, 4:** Dirk Meier/ Tischlerei Meier; **p. 278, 5:** BBR/Thomas Bruns; **p. 282, 1, 2:** BBR/Marcus Ebener;

p. 286, 1–5: BBR/ProDenkmal GmbH;
p. 288, 2: Staatliche Museen zu Berlin/
Zentralarchiv/Reinhard Friedrich; p. 291, 3:
Jürgen Liehr; p. 291, 4: Constanze von
Marlin; p. 291, 5: Bettina Bergande/TOPOS;
p. 296, 1: Staatliche Museen zu Berlin/
Zentralarchiv/Reinhard Friedrich; p. 299, 2,
3: SMB/Thomas Bruns; p. 299, 4, 5:
Thomas Lucker/Restaurierung am Ober-
baum GmbH; p. 301, 6: SMB/Thomas Bruns

Artworks

Ludwig Mies van der Rohe, VG Bild-Kunst,
Bonn 2021
p. 55, 2: Peter Gut, VG Bild-Kunst, Bonn
2021; p. 79, 1: Piet Mondrian, p. 79, 2:
Großer Boss 1972 von Bernhard Luginbühl;
p. 85, 1: Rudolf Stingel; p. 88, 1: David
Chipperfield; p. 252, 1: J. M. W. Turner;
p. 260, 1: Wilhelm Lehmbruck; p. 296, 1: ©
2021 Calder Foundation, New York/Artists
Rights Society (ARS), New York; p. 299, 2,
3: © 2021 Calder Foundation, New York/
Artists Rights Society (ARS), New York;
p. 301, 6: © 2021 Calder Foundation, New
York/Artists Rights Society (ARS), New York

Plans

p. 111, 1: Staatliche Museen zu Berlin/
Kunstbibliothek/Dietmar Katz; p. 111, 2:
Digital image © 2021, The Museum of
Modern Art, New York/Scala, Florence;
p. 123, 2, 3: David Chipperfield Architects;
p. 132–135, 1–5: David Chipperfield
Architects; p. 137, 7, 8: David Chipperfield
Architects; p. 143, 2: David Chipperfield
Architects; p. 145, 5: Arge Ingenieurge-
sellschaft W33/Domann Beratende
Ingenieure; p. 148, 2: HPP West Beratende
Ingenieure GmbH; p. 208–209, 4–6: David
Chipperfield Architects; p. 225, 2: Arup;
p. 253, 2, 3: Arup; p. 260, 3: David Chipper-
field Architects; p. 288, 1: bpk/Staatliche
Museen zu Berlin, Kunstbibliothek/Dietmar
Katz; p. 292–293, 6: TOPOS; p. 304–309:
David Chipperfield Architects

Imprint

Published by
Arne Maibohm for the Federal Office
of Building and Regional Planning

Bundesamt für Bauwesen und
Raumordnung (BBR) Referat IV 5
Straße des 17. Juni 112
10623 Berlin

Idea and concept
Arne Maibohm (BBR)

Conceptual collaboration
Dr. Constanze von Marlin (schmedding.
vonmarlin.), Martin Reichert (David
Chipperfield Architects)

Project management
Arne Maibohm, Dr. Constanze von Marlin

Editorial team
Dr. Constanze von Marlin with Hannah Butz;
Jana Galinowski (BBR)

Translation into English
Benjamin Liebelt

Translation proofreading
Tatyana Pugacheva

Layout and graphics
StudioKrimm, Berlin
Björn Streeck

Lithography
Bild1Druck, Berlin

Printing and binding
optimal media GmbH, Röbel/Müritz

Bibliographic information published by
the Deutsche Nationalbibliothek
The Deutsche Nationalbibliothek lists
this publication in the Deutsche
Nationalbibliografie; detailed bibliographic
data are available on the Internet at
http://dnb.d-nb.de

jovis Verlag GmbH
Lützowstraße 33
10785 Berlin

www.jovis.de

jovis books are available worldwide
in select bookstores. Please contact your
nearest bookseller or visit www.jovis.de
for information concerning your local
distribution.

ISBN 978-3-86859-688-5